Four Crises *and a* Peace Process

Four Crises *and a* Peace Process

American Engagement in South Asia

P. R. Chari
Pervaiz Iqbal Cheema
Stephen P. Cohen

HarperCollins Publishers India

First published in India by
HarperCollins *Publishers* in 2007
A-75, Sector 57, Noida, Uttar Pradesh 201301, India
www.harpercollins.co.in

First Published in the United States by The Brookings Institution in 2007

2 4 6 8 10 9 7 5 3

ISBN 978-81-7223-731-8

Typeset in Minion

Cartography by Meridian Mapping
Minneapolis, Minnesota

Printed and bound at

Manipal Technologies Limited, Manipal

Contents

Foreword

The partition that accompanied the end of the British Raj in 1947 created two newly independent states that today account for almost 1.3 billion people, about one-fifth of all mankind. But India and Pakistan spent the next quarter century in a more or less permanent crisis that has escalated into three major wars—in 1947, 1965, and 1971. When fighting erupted again near the border town of Kargil in the Himalayas in 1999, the stakes were higher than ever, since both countries had tested nuclear weapons the year before.

Tensions have flared more recently as well, especially in 2001–02. By then the world had entered the post-9/11 era, and South Asia had acquired, in American eyes, a new significance. Pakistan was a militarily powerful but structurally fragile Islamic state whose porous frontier with Afghanistan was a refuge for al-Qaeda. India—itself the victim of a series of terrorist attacks—was seeking to cultivate what its leaders called a "natural alliance" with the United States. The American government, loath to choose sides between the two, sought instead to encourage a peace process. That was no easy task, given the combatants' profound lack of trust in each other and their aversion to third-party mediation (even though the Pakistanis often claim to want precisely that).

This book—the fourth in a series of joint studies of South Asian crises—is a testament to the knowledge, prescriptive persuasiveness, and collaborative skill of P. R. Chari, research professor at the Institute of Peace and Conflict Studies; Pervaiz Iqbal Cheema, president of the Islamabad Policy Research

Institute; and my colleague at Brookings, Stephen P. Cohen. If only their diplomatic counterparts were able to collaborate so well!

Having been involved in the American effort to defuse one of the four crises they examine—the one near Kargil in 1999—I can testify to the value of this book. Chari, Cheema, and Cohen dissect each episode carefully and clearly, comparing and contrasting their causes, the attitudes and actions of the key characters who squared off against each other across the no-man's-land, and the decisionmaking dilemmas that confronted national leaders in their capitals.

Maintaining throughout a balanced, objective approach and combining their knowledge of the inner workings of the three governments involved, the authors take full account of the changing international environment, from the late cold war to the onset of George W. Bush's "war on terror." More generally, their research and conclusions helps us better understand the underlying dynamics of the fraught relationship between India and Pakistan.

The good news in the story told here is that three of the crises featured stopped short of war, while the fourth—Kargil—remained "subcritical" (that is, it did not go nuclear). The bad news is that the Indian and Pakistani combatants did not always learn from their mistakes. Worse, the lessons were often misunderstood, sometimes in ways that precipitated another showdown. The right lessons are to be found in these pages. If policymakers in New Delhi, Islamabad, and Washington were to study this book carefully, there might be less danger that the authors will have to write a sequel.

STROBE TALBOTT
President

Washington, D.C.
November 2007

Acknowledgments

This book—based in part on our collaborations with others on the 1987 "Brasstacks" crisis, our book on the 1990 crisis, and subsequent reports for the U.S. Institute of Peace—owes much to many individuals. First and foremost are Mallika Joseph, Tanvi Madan, and Dhruva Jaishankar, who helped manage this project from New Delhi and Washington, respectively, and who contributed much to its intellectual development. Second, we wish to thank Zoe Konovalov, who helped develop the methodology for comparing elite press coverage of the four crises and who measured the American papers, and B. Rajeshwari and Syeda Talat Yasmin Kazmi, who, respectively, measured the Indian and Pakistani press. In the final stages, we received the expert help of Ryan Kaminski of the University of Chicago and Moeed Yusuf of the Fletcher School, Tufts University.

We also wish to acknowledge the contribution of other individuals associated with this project who provided timely and critical help: Sidney Kwiram and Anit Mukherjee of the School of Advanced International Studies, Washington, D.C., and Arti Trehan of the University of Michigan.

The International Institute for Strategic Studies (IISS) helped us organize a meeting of key American, British, Indian, and Pakistani officials to discuss the 1999 and 2001–02 cases. We are particularly grateful to Gary Samore and Rahul Roy Choudhury of IISS for their hospitality. We are also appreciative of the cooperation of many former and serving officials from these and other countries who shared with us their understanding of what happened over the past twelve years in the United States, India, and Pakistan, and at meetings in

London, Bellagio, Colombo, and elsewhere. Some of our respondents were interviewed several times, as we went back to check facts, dates, and perceptions.

Finally, we wish to express our gratitude to our wives—Chandra Chari, Asma Pervaiz Cheema, and Roberta Cohen—for their patience and support of the project.

Funding for this book came from a variety of sources, notably the Brookings Institution, the U.S. Institute of Peace, and the U.S. Department of Energy.

Four Crises *and a* Peace Process

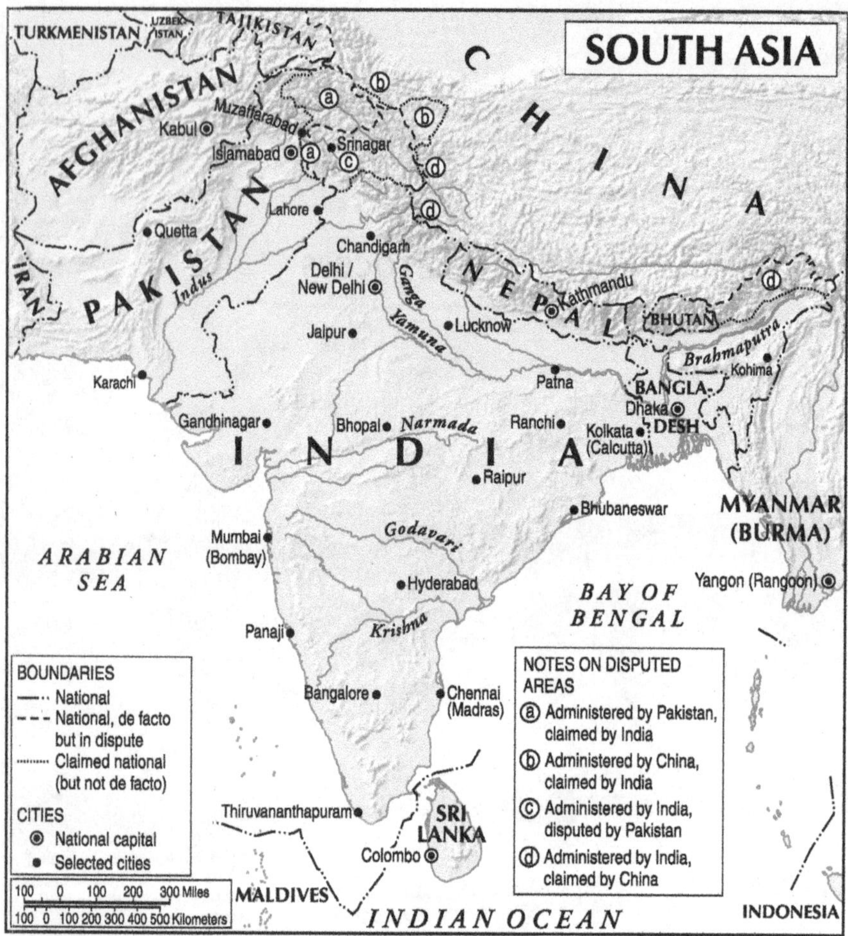

This map is indicative and not to scale. The disputed areas shown in the map reflect the authors' judgement. The boundaries shown in the map may not confirm to the official boundaries of India. The printer and publisher bear no responsibility on the accuracy or otherwise of this map.

CHAPTER ONE

Fifteen Years, Four Crises

Sometimes events move so rapidly that no one has time to be surprised. That was the case in South Asia in the years between 1987 and 2002. Developments were rapid and unpredicted—perhaps unpredictable—coalescing in what seemed one long India-Pakistan crisis punctuated by periods of peace. The crises approached serious proportions on four occasions: during India's "Brasstacks" military maneuvers (1986–87), increased turmoil in Kashmir (1990), the Kargil conflict (1999), and a subsequent border confrontation (2001–02). Each could have escalated to large-scale conflict. Each was also linked, in one way or another, to the introduction of nuclear weapons into the arsenals of India and Pakistan that took place after their 1998 nuclear tests (but that may have occurred as early as 1990). The goal of this book is to examine the underlying causes and effects of these four crises, along with the subsequent peace process.

Each crisis had a distinct history. Briefly:

—The crisis of 1987 was sparked by a massive Indian military exercise named Brasstacks that took place just as Pakistan, the United States, and other states were engaged in countering the Soviet occupation of Afghanistan. Pakistan responded with a countermove, and the crisis escalated to a point just short of war. Although India eventually retreated from its provocative stance, Pakistan asserted that India had been deterred. In retrospect, it is clear that the crisis accelerated the nuclear programs of both states. Misreading these events, the United States reassured both sides that there was nothing to be alarmed about.

—The 1990 crisis over Kashmir was a multifaceted affair related not only to some movement of military assets but also to political turmoil in both

India and Pakistan. No less important was a massive uprising against Indian misrule in the Indian parts of Kashmir, which drew Pakistan's support. Played out in the international context of a fading Soviet Union, uprisings in Eastern Europe, and the Palestinian Intifada, the crisis ended, with some American facilitation, when both sides recognized that no significant military activity was likely.

—The 1999 Kargil conflict originated when Pakistani-supported *jihadis* (Islamic militants) and regular units moved across the Line of Control (LOC)—the de facto border—in the contested state of Jammu and Kashmir. The two militaries fought from May to July in the mountainous Kargil sector northeast of Srinagar, Kashmir's capital. Tensions mounted over the question of when and how India might escalate the mini-war, which put the world on alert since both India and Pakistan had tested nuclear devices in May 1998 and subsequently declared themselves to be nuclear weapon states. The crisis was defused, and significant escalation across the LOC was averted in part because of U.S. President Bill Clinton's personal intervention.

—The 2001–02 border confrontation, from December 2001 to October 2002, was precipitated by a massive Indian military mobilization following two major terrorist attacks. India and Pakistan were close to war on at least two occasions, although no organized fighting took place. The crisis ended when India announced the withdrawal of its forces from the border and claimed that its demands on Pakistan had been met; the United States contributed to its resolution in some measure, through sustained talks with both India and Pakistan.

These crises have important global implications, the first and most alarming being their nuclear dimension. The nuclear tests of 1998 and declaration of nuclear power by both states persuaded many outsiders that South Asia, especially Kashmir, had become a nuclear flashpoint and the most "dangerous place in the world."[1] Second, the crises contradict several important theories of international politics, notably the notion that democracies and nuclear weapons states are reluctant to go to war against each other. Third, in view of India's and Pakistan's respective positions as a rising Asian power and a militarily powerful Islamic state—and hence their potential role in shaping the world order—their management of these crises could serve as one indicator of their future relationship with one another as well as with other states. And fourth, these crises yield some important doctrinal and strategic lessons, not only for the two South Asian states but also for other regions and potential pairs of nuclear-armed rivals. Indeed, South Asia provides at least three, perhaps more, examples of crisis behavior between nuclear-armed states, to add to the few case studies of such behavior thus far.

An objective record of these crises and analysis of their consequences can go a long way toward improving "learning" from crisis to crisis and enhance the institutional memory of regional policymakers and also outsiders. An understanding of these still-recent events will help the policy community and wider public, present and future, avoid repeating the mistakes of others, accepting the possibility that they may always invent new mistakes.

Whether India, Pakistan, and sympathetic outside powers actually "learn" the lessons of each crisis, they cannot help but be influenced by the experience of having gone through four different ones. As Kierkegaard wrote, history is lived forward but understood backward: the four crises form part of the very identities of India and Pakistan, identities that have changed since they became nuclear weapons states, especially since the Kargil and 2001–02 crises.

Several scholars, notably Sumit Ganguly and Devin Hagerty, have taken a somewhat different approach to India-Pakistan crises, expanding the list of critical events.[2] They include Pakistan's claim in 1982 that India might launch a preventive attack against Islamabad's nuclear program and the diplomatic flap surrounding the 1998 nuclear tests. While these events are discussed in this book, we do not consider them as critical as the four crises of 1987, 1990, 1999, and 2001–02.

This book is our fourth in a series of studies of crises in South Asia. The first two dealt with the Brasstacks crisis and the Kashmir-related 1990 crisis; the third, a report written under the auspices of the United States Institute of Peace (USIP), examined the Kargil crisis of 1999 and the subsequent border confrontation crisis of 2001–02.[3] The singular feature of these studies is our attempt to both reflect and reconcile different perspectives of the same crises. The Brasstacks project followed a chapter-by-chapter, country-by-country approach, informed by the methodology of Akira Kurosawa's film, *Rashomon*, in which the same incident is narrated in different ways by different observers from different vantage points.[4] In tackling the Kashmir-related 1990 crisis, we had more ambitiously sought to mold our various perspectives into a synthesized account. The USIP study reverted to the format of the Brasstacks book.

In this volume, we summarize the regional conflict and attempts at peacemaking (chapter 2), synthesize the separate perspectives on each crisis (chapters 3–6), and then examine the subsequent peace process and policy implications (chapter 7). Box 2-1 (in chapter 2) provides a chronology of the four crises and other important regional events. The rest of this chapter sets out a taxonomy of crisis and a set of related questions, which together provide a comparative framework for examining South Asia's multiple crises.

What Is a Crisis?

The term "crisis" derives from the classical Greek *krisis*, meaning "judgment" or "decision." Some trace its sense of impending danger to the Chinese pictogram for "crisis," erroneously believed to contain the symbols for "danger" and "opportunity." Without doubt, the 1962 Cuban missile crisis reinforced this meaning of the term, linking it to a period of acute tension between states that threatens to break out into major war. As defined by scholars Glenn Snyder and Paul Diesing, "an international crisis is a sequence of interactions between the governments of two or more sovereign states in severe conflict, short of actual war, but involving the perception of a dangerously high probability of war."[5]

Crises need to be distinguished from "emergencies." In the social sciences, the latter term, along with the related form "complex emergency" introduced in the late 1980s, usually carries humanitarian overtones. Furthermore, writes the distinguished social scientist Craig Calhoun, "the idea of crisis suggests a determinant turning point that, commonly, the idea of emergency does not. Emergency suggests instead a similar urgency, but not a similar directionality or imminent resolution."[6]

As interpreted by policymakers, crises begin with an action or threatened action by a given party that could imperil an important national interest, a country's status in the international community, or their own office, thus creating an environment of high risk. In such circumstances, they believe time is of the essence in their response, which makes crisis decisions qualitatively different from their other decisions.[7]

Thus far a comprehensive definition has eluded scholars, most of whom have tackled single cases rather than attempting to *compare* crises. As Charles Hermann pointed out in one of the earliest and most sophisticated crisis studies, the term can refer to the state of mind of decisionmakers at a particular moment as well as to the potential consequences for a political system or even for the international order.[8] In Hermann's view, "a crisis is a situation that creates an abrupt or sudden change in one or more of the basic systemic variables," such variables being an alliance, or a state-actor, or the international system itself.[9]

For Michael Brecher and Jonathan Wilkenfeld, a crisis is the perception by seniormost decisionmakers of "a threat to one or more basic values, along with an awareness of finite time for response to the value threat, and a heightened probability of involvement in military hostilities."[10] When two or more adversaries are in such a situation and engage in disruptive interaction, Brecher notes, there is an international crisis.[11] By these definitions, surprise is not a necessary component of crisis, and the time span involved is only very loosely of a limited nature (perhaps months or even a year), because the key determinant of an international crisis is a heightened perception of the possibility of an armed clash between two (or more) states. Brecher also merges state and international crises into a unified model consisting of four stages or periods: onset, escalation, deescalation, and post-crisis consequences. Movement from one stage to another, he says, is a change in level that can be triggered by an act, event, or environmental development that alters (that is, increases or decreases) an actor's perception of threat, time, or likelihood of war. Using this model and his crisis data set, Brecher investigated the impact of factors such as decisionmaker stress, regime type, and geography on how crises unfold.

Another useful distinction to consider, noted by Israeli scholar Yehezkal Dror, is that between policymaking in an adverse environment and policymaking in normal circumstances.[12] On that basis, the India-Pakistan relationship might be considered a protracted conflict of the sort between the United States and the Soviet Union during the cold war and between the Arabs and Israelis since 1947. While a protracted conflict does not equate with a crisis or a war, it does contribute to the "proneness" to crisis or war.

Needless to say, one cannot ignore the effect of new technologies, especially the globalization of media (such as CNN, Al-Jazeera, and the BBC), on the perceptions and management of international crises. These developments have revolutionized not only the reporting of international crises but also the interactions of governments in crises. According to Carnes Lord, "*The* problem of the post–Cold War security environment from the perspective of crisis management may be said to be the relaxed level of tensions between all the major powers. The effect of this is to widen the gap between normal and crisis modes of national security decisionmaking, making it more difficult both to anticipate crises and to take them seriously as they develop."[13] However, he also points out, in South Asia the incentives to do so are lower, and the United States cannot be expected to bring to the table a comparably sophisticated strategic assessment. As demonstrated by U.S. intelligence's surprise at India's nuclear tests in the spring of 1998, little can be taken for granted. Lord's conclusion may be less relevant in a post-9/11 environment since American interest in the region has grown dramatically as a result of the tests, 9/11, the 2001–02 crisis, a new strategic engagement with New Delhi, a revived one with Pakistan, and a military presence in Afghanistan.

Some attempts have also been made to *measure* a crisis quantitatively and qualitatively. Brecher and Wilkenfeld's International Crisis Behavior (ICB) project included accounts of 412 crises that occurred between 1929 and 1992, a list of their sources, a table of the beginning and end dates for each crisis, the participants (including third parties involved), and the highest level of violence.[14] The authors examined several other variables as well, including which state initiated or "triggered" the crisis, the triggering event, the most salient threat perceived during the crisis, the principal conflict-management technique employed by each participant, the type of outcome, and each state's satisfaction with the outcome.

Important data have also been compiled by the Correlates of War (COW) Militarized Interstate Dispute (MID) project.[15] To ensure high reliability, the COW project followed strict operational definitions of indicators. For example, its definitions of militarized disputes (and militarized interstate crises) are based on the observed presence of threats, displays, or uses of force, and its variables are limited to directly observable phenomena: beginning and end dates, participants, incidents depicting the threat, display or use of force, highest level of force used, and outcome.

Employing a comparative approach, we drew upon such data where possible to measure crisis intensity and duration.[16] We used an index that measures press coverage in two English-language papers in the United States, India, and Pakistan (see chapter 3 and the appendix). In detecting the presence of a crisis, we have also taken into consideration the views of contemporaneous policymakers and political elites, an approach that captures different judgments of whether there was a crisis, its severity, and the policy implications for the states involved.

Crisis Taxonomy

A book on the evolution, resolution, and consequences of regional crises cannot avoid some discussion of their taxonomy. We distinguish between simple and compound crises, for example, a notion introduced in our earlier study of the events of 1990. A simple crisis is one in which a commanding strategic idea prompts one side or the other to take deliberate, perhaps provocative, action. By contrast, compound crises grow out of several simultaneous subcrises, which in concert lead policymakers in one or more countries to believe that they are on the verge of a real crisis and hence to respond accordingly.

One notable quality of simple crises is that the side taking the initiative may or may not intend to create a crisis, and furthermore that the result may be of a different magnitude than anticipated, as in some of the crises examined in this book. In a compound crisis, one side or the other (or both) may reach a point at which they conclude that even though no major crisis was intended, there is some advantage in pressing forward. The classic fictional depiction of such an event is found in Stanley Kubrick's film *Dr. Strangelove,* in which a U.S. Air Force general sees an inadvertent crisis as an opportunity to destroy the Soviet Union's nuclear capability. As this book shows, South Asia has had unintended crises that have been overtaken by events, with things getting out of hand in a near replay of the "Guns of August" syndrome.

It is well to remember that compound crises result from a combination of many variables or events—often domestic political events, but also intelligence errors, systemic perceptual distortions, technical breakdowns, and accidents. Compound crises would thus seem more likely to occur under inefficient and highly complex political and military systems. In "tightly coupled" political and military systems, observes Scott Sagan, a break in one link of the chain might trigger a catastrophic event—perhaps an accidental release of a nuclear weapon, or even a nuclear war.[17] However, very loose systems have their risks as well, and the cumulative effect of several small mistakes in a loosely coupled political/strategic system can also lead to a crisis, as may have been the case in 1990.

For policy purposes, it is important to know whether a crisis is inadvertent or deliberate, and also whether it is likely to have wider ramifications. Different kinds of crises are also more (or less) apt to draw outsiders into playing the role of go-between or facilitator. Generally, compound crises can be more readily defused if properly understood, although figuring out exactly what went wrong may be exceedingly difficult. To complicate their resolution, crises are not necessarily bilateral. In the several India-Pakistan crises over Kashmir, for example, various Kashmiri groups (on both sides of the LOC) have been parties to the crisis, which on closer examination are not monolithic entities either.[18] Once able to distinguish between a simple and compound crisis, policymakers would surely be in a better position to develop a strategy to ameliorate or terminate it.

Some types of crises, as just mentioned, draw the attention of the international community. The most alarming aspect of South Asia's crises to outsiders has been the nuclearization of India and Pakistan, which from 1990 onward has made all of the region's crises inherently "nuclear," whatever their origin. Some outsiders have also been stirred to respond to crises involving terrorism, religious identity, or sectarianism. Turmoil in Kashmir after 1989, for instance, persuaded radical Islamists to place the region on their agenda and drew jihadis from around the world into the conflict. Terrorism has had less impact than nuclearization, however, with the result that India was initially unsuccessful in persuading outsiders to see it as a legitimate basis for a crisis response—particularly during the 2001–02 crisis.

Seven Lines of Inquiry

The case studies of this book follow seven lines of inquiry. However, the questions are handled somewhat differently in each case, as appropriate to their relevance to the structure of the crisis.

Origin and Typology

When we categorize these crises by origin, development, and termination, we find the crisis of 1990 stands apart from the others: it was a surprise to those involved and comprised several elements, whereas the others were more the product of calculation or a response to a dramatic episode. This line of investigation raises a number of questions. To what degree did these crises have a common origin, such as the participants' long-standing strategic rivalry or their Kashmir dispute? Were some more idiosyncratic than others; and did different factors, such as domestic political developments or the emergence of new technologies or doctrines, play a different role in each crisis? As the crises evolved, how did decisionmakers, operating under time constraints, identify specific political and strategic concerns, and what actions did they think were necessary to protect and advance these important interests even as they were calculating the gains and risks that might flow from crisis escalation? Finally, why did these crises end? Was it because policymakers became exhausted, outsiders intervened, or the parties involved arrived at a calculated assessment of gains and losses?

In brief, we are interested in whether these four crises followed similar or different trajectories. If crises have different origins, and perhaps different life cycles, are different strategies available to anticipate or understand them, and to formulate policies to resolve them?

Perception and Crisis

Perceptions of these crises differed across India, Pakistan, and other states and in some cases changed as the crisis evolved. For example, some regional policymakers railed against the characterization of South Asia as the most dangerous place in the world or Kashmir as a "nuclear flashpoint," whereas others were quick to apply such terms after only a single event had occurred. Since the four crises took place over a relatively short period, a comparative analysis could lead to a more refined theory of crisis and make it possible to recognize an actual "flashpoint." Suppose that one or both parties in a crisis differ as to the seriousness of the events at hand, and that outsiders view them still differently. If there is a "flashpoint," however defined, does it have discrete implications for the detection and management of a crisis in such a region?

The Strategic Environment

These four crises took place in the context of *three* different international environments: (a) for Brasstacks, the backdrop was the cold war; (b) for the 1990 and Kargil conflicts, it was the immediate post–cold war period, and (c) for the border confrontation crisis, it was the post-9/11 world. Did the changing international environment have a direct bearing on these crises? Specifically, were they connected in any way with America's changing relations? In 1987 Washington was a close ally of Pakistan, but by 1990 it had distanced itself from the region. Then in 1999, after the nuclear tests, it began a new rapprochement with India, and by 2001–02 it again saw Islamabad as an important ally, this time in the "war on terrorism."

"Going Nuclear"

Another important line of inquiry pertains to the nuclear factor. These crises took place at very different stages of South Asia's nuclearization: Brasstacks (1987), *before* India and Pakistan had manufactured nuclear weapons; the 1990 crisis, *just as* both countries were beginning to develop crude nuclear devices; and the 1999 and 2001–02 crises, *after* both had declared, tested, and perhaps deployed nuclear weapons. Several of these crises involved the threat of the use of nuclear weapons, and one—Brasstacks—had a major impact on nuclear planning in the region. Did nuclear weapons lead to any of these crises or cause it to intensify? Did they help to resolve the crisis or temper state behavior? How did the introduction of nuclear weapons shape outsiders' perceptions of South Asia as a crisis zone and thus their involvement? Also, did the possession of nuclear weapons enhance the political authority of the governments that controlled them, and how were nuclear weapons (and missiles) symbolically deployed by India and Pakistan?

Some other factors to consider here are the fear of conventional retaliation, the costs of escalation, obstacles to increasing the ante created by outsiders, and policymakers' inherent cultural, moral, or political resistance to intensifying the crisis. It is also important to determine whether the crises precipitated a process of *learning* about the strategic character of nuclear weapons, and how this learning affected the course of the crises. The great paradox surrounding nuclear weapons is that it is very hard even to imagine them being used, yet their effectiveness as instruments of deterrence depends on the credibility of a state's capability (and willingness) to employ them. How do decisionmakers and strategic communities come to learn this ground truth of the nuclear era? Did the crises accelerate this learning process?

Further, how did these crises shape Indian and Pakistani attitudes toward their obligations as a nuclear weapons power? If an international norm regarding such obligations exists, it does not countenance threats, confrontation with other nuclear weapons states, or a provocative policy toward states without such weapons. Equally important, it suggests active engagement with the arms control process and a commitment to transparency.

Limited War and Escalation

South Asia is clearly a useful test-bed for theorizing about the transition from crisis to conventional and nuclear conflict and about escalation control. Events there seem to have followed the cold war model of deep and persistent conflict, nuclearization, and limited war. Despite the apparent danger that India-Pakistan crises might cross the nuclear threshold, the idea that limited wars can be fought within the framework of nuclear deterrence has gained currency in India. According to George Fernandes, India's defense minister at the time of two of the crises, "Pakistan did hold out a nuclear threat during the Kargil War last year. But it had not absorbed the real meaning of nuclearisation; that it can deter only the use of nuclear weapons, but not all and any war. . . . [S]o the issue was not that war had been made obsolete by nuclear weapons, and that covert war by proxy was the only option, but that conventional war remained feasible though with definite limitations."[19]

India and Pakistan have conducted proxy wars and sub rosa operations against each other and fought a limited war. Hence the widespread convictions regarding the irrationality of the other side has not dampened the belief that limited conflicts can be fought and will not escalate to general war and a nuclear exchange. Is this optimism justified? Did nuclear weapons act as a deterrent, inhibiting the two nations from escalating their conflict to all-out war? Is there, as some have argued, a strategic space for conventional conflict between nuclear use and low-intensity conflict?

Specifically, what do these cases reveal about India's and Pakistan's understanding of the relationship between nuclear and conventional weapons, especially about their conception of the escalatory process—how many rungs do they see on the escalatory ladder, in what order, and pertaining to what risks? How do they view "firebreaks" or even "redlines"? Although to outsiders the two may appear to be a tightly coupled nuclear pair willing to rush up the escalation ladder once a conflict begins, both seem confident that they can manipulate and manage this process, that they understand each other well, and that escalation is controllable.

Politics and Decisionmaking

The often-blurred link between domestic politics and foreign policy also merits attention. What impact did domestic politics have on the origin or evolution of the four crises? Did thc crises in turn affect domestic politics?

During the research for this book, we often heard key decisionmakers complain that they "were driven by events." Was this true of *all* of the parties to the crises, and what do these crises reveal about national decisionmaking styles? Who actually made the decisions during these crises? Was the crisis the product of a calculated decision initially focused on strategic or tactical goals? Did closed and restricted decisionmaking invite errors of perception and analysis? Did the decisionmaking system of military-dominated Pakistan differ significantly from that of civilian-dominated India? In a crisis, the quality and timeliness of intelligence is disproportionately important—how good was Indian and Pakistani intelligence, and that of other countries, notably the United States? Answers to these questions might inform the long-standing academic debate over the conditions under which democracies go to war, especially since one of these crises (Kargil, 1999) did involve a limited war.

Policy Implications

Finally, did these crises make it easier for India and Pakistan to embark upon a process of normalization? Obviously, the lesson a state "learns" from a crisis may not necessarily be the right one or may not be one that advances its own security without creating a more unstable or insecure environment. Did India and Pakistan learn the right lessons, or does South Asia's nuclear balance remain fragile—a point in dispute between American and South Asian security analysts? Since the two countries remain at odds, one or the other (or conceivably both) must have learned the wrong lessons from the 1998 tests and subsequent events. All in all, some might be tempted to ask whether it is even realistic to expect generic "one-size-fits-all" recommendations for crisis resolution and management that transcend the banal and the obvious.

CHAPTER TWO

South Asia's Crises

South Asia has had more than its share of crises and wars, their causes ranging from national identity and irredentism to mutual meddling in each other's politics, the unfinished business of a botched partition, and conflicting territorial claims. Some, as discussed later in this book, were affected by India's and Pakistan's gradual nuclearization. Also notable, few of the major clashes were of a bilateral nature; the United States, in particular, played a steadily increasing role as a conflict manager, attempting to defuse crises and bring the wars to a quick conclusion. These and other factors make for a complicated crisis history marked by an assortment of events beyond the four of central concern in this volume.

Other Conflicts

Of the crises that occurred outside the India-Pakistan context, several involved the use of armed force and a few did not.

—In 1948 India absorbed two princely states, Junagadh and Hyderabad, when their rulers hesitated to sign the instrument of accession (both had a Muslim ruler and a majority Hindu population) and it appeared that Hyderabad might seek independent status. These actions put considerable strain on India-Pakistan relations.

—In December 1961 Prime Minister Jawaharlal Nehru ordered the Indian army to seize the Portuguese colony of Goa in response to strong domestic pressures to eliminate this last vestige of European colonialism on Indian soil (France had peacefully yielded up its tiny colony of Pondicherry).

—In late 1962 Chinese forces swept away Indian army units in the Aksai Chin region of Kashmir and the North East Frontier Agency (NEFA) after India's probing along the contested border. When New Delhi sought Western military assistance, the U.S. government considered, but rejected, the idea of using nuclear weapons should there be a second Chinese attack. The United States and Great Britain endeavored to mediate in Kashmir, but without success. Although China returned much of the territory it had seized and interim agreements were reached in 1993, 1996, 2003, and 2005, the India-China border and associated territory remain in dispute.

—In 1974 India's "peaceful nuclear explosion" triggered widespread concern about the prospect of nuclear proliferation and led directly to American legislation aimed at India.

—In 1975 Sikkim, a semi-independent Himalayan kingdom, was incorporated into the Indian union in response to a referendum and strong Indian pressure.

—Between 1979 and 1988 the first contemporary Afghan war was fought on Pakistan's borders in reaction to the Soviet invasion and occupation of Afghanistan. With the strong support of Pakistan and the United States, anti-Soviet forces gained the upper hand, but in a subsequent factional conflict, power shifted to the Taliban. A second Afghan war was fought in 2001–02 when the United States returned to remove the Taliban and al-Qaeda.

—In 1987 there was a minor crisis at Somdurong Chu, along the disputed McMahon Line between India and China. Chinese troops, reinforced by an expanded presence in Tibet, once again faced the Indian army. India initiated Exercise Checkerboard in March, and China vehemently protested. Indian officials made light of the event, and a confrontation was averted. Strong American and Soviet diplomatic representations to both sides urged restraint, but the full story of the disengagement of the two sides has yet to be made public.

—In 1987–88 India dispatched an Indian "peacekeeping force" (IPKF) to the northern areas of Sri Lanka. Originally intended to disarm the rebels, the IPKF came under attack by the Tamil Tigers, a group that it had once supported. Unprepared militarily or psychologically, it retreated in humiliation from what came to be known as India's Vietnam. In perhaps a related event, in May 1991 vengeful Tamils murdered former prime minister Rajiv Gandhi in a suicide attack.

—In the summer of 1998 first India, and then Pakistan, tested a number of nuclear weapons, even as they were engaged in competitive missile tests. Washington imposed sanctions on both countries, which were soon relaxed by the Clinton administration and then lifted by the George W. Bush administration.

The India-Pakistan Conflicts

India and Pakistan have had approximately fifteen conflicts and crises of varying severity (box 2-1). They can also be categorized according to source: some are rooted in border disputes, some in nuclear concerns, and some in ethnic, religious, and irredentist issues. The dispute over Kashmir is a special case because of its many facets and long history (it has been both a cause and consequence of India-Pakistan hostility for more than fifty years). In addition, the crises can be divided into minor incidents and those short of war (or in the case of Kargil, a limited war).

The Wars

In the period 1947–87 India and Pakistan fought three sizable wars and experienced three major border clashes; there were also innumerable exchanges of fire across the Line of Control (LOC).

1947–48. Between October 1947 and January 1, 1949, India and Pakistan fought a small-scale war in Kashmir. With British officers present in both armies and the international community urging restraint, the conflict ended in a tactical and strategic stalemate. Approximately 1,500 soldiers were killed on each side, a small figure when compared with the estimated million or so who perished during the partition of British India and the incorporation of the Indian states into India and Pakistan. This mini-war had the effect of militarizing relations between the two dominions. Each sought outside support and allies and for several years pressed its case in the United Nations, where the dispute remains.

1965. By 1965 India appeared (in Pakistani eyes) to be pulling ahead in the regional arms race, thanks in part to increased support from the United States, Great Britain, and the Soviet Union. When Pakistan tried without success to foster an armed uprising of the Kashmiri people, India decided to cross the international border with regular forces, and the two states fought a small-scale land, sea, and air war, which featured the first-ever dogfights between supersonic jet aircraft. There were few civilian casualties, but approximately 3,000 and 3,800 soldiers were killed in India and Pakistan, respectively. The military action was inconclusive but left the eastern and western wings of Pakistan at odds, contributing to the growth of separatist sentiments in the east that led directly to another war between India and Pakistan.

Box 2-1. *India-Pakistan Conflicts*

1947–49: First Kashmir War

Proximate origin and type

Escalation to war between India and Pakistan after raiders enter Jammu and Kashmir; a struggle for control over Kashmir state.

Resolution

None; semi-permanent division of the state; international reconciliation efforts ineffective; the oldest conflict still before the United Nations.

Consequence

Still in dispute.

April 1965: dispute over Rann of Kutch

Proximate origin and type

Reached crisis stage; limited use of force; border dispute.

Resolution

Resolved in 1968 by International Court of Justice.

Consequence

Followed immediately by India-Pakistan war in September 1965.

September 1965: India-Pakistan war

Proximate origin and type

Initiated by Pakistan in an attempt to contain rising Indian power and internationalize Kashmir dispute; strategic preemption.

Resolution

Military standstill; U.S.-U.K. pressure to stop fighting, followed by partly successful Soviet effort at mediation in Tashkent.

Consequence

Contributed to East Pakistani resentment; no change in status of Kashmir; captured territory returned by both sides.

1971: India-Pakistan war

Proximate origin and type

Indian support for East Pakistani separatist movement.

Resolution

Military standstill in west; complete Indian victory in east, followed by ceasefire; U.S. and Soviet engagement with India and Pakistan.

Consequence

Strategic division of Pakistan; independent state of Bangladesh established normal relations with India and subsequently with Pakistan.

1974: Indian "peaceful nuclear explosion"

Proximate origin and type
Covert Indian program to build a nuclear device culminated in one test.

Resolution
None; severe U.S. and international sanctions against India.

Consequence
Indian program recessed until late 1980s, stimulated Pakistani bomb program; U.S.-Indian strains resolved only by 2005 India-U.S. agreement.

1984–present: Siachen Glacier dispute

Proximate origin and type
Indian military commander seizes glacier.

Resolution
Unresolved, but escalation limited by human and material costs and secondary strategic importance of territory; agreements concluded in 1989 and 1992, not endorsed by political leadership.

Consequence
Siachen importance largely symbolic; many studies show that technical verification of a pullback is possible; also schemes to turn Siachen into a high-altitude "peace park" have been suggested.

1984–92: separatist Sikh "Khalistan" movement

Proximate origin and type
Some Sikh dissidents launched a separatist movement; Indira Gandhi assassinated; some Sikh army units revolted.

Resolution
Tough Indian measures against separatist movement; Pakistan reduces support for Khalistanis.

Consequence
Restoration of normalcy by 1992.

1984–85: Pakistan suspicion of Indian attacks on nuclear facilities

Proximate origin and type
Threat raised with Americans by Pakistan government; atomic-radiation-release alarm.

Resolution
Indian denial; no credible evidence of preparation for an imminent attack.

Consequence
Led to a confidence-building measures (CBM) agreement not to attack nuclear facilities/installations.

(continued)

1986: suspicion of likely Indian attack on Kahuta

Proximate origin and type
Threat raised with Americans by Pakistanis; nuclear alarm.

Resolution
Denied by India; no evidence.

Consequence
Resolved at pre-crisis stage.

1987: Brasstacks

Proximate origin and type
Massive Indian military maneuver escalated into full-fledged crisis; no military action.

Resolution
India reoriented provocative military exercise; United States reassured both sides there was nothing to be alarmed about.

Consequence
Nuclear programs accelerated in India and Pakistan; no resolution of India-Pakistan tensions, but some minor CBMs agreed to.

1990: multifaceted Kashmir conflict

Proximate origin and type
Combination of domestic political weakness in both India and Pakistan; Kashmiri uprising, support by Pakistan for Kashmiri separatists; compound crisis complicated by nuclear alarm.

Resolution
Mutual realization that no significant military activity likely; U.S. intervention and reassurance to both sides.

Consequence
Led to establishment of important military CBMs regarding pre-notification of military exercises and preventing airspace violations.

1993: mounting tension

Proximate origin and type
Multiple blasts in Bombay; accusations of Pakistani culpability; subsequent atrocities in Kashmir.

Resolution
Pakistan denied role in Bombay and Kashmir episodes.

Consequence
None; repeated terrorist attacks in India in subsequent years, but cross-border movement apparently tapered off after 2002 crisis.

1998: nuclear tests

Proximate origin and type
Major diplomatic crisis after India and Pakistan tested nuclear devices and set themselves forth to be nuclear weapons states; no evidence of any threat to attack.

Resolution
Both countries sanctioned and begin extended series of negotiations with the United States about their adherence to precepts of global nonproliferation regime.

Consequence
Sanctions relaxed by Clinton; most of them lifted by Bush.

1999: Kargil mini-war

Proximate origin and type
Pakistan-sponsored jihadis and regular units occupy territory on the Indian side of the LOC; border crisis, with strategic undertones; gross Pakistan miscalculation of Indian response.

Resolution
War fought from May to July but limited to Kargil sector; American pressure on Pakistan to withdraw back to own territory behind LOC.

Consequence
LOC begins to assume permanent status.

2001–02: border confrontation

Proximate origin and type
Indian buildup of armed forces after terrorist attacks; direct pressure on Pakistan, indirect pressure on United States to force Pakistan to stop/reduce support for jihadis and terrorists.

Resolution
Lasted ten months; resolved by American pressure on Pakistan to reduce cross-border terrorist attacks and Pakistani assurances.

Consequence
Major effort to start a new peace process initiated by Prime Minister Vajpayee in April 2003; continued by Congress-led coalition since 2004–05.

1971. In terms of outcome, the 1971 war reached a new order of magnitude: it led to the vivisection of Pakistan and the creation of a new state, Bangladesh. From India's perspective, this may have been a partial victory, since the government achieved its objective of returning several million East Pakistani refugees who had fled to India. For Pakistan, however, it was a traumatic conclusion, amounting to a complete defeat.

In late 1971 the Indian army moved into East Pakistan and joined with local separatists and guerilla fighters. India had been covertly aiding these groups for many months, and the final battles were quick and decisive, with 2,000–3,000 Indian and 8,000 Pakistani casualties and more than 90,000 Pakistani army prisoners of war. There were also a number of civilian casualties, most of them a by-product of the savage fighting between Pakistani forces and East Pakistanis. Estimates of the civilian casualties, which tend to be notoriously unreliable generally, range from the hundreds of thousands to 1 million or 2 million. Pakistan insisted that India violated international law when it crossed into East Pakistan, with the malevolent intention of dividing Pakistan. This provided a major impetus for Pakistan to take up a nuclear weapons program. Furthermore, the postwar chaos made it possible for Zulfikar Ali Bhutto to come to power. Ironically, Bangladeshi history gives India scant credit for that country's creation. The Bangladesh interpretation of events is that the Bengalis fought their own liberation war, and that India provided assistance only toward the end.

The Border Conflicts

Although separated by twenty years, the border clashes in the Rann of Kutch (1965) and Siachen (1984–89) have much in common. They were both fought with limited means for limited objectives in a geographically confined area, from which the clashes take their name.[1] They also share some features with the Kargil crisis (see chapter 5).

THE RANN OF KUTCH, 1965. Like Kashmir, the Rann of Kutch (an area of roughly 3,500 square miles) became a disputed territory after partition. Even before partition, its boundary was not clearly defined and the region was a bone of contention between the princely state of Kutch and the British Indian province of Sindh.[2] India and Pakistan inherited this problem and first exchanged diplomatic notes on the issue in 1948; since then, it has been part of an all too familiar blame game between the two countries.

The Rann is a marshland adjacent to the Arabian Sea.[3] Viewing the marshes as a landlocked sea because of flooding during the monsoons, Pakistan argued that the boundary should lie in the middle rather than along the northern edge and in 1954 staked a claim to half the area. India countered that a marshland was not a sea and hence the boundary should remain in its northern location. On April 9, 1965, fighting broke out between probing patrols sent out by Pakistani and Indian ground troops positioned in the area, rapidly escalating to a brigade-sized battle. On April 27, India withdrew its troops, by then in danger of becoming isolated by monsoon flooding. At the end of June, the two sides agreed to a formal cease-fire, largely because of the diplomatic efforts of Prime Minister Harold Wilson of Britain. Washington opted to stay out of these negotiations since Pakistan's use of American-supplied weapons and equipment had raised some question about whether this was a transgression of their terms of supply by the United States. Following the cease-fire, Pakistan and India agreed to submit the dispute to arbitration and later accepted the award made in 1968 by the tribunal that adjudicated the matter.

SIACHEN, 1984. The second major border clash took place in 1984 on the world's highest battlefield: the Siachen Glacier and environs, situated at the extreme northwestern edge of the subcontinent south of the Chinese border at an altitude of more than 22,000 feet. Temperatures in the area reach minus 40° Centigrade. The conflict over Siachen (the "place of roses") is rooted in the UN-supervised Karachi Agreement of 1949, with the support of the Simla Agreement of 1972, not to extend the India-Pakistan cease-fire line (later the LOC) north of map grid point NJ 9842 on the assumption that human habitation was not feasible beyond that point. This left a large stretch between NJ 9842 and the Chinese border undemarcated. Before 1984 neither India nor Pakistan had any permanent presence in the area.

In the 1970s and early 1980s a number of international mountaineering expeditions climbed Siachen via Pakistan. When the Indians discovered this through international mountaineering journals, they launched Operation Meghdoot (Cloud Messenger) on April 13, 1984, prompting Pakistan to deploy its own troops. While the fighting has been limited (many more soldiers have been killed on each side by frostbite and accident than in combat), the two parties remain at a military and political stalemate. Estimates of combat deaths vary widely depending on the source, but at least 1,500 Pakistani and 2,000 Indian soldiers have died at elevations of 18,000 to 24,000 feet. The Indian army is unable to advance from its position on the glacier, and the Pakistan army is unable to dislodge the Indians. The number of deployed troops is unclear and may well be in the thousands, though probably less than 10,000 on each side. Siachen is perhaps the most striking example of India-Pakistan miscalculation and misjudgment: such a remote region at that elevation seems an unlikely battlefield for a major conflict. Both sides have expanded their support infrastructure, however, and the possibility that Siachen will be a battleground cannot be ruled out.

Pakistan asserts that international maps and even statements by Indian officials—notably a speech in parliament after the Simla Summit by then foreign minister Swaran Singh—indicate the glacier falls within Pakistani-administered territory.[4] The Indian government maintains that the accession of the Maharaja of Kashmir and the subsequent Karachi Agreement give it control of the glacier. It also insists that the Actual Ground Position Line (AGPL), meaning the current line of occupation of the Siachen Glacier by India and Pakistan on the ground, be recognized in some fashion before troops from both sides withdraw to mutually agreed positions.

According to Robert Wirsing, who has studied the dispute in detail, there is little evidence to suggest either of the parties was the aggressor in Siachen: "Precisely who shot first is probably impossible to determine. Which of the two armed forces had the right to be on the glacier—because the question of legitimacy of the two sides' territories claims has never been submitted to impartial adjudication—is a matter obviously open to disagreement."[5] At the same time, Wirsing notes, "ample evidence points to the Indian armed forces as being the first to establish permanent posts on the glacier and that they had prepared themselves long and well for the task."[6] The principal actor in precipitating the crisis was an Indian lieutenant general, M. L. Chibber, then head of India's Northern Command, but while Chibber's account of the buildup as a military venture may be accurate, it clearly had some political sanction in that it received the prior approval of Indira Gandhi.[7]

India appears to have had no clear idea of what strategic advantage it saw in possessing the glacier. Subsequent explanations that Pakistan had to be stopped from coming down to Leh from Baltistan/Northern Areas are ex post facto rationalizations, although some officials may well have believed if the glacier went to Pakistan, it would create a link between the Baltistan/Northern Areas in Pakistan and the Shaksgam Valley ceded by Pakistan to China. Strategically, India claims that it needed to control the glacier because it was a gateway to Ladakh, the Buddhist part of Jammu and Kashmir, the state contiguous to the disputed border with China. Pakistan wanted Siachen on the grounds that India could use it to deny them access to the Northern Areas. Both claims are greatly exaggerated; the simple truth is that each side feared the other would gain control of the area and they could not agree on a mechanism whereby the dispute could be peacefully resolved.

At a meeting in 1985 Prime Minister Rajiv Gandhi and President Zia ul-Haq agreed in principle to discuss Siachen. By 1993 six rounds of foreign secretary talks had taken place. The fifth round, in 1989, appeared to reach a breakthrough, but it was never announced, perhaps because Rajiv Gandhi and India's Congress Party may have felt that any perception or suggestion of weakness could affect their electoral prospects in the general elections to be held later in the year.

There was another attempt to resolve the Siachen dispute at a meeting of foreign secretaries in 1992, culminating in an announcement that troops would not only be pulled back but that the glacier would be demilitarized by the end of October 1992. No move was made to this end, however. After the onset of the peace process in 2003, talks were again held, and in 2005 the two sides announced (unspecified) progress on Siachen. Remarkably, both have agreed to resolve Siachen yet cannot see eye to eye on implementation. Siachen is vastly complicated by the fact that it lies within the territory of the contested state of Jammu and Kashmir. Since this location has a logistics advantage for India and thus strengthens its relative position—not to mention the fact that Siachen is closely linked to questions of status, prestige, and honor, as well as the larger Kashmir problem—a breakthrough does not seem likely in the absence of basic political decisions on both sides, even as talks continue.

Parenthetically, Siachen has been the subject of a number of studies, some sponsored by the Cooperative Monitoring Center (CMC) of Sandia National Nuclear Laboratory in Albuquerque, New Mexico.[8] The CMC website is now the repository of several detailed studies of how Siachen might be turned into a science park, how the two armies can gracefully exit the scene, and how their strategic concerns can be accommodated.

The Neonuclear Crises

During the 1980s Pakistan's nuclear installations raised alarm on three occasions, and at the time of the 1998 nuclear tests there was again talk of a preemptive Indian strike. Some of these events have been treated as crises in their own right.[9]

As early as 1982, reports in the American press suggested that India might attack Pakistan to destroy its nuclear facilities.[10] These reports were by and large inspired by the example of the Israeli attack on the Osirak reactor in 1981, which also had a powerful impact on Pakistani thinking. There is no evidence, however, of plans for such an attack, although Indian officials certainly discussed it and Pakistan definitely raised it with the Americans.

Two years later, in 1984, a minor diplomatic crisis erupted owing to suspicions of an impending Indian attack on the nuclear facility in Kahuta. Citing intelligence reports from Canada and Europe, Pakistan believed that Israel was also planning an attack on Kahuta. The Pakistani military leadership concluded that Israel could not go it alone and would need the assistance of Indians or of Soviet forces, then in Afghanistan. In a speech to Pakistan's federal legislature, the Majlis-i-Shura, on July 12, 1984, Zia made public the suspicion that India might attack Kahuta, repeating it in an interview with the *Wall Street Journal* and adding that India might launch an air strike as the Israelis had in Iraq.[11]

A very hawkish speech by Rajiv Gandhi, then a senior official in the Congress Party, might have made the situation worse, although he did state that Pakistani military maneuvers were undoubtedly a prelude to an invasion of Kashmir and called on India to issue a stern response. Alleging that Pakistan was using its army and air force exercises to influence the internal situation in Kashmir, he openly criticized both the state government of Farooq Abdullah and the governor of Jammu and Kashmir (his uncle, B. K. Nehru) for failing to properly assess intelligence reports on these maneuvers. Rajiv even predicted the spot at which the "invasion" would come: the "Chicken's Neck" near Jammu, "which is our most vulnerable point on the border."[12]

Approached by Pakistan with the intelligence information, Washington checked with Israel, which assured Pakistan that it was not planning any such attack. However, senior American officials (who had developed a close relationship with Pakistan because of the joint American-Pakistani efforts to evict the Soviet forces from Afghanistan) viewed the reports and the rhetoric with alarm. They concluded in mid-1984 that a war between India and Pakistan was possible, or at least that an Indian attack on Pakistan was imminent. They based their assessment on two factors.

First, the location of relevant aircraft—particularly the twin-engined Jaguar fighter-bombers that India had acquired from Britain in the 1970s to serve as "deep-penetration strike aircraft"—was uncertain since American intelligence had "lost sight of them" because of monsoon cover. Their chief operational feature, as discussed in India at that time, was that they could reach any part of Pakistan, deliver an appreciable bomb load, and return to their bases. Their acquisition had been seen as part of a larger Indian effort to achieve strategic dominance over Pakistan. Some suspected that they had been moved to forward attack bases and grew fearful of enhanced Indian military capabilities, especially when backed by doctrinal announcements of a Pakistani strategy of "offensive defense," that is, a preemptive war. Second, the suspicion of imminence was reinforced by Pakistani intelligence and military information: some from U.S. sources indicated that the Jaguars were in Kashmir practicing "toss-bombing" and would soon be redeployed for an attack on Pakistan. Others emphasized the Indian-Soviet connection, claiming that a joint pincer attack on Pakistan was in the works.

While some intelligence analysts discounted the possibility of an attack, a policy-level review took a graver view, and the United States engaged in conversations with both India and Pakistan to avert a crisis. Prime Minister Indira Gandhi promptly denied that an attack was imminent, but in ambiguous language. Subsequently, the *New York Times*, drawing on information presented to the U.S. Senate Intelligence Committee, reported that she had considered such an attack.[13] The United States soon made its position known. On September 16, 1984, its ambassador to Pakistan, Dean Hinton, told President Zia that if the United States were to see signs of an imminent Indian attack, it would notify Pakistan immediately and reaffirmed this "responsive" stance in a public lecture in Lahore. James Buckley, the U.S. under secretary of state, repeated this assurance in Islamabad. This led Indira Gandhi to seek verbal assurances from the Soviet Union, which agreed that the U.S. actions posed a threat to India and itself.

The U.S. decision to deliver an early warning to Pakistan was the one concrete outcome of this non-crisis, although there is no evidence that any such notification was ever issued. Subsequently, according to one of his closest advisers, Zia concluded that either the attack had been called off or that the intelligence had been inaccurate.[14] On the Pakistani side, there was undisguised pleasure at having faced down the Indians; A. Q. Khan, the scientist responsible for the enrichment facility at Kahuta, even boasted that his own public statement in February 1984, to the effect that Pakistan could enrich uranium, had later deterred Mrs. Gandhi from ordering an attack on Pakistan.[15]

Meanwhile, American officials were becoming more deeply involved in an attempt to prevent Pakistan from developing nuclear weapons. One of the major policy objectives of their military aid package to Pakistan was to enhance its conventional security so that it would not need to press ahead with nuclear weapons. Pakistan took the aid and bought American weapons, but also made steady progress on the covert nuclear program.

In mid-1985, the entire exercise was repeated. The scenario of an Indian attack on Kahuta again captured attention in Washington and Islamabad. Following unsubstantiated reports that Indian aircraft were flying reconnaissance missions over Kahuta in preparation for bombing it, Pakistan's minister of state for foreign affairs, Zain Noorani, warned that an attack upon the Kahuta uranium enrichment plant would be construed as an act of war.[16] Again, diplomatic representations were made to New Delhi, and (it is believed) Moscow and Beijing were included in an effort at preventive diplomacy. However, since nothing had happened in 1984, and the evidence was so circumstantial and indirect, discussion of the second "war-that-never-was" quickly dissipated within the American foreign policy bureaucracy.[17] In both cases, U.S. military intelligence was reluctant to treat these reports as firm evidence of an Indian plan to attack, while the CIA, which had its own links to Pakistani intelligence because of their joint operations in Afghanistan, seemed to be pressing the case hardest, despite the skepticism of many competent analysts.

One year later, in June 1986, a *third* diplomatic nuclear flap demonstrated Washington's great sensitivity to threats to Pakistan. Pakistani officials informed their American counterparts that the Soviet Union had issued a démarche stating Moscow would take retaliatory steps if Pakistan were to acquire a military nuclear capability. On the basis of this report, the United States delivered a tough démarche to the Soviet Union, pledging continued American support for Pakistan's integrity. Responding with some asperity, Soviet officials claimed their message to Pakistan had not been in the nature of a threat and was merely echoing American concerns about proliferation in South Asia. Subsequent conversations with Soviet scholars and officials suggest that Soviet officials may not have intended to threaten, and that Pakistan may have misinterpreted (or misrepresented?) their terminology. The whole episode quickly died down, with American officials reiterating their concern about Pakistan's nuclear program to the Pakistanis, while pledging their continued support for Pakistan against future Soviet threats. This false claim may have shaped American responses to Brasstacks one year later.

These three mini-crises were possibly triggered by calculated Pakistani alarmism, designed to put the Americans on the defensive at a moment when Washington was pressuring Islamabad to restrain its nuclear program and the two countries were closely cooperating in Afghanistan. It was a difficult balancing act. By claiming that it was under unprovoked threat from India or the Soviet Union (or the two acting together, according to some Pakistanis and Americans), Islamabad forced Washington to support it again and again and, ironically, become involved in the business of inadvertently protecting the very nuclear programs that so concerned Washington.[18]

These episodes thus fit into a larger Pakistani strategy: that of linking its own nuclear program (at the highest policy level) with an American commitment to defend Islamabad from an Indian attack or an envisaged conventional attack from Soviet forces (then based in Afghanistan). With American naval vessels (such as the USS *Vinson* and an accompanying battle group) making routine port calls in Pakistan and major U.S. forces in the vicinity, U.S. military officials wondered whether they would indeed be called upon suddenly to help Pakistan in a war. The Pakistanis repeatedly demanded strong security guarantees from Washington, arguing that they would obviate the need for a nuclear program (although the Pakistanis also maintained the fiction that their program was entirely peaceful). U.S. officials, however, were not at all inclined to provide such assistance on terms dictated by regional allies, at least at short notice and without consideration of American strategy.

Subsequently, in the aftermath of the 1998 nuclear tests, Pakistan again raised the possibility of an attack on its nuclear facilities. This time the suspects were the Israelis, and Pakistani officials went so far as to informally contact Israeli officials to determine whether Israel was indeed contemplating action against the nuclear installations of Pakistan.[19]

These incidents cannot be categorized as nuclear crises except in the sense that attacks on nuclear facilities and installations were discussed (neither state had a nuclear weapon at the time). Furthermore, India was aware that an attack on Pakistan's nuclear assets would be feckless for several operational reasons: intelligence had failed to pinpoint the location of Pakistan's relevant nuclear facilities; India was not certain that a preventive/preemptive strike could destroy them; and its own nuclear facilities and installations were equally vulnerable to Pakistani air attacks. Thus a state of virtual deterrence already existed, even though no nuclear weapons were deployed or were probably even available at the time.

The United States played an ambiguous role in these crises—at times trying to douse the flames, at times adding fuel to the fire. On the one hand, the U.S. government, led by President Ronald Reagan, exercised constant pressure on both countries to moderate their competition. On the other hand, during the crisis in 1984, statements of Senator Daniel Patrick

Moynihan, Ambassador Hinton, and Under Secretary of State James Buckley, made on the basis of limited evidence, fanned suspicions that India might attack Pakistan's nuclear assets. This sequence of events fails to make clear whether U.S. policy was being orchestrated to dissuade India from contemplating a preventive strike. Ironically, fifteen years later India was to implement the strategy developed so successfully by Islamabad, when it succeeded in getting the Americans to put pressure on Pakistan during the Kargil mini-war.

Ethnic, Religious, and Irredentist Crises

Almost every India-Pakistan crisis has revolved around overlapping ethnic and religious issues. In the next section, several involving Kashmir are discussed in that context. Three others of this nature are also notable, the most important fanned by massive Indian support for the East Pakistani separatist movement. As already mentioned, it erupted in a major war and concluded with the creation of Bangladesh.

Of the other two, one was related to a Khalistan/Sikh separatist movement raging between 1984 and 1992, which caused enormous disruption in several north Indian cities (including Delhi), fomented a military uprising of Sikh soldiers, and led to the assassination of Indira Gandhi at the hands of her Sikh bodyguards. During that period, Sikh separatists received substantial support from Pakistan, which included training in Pakistani camps. By 1992 a combination of exhaustion, tough Indian police countermeasures, and political accommodation with Sikh moderates had put an end to the movement.

The third crisis, in April 1993, was triggered by multiple terror bombings in Bombay following extensive communal rioting in the wake of the demolition of the Babri Mosque in Ayodhya in December 1992. India promptly accused Pakistan of masterminding these attacks and providing sanctuary to the main suspects.[20] Equally promptly, Pakistan denied the allegations. A verbal duel ensued, heightening tensions between the two countries. The United States cautioned India against taking military steps and advised Pakistan to help India with its investigations.[21]

Kashmir: The Protracted Conflict

The most enduring and perplexing conflict between India and Pakistan (see box 2-2) is the chronic, multifaceted dispute over the former princely state of Jammu and Kashmir, often referred to simply as Kashmir. With roots

Box 2-2. *Terminology*

The political status of Kashmir is an intensely emotional issue, and different parties have described it in different terms. American, British, and other international observers look upon both the Indian- and Pakistani-controlled parts of the former princely state as "administered" territories. Many Pakistanis, including the government, refer to the areas under Indian control as "held Kashmir" or "Indian-held Kashmir" (IHK), and the Pakistan-controlled areas as "Azad (free) Kashmir." On the Indian side, the latter territory is termed "Pakistan-Occupied Kashmir" (POK). In a similar vein, Pakistan tends to view Kashmiris (and others) who battle Indian forces as freedom-fighters, while Indians commonly refer to them as terrorists, separatists, ultras, or militants. In our approach to the Kashmir problem, we have used the relatively neutral terms "administered" and "militant" to describe the territory and the groups involved in this long-running conflict.

going back many decades, it is widely acknowledged to be one of the world's most intractable conflicts. The central issues range from a struggle over territory to a clash of identities and the fate of more than 15 million Kashmiris, approximately 10 million of whom live under India's control and 4 million under Pakistan's.[22]

Jammu and Kashmir consists of five regions: (1) Jammu, with a Hindu majority; (2) Ladakh, where Buddhists and Muslims are almost in equal proportion; (3) Mirpur and Muzaffarabad, with a Muslim majority (this region constitutes Pakistan-administered Kashmir); (4) Baltistan, Hunza, and the Gilgit Agency, all predominantly Muslim territories with a special but ambiguous status in relation to Pakistan; and (5) the "Vale" or Valley of Kashmir, centered around Srinagar and containing most of the state's population (it constitutes what is referred to as Indian-administered Kashmir).

The dispute consists of many layers: as each is peeled away, new ones appear. Small conflicts are nested within larger ones, and most are interconnected. The following factors have played a large role in the conflict:

—A truly separatist Kashmiri movement that seeks independence from both India and Pakistan.

—Federal tensions between the dominant Valley and other regions in the state.

—Several minority rights struggles, involving minority sect Muslims (in the northern territories), Hindus (in the Valley), Shia Muslims, and Buddhists (in Ladakh).

—The link between Kashmir and global Islamist issues and the presence of jihadis from around the world seeking to liberate by force what they regard as oppressed Muslims.

While granting dominion status to both India and Pakistan, the British denied independence to princely states and instead asked them to accede to either country, keeping in mind geographical contiguity and the wishes of each state's people. Contemplating independence, the Maharaja of Kashmir delayed the decision of whether to accede to one country or the other.

Pakistan's chief proponent, the Muslim League, had not made Kashmir an issue before partition, as it assumed that the state would inevitably join Pakistan because of its Muslim majority. Sheikh Abdullah, the dominant (and secular) political figure in Kashmir, probably wanted independence for Kashmir but did not think it was attainable.[23]

In October 1947 India alleged that tribesmen from the North West Frontier Province had perpetrated unprovoked aggression as part of a Pakistani plot to seize Kashmir by force. In its view, the state of Jammu and Kashmir had been legally joined to India when the Maharaja (the princely ruler) signed the instrument of accession. Therefore India was justified in using force to defend the state. On January 1, 1948, after a UN-brokered cease-fire, India took the Kashmir dispute to the United Nations under article 35 of the UN Charter. It charged Pakistan with assisting the tribesmen and other invaders, in violation of India's sovereignty. Pakistan, in turn, denied the allegation and claimed the raiders were provoked by anti-Muslim atrocities committed in Kashmir by the Maharaja's predominantly Hindu army. It lodged a countercomplaint accusing India of organized genocide of Muslims in East Punjab, Delhi, and other places in India, as well as the forcible occupation of Junagadh (whose Muslim ruler had acceded to Pakistan) and the manipulation of Kashmir's accession by fraud and violence.

On January 17, 1948, the United Nations Security Council (UNSC) passed a resolution asking the parties not to aggravate the situation and do everything to improve it. A second UNSC resolution, passed on January 20, 1948, established a mediatory commission known as the United Nations Commission on India and Pakistan (UNCIP). After comprehensive consultations with the parties involved, the UNCIP tabled two resolutions on August 13, 1948, and January 5, 1949, which were accepted by both parties and endorsed by the UNSC. These resolutions provided for a cease-fire, demilitarization of the state, and a free and impartial plebiscite to be conducted by the United Nations to determine the state's accession to either India or Pakistan. Although the cease-fire was quickly attained, the issue of demilitarization could not be resolved, and the third stage, with a plebiscite under UN auspices, was never implemented.

On this point, Indian and Pakistani positions are poles apart. As far as India is concerned, the Maharaja's accession to India was final and legal, and the UN resolution calling for a plebiscite in Kashmir could not be fulfilled because Pakistani forces were present in the state—and in any case, a plebiscite is made irrelevant by successive Indian elections there. According to Pakistan, the accession took place under pressure and violates international law, and India is afraid to live up to its promise of a plebiscite; furthermore, it points to human rights violations by Indian forces in Kashmir, to which India replies that such violations are caused by the presence of an illegal and now terrorist separatist movement funded and supported from Pakistan.

After the cease-fire, Pakistan controlled about a third of the state, including the Mirpur and Muzaffarabad areas and the northern territories of Gilgit, Hunza, and Baltistan. It should be emphasized that the exact link between Kashmir and Gilgit and Hunza remained controversial, and that India controlled most parts of Ladakh, all of Jammu, and the crucial Valley of Kashmir.

Subsequently, both India and Pakistan claimed to speak on behalf of the people of Kashmir, but neither has been prepared to discuss the demand of many Kashmiris for independence. India maintains that Kashmir is an undisputed part of its territory, Pakistan that the accession to India and subsequent ratification by the Jammu and Kashmir State Assembly had no firm basis in law and was never accepted by the United Nations. Moreover, many major powers—notably Great Britain, the United States, and China—agree that Kashmir is "disputed." According to Pakistani officials, Kashmir remains the unfinished business of the 1947 partition, and India's control of the Muslim majority areas in J&K went against the overall logic of the partition. Pakistan believes that a peaceful solution can be found only if India yields on these points instead of refusing to accept the reality of Pakistan and its hegemonic aspirations.[24]

After the 1962 India-China conflict, the United States and Britain launched a concerted effort to bridge the gap between Islamabad and Delhi, yet six rounds of talks between 1962 and 1963 failed to produce any result. Kashmir was the site of a second India-Pakistan war, a short conflict fought in 1965. A UN-sponsored cease-fire became effective on September 23, 1965, and both countries retreated to their earlier positions, subsequently after a summit meeting in Tashkent brokered by the Soviet Union. After the 1971 war, a dominant India sought to reach a bilateral understanding with Pakistan without the participation of outside powers. In late June and early July 1972, Zulfiqar Ali Bhutto and Indira Gandhi met in the Indian hill-station of Simla and signed an agreement envisaging a bilateral settlement of all outstanding disputes, including Kashmir. Under the terms laid out in the first paragraph, the two countries agreed that the principles and purposes of the charter of the United Nations would govern their future relations. In interpreting the Simla Agreement, Pakistan emphasizes this clause, whereas India dwells on the second paragraph, dealing with the principle of bilateralism. These differences have persisted.

However, Kashmir was not a subject of many subsequent bilateral discussions. Between 1972 and 1994, India and Pakistan held forty-five bilateral meetings but devoted only one, in January 1994, to Kashmir. India began to view the LOC as a more or less permanent border, while Pakistan felt the Simla Agreement did not replace the UN resolutions and the LOC based on the cease-fire line was not a permanent international border.

The Kashmir dispute continues to spin off crises on a regular basis, five of which bear special mention:

—In November 1963, following rumors that a holy relic, a hair of the Prophet's beard, had been stolen from the Hazratbal shrine near Srinagar, the state plunged into violence. It spread throughout India, as far south as Orissa, and there were attempts to force Indian Muslims across the international border from West Bengal to East Pakistan.

—In 1989–90 Kashmir was the scene of a major uprising in protest against the rigged state elections of 1989. This contributed directly to the serious 1990 crisis discussed in chapter 4.

—In 1992–93 activists based in Pakistan-administered Kashmir made three attempts to launch protest marches across the LOC into Kashmir and press for an independent state. India placed its troops along the LOC on high alert to repel these intrusions by force, if necessary, and tensions flared along the border. Sensitive to the escalatory potential of the activists' deliberate border infractions, the Pakistan army took harsh steps, even firing on the marchers to prevent them from crossing the border.

—In October 1993 two battalions of the Indian army laid siege to the Hazratbal shrine to flush out some forty militants who had occupied it, including several foreigners. It was later discovered that only seven militants belonging to the JKLF were present. A report was also circulated that the hair of the Holy Prophet's beard, the relic in question earlier as well, had been stolen, which greatly inflamed passions. Negotiations between the governor and Hurriyat leaders yielded a settlement allowing the militants to leave the shrine, surrender their weapons, and be taken into custody, interrogated, and released early. The militants finally vacated the shrine on November 16.

—In April 1995, the Indian army laid siege to the Charar-i-Sharif shrine dedicated to Sheikh Nooruddin Wali, a revered saint in Kashmir, in order to apprehend several militants who had taken refuge there. In the ensuing clash between the Indian army and the militants, the shrine was burned down, leading to considerable resentment in the Valley and a flurry of accusations between India and Pakistan, again escalating tensions between the two countries.

It is also important to take note of the various perpetrators of violence in Kashmir, as they could trigger a new India-Pakistan conflict. One group would be Indian security forces, notably the paramilitary units, which sometimes used excessive force while undertaking operations against suspected militants and separatists, both Kashmiri and non-Kashmiri alike. According to unofficial Kashmiri sources, these units have killed more than 80,000 Kashmiris and maimed countless others, destroyed properties, burned shops, and frequently raped women, all in the name of security. Official Indian estimates are almost half this figure, with casualties in Kashmir due to terrorism from 1990 to the end of January 2005 totaling 38,883 (12,542 civilians, 4,116 security forces personnel, 18,589 terrorists, and 3,636 foreign terrorists).[25] Similarly, a well-informed unofficial Indian website, the "South Asia Terrorism Portal" managed by K. P. S. Gill's Institute of Conflict Management, puts the total number of casualties from 1988 to July 10, 2005, at 39,014 (13,673 civilians, 5,347 security forces personnel, and 19,994 terrorists).[26] It is difficult to account for the large difference between these totals and the local estimates since one does not know how they were calculated.

Another group would be the local/indigenous separatists who—especially in the early stages of the uprising (many have since been infiltrated, turned, or killed by Indian intelligence)—have attacked both military targets and fellow-Kashmiris suspected of being informers. They have committed torture for "the cause" but also for personal ends.

According to some sources, mostly Indian, the infiltrators who cross from Pakistan to the Indian side of the LOC fall into two categories: militants under the control of the Inter-Services Intelligence (ISI) and militants who feign allegiance to the ISI but often carry out their own agenda once they cross the LOC. The latter are truly a wild card and have the potential and the incentive to disrupt any agreement that India and Pakistan might reach. In recent years Pakistan has tightened its grip on these infiltrators, and their number has declined. Since 2005 both Pakistani and

Box 2-3. *Relevant India-Pakistan Diplomacy and Dialogue, 1986–2007*

Brasstacks and Beyond

November 1986: Prime Ministers Rajiv Gandhi and Mohammad Khan Junejo meet in Bangalore at the South Asian Association for Regional Cooperation (SAARC) summit.

February 1987: General Zia ul-Haq travels to India, ostensibly for a cricket match in Jaipur; meets Rajiv Gandhi in New Delhi ("Cricket Diplomacy I").

November 1987: Rajiv Gandhi and Junejo meet in Kathmandu at the SAARC summit.

August 1988: Presidents Ramaswamy Venkataraman and Ghulam Ishaq Khan meet at General Zia's funeral.

December 1988: Prime Ministers Benazir Bhutto and Rajiv Gandhi meet at the SAARC summit in Islamabad; India and Pakistan sign the Agreement on Non-Attack of Nuclear Facilities and Installations; agreements are also reached on cultural cooperation and "avoidance of double taxation on incomes derived from international civil aviation transactions."

July 1989: Benazir Bhutto and Rajiv Gandhi meet in Islamabad; a joint communiqué is issued expressing their countries' desire to work toward a comprehensive settlement to reduce the chances of conflict and promote the avoidance of the use of force; first prime ministerial hotline set up.

Post-1990: Confidence Building Is Highlighted

November 1990: Prime Ministers Chandra Shekhar and Nawaz Sharif meet at SAARC summit in Male; India and Pakistan decide to resume talks at the foreign secretary level.

December 1990: India and Pakistan agree to reestablish the Directors General of Military Operations (DGMO) hotline and to use it on a weekly basis; the foreign secretaries work out a code of conduct to protect diplomatic personnel.

April 1991: Agreement on Advance Notice of Military Exercises, Maneuvers and Troop Movements; Agreement on the Prevention of the Violation of Airspace.

May 1991: Chandra Shekhar and Nawaz Sharif meet at Rajiv Gandhi's funeral.

October 1991: Prime Ministers Nawaz Sharif and P. V. Narasimha Rao meet at the Commonwealth Heads of Government Meeting (CHOGM) in Harare.

December 1991: Nawaz Sharif and Narasimha Rao meet at the SAARC summit in Colombo.

February 1992: Nawaz Sharif and Narasimha Rao meet in Davos at the World Economic Forum meeting.

April 1992: Nawaz Sharif and Narasimha Rao meet in Dhaka at the SAARC summit.
August 1992: Joint Declaration on the Prohibition of Chemical Weapons.
September 1992: Nawaz Sharif and Narasimha Rao meet in Jakarta at the Non-Aligned Movement summit.

Composite Dialogue Emerges

January 1994: Non-papers exchanged between the two countries.
May 1995: Prime Minister Narasimha Rao and President Farooq Ahmed Leghari meet briefly at the SAARC summit in Delhi.
May 1997: High-level talks resume; Prime Ministers I. K. Gujral and Nawaz Sharif meet at the SAARC summit in Male; they pledge to reinstate the prime ministers' hotline and decide to constitute joint working groups on various issues between India and Pakistan—this would constitute the "composite dialogue."
June 1997: Foreign secretaries identify eight "outstanding issues" on which the joint working groups would focus: Kashmir, peace and security, Siachen, Wullar Barrage, Sir Creek, terrorism and drug trafficking, economic cooperation, and promotion of friendly ties.
September 1997: Talks break down after Pakistan insists that Kashmir be the core issue; Prime Ministers I. K. Gujral and Nawaz Sharif meet in New York at the U.N. General Assembly (UNGA) meeting.
October 1997: I. K. Gujral and Nawaz Sharif meet in Edinburgh at the CHOGM.
January 1998: I. K. Gujral and Nawaz Sharif meet in Dhaka for a trilateral business summit.
July 1998: Prime Ministers Atal Bihari Vajpayee and Nawaz Sharif meet in Colombo at the SAARC summit.
September 1998: Vajpayee and Nawaz Sharif meet in New York at the UNGA meeting. Foreign secretaries agree to commence "substantive dialogue" on the eight issues; meetings held over the next few months.
February 1999: Vajpayee and Nawaz Sharif meet in Lahore; Lahore Declaration and Memorandum of Understanding signed.

Post-Kargil

November 2000: Vajpayee declares a Ramadan cease-fire.
July 2001: Vajpayee and President Pervez Musharraf meet in Agra for a summit.

(continued)

After the 2001 Confrontation

April 2003: Prime Minister Vajpayee extends a "hand of friendship" to Pakistan in Srinagar.
May 2003: India and Pakistan restore full diplomatic relations and announce the resumption of the Lahore bus service.
October 2003: India proposes twelve confidence-building measures (CBMs); Pakistan conditionally accepts them and contributes an additional one.
November 2003: Prime Minister Mir Zafarullah Khan Jamali announces a cease-fire.
December 2003: The two countries agree to resume direct air links.
January 2004: Vajpayee and Musharraf meet in Islamabad at the SAARC summit; the joint press statement indicates that the composite dialogue will be resumed; rail services resumed between the two countries.
February 2004: Foreign secretaries reach understanding on modalities of resuming the composite dialogue.
March 2004: The Indian cricket team tours Pakistan for a full set of matches for the first time since 1989 ("Cricket Diplomacy II").
June 2004: Foreign Ministers Kurshid Kasuri and Natwar Singh meet in China; experts meet in Delhi to discuss nuclear CBMs; foreign secretaries meet to discuss "peace and security" and "Jammu and Kashmir."
July 2004: Kasuri and Singh meet twice; schedule of meetings drawn up to discuss the six other elements of the composite dialogue.

Indian officials have acknowledged that the incidence of cross-border infiltration has decreased, although they disagree as to whether it has actually stopped. In India's view, cross-border terrorism will not cease until Pakistan dismantles the extensive jihadi infrastructure within its borders, which allegedly continues under its patronage.

Yet another group comprises the surrendered militants, locally called Ikhwans, who enjoy the patronage of the Indian security forces. They have often been accused of blackmailing the local population and committing atrocities, ostensibly while discharging their duties. Human Rights Watch has severely criticized the Indian armed forces for making use of these individuals.[27]

A Very Brief History of Peace in South Asia

Multiple wars, major crises, and innumerable exchanges of fire along the LOC over sixty years of independent coexistence constitute an unenviable

September 2004: Following the discussions on these other elements, the foreign secretaries meet in Delhi to assess and review the composite dialogue; Prime Minister Manmohan Singh and President Musharraf meet in New York at the UNGA summit and release a joint statement.
October 2004: Musharraf announces his three-point basis on which to solve the Kashmir dispute.
November 2004: Prime Ministers Manmohan Singh and Shaukat Aziz meet in Delhi at the SAARC summit; India releases its nine-point strategy for Kashmir.
December 2004: Bilateral meetings held to discuss various elements of the composite dialogue; foreign secretaries review progress at the commencement of the second round of dialogue.
February 2005: Foreign Ministers Natwar Singh and Kurshid Kasuri meet in Islamabad.
March 2005: Pakistani cricket team travels to India for a full tour after a gap of six years.
April 2005: Srinagar-Muzaffarabad bus service begins; Musharraf travels to Delhi for a cricket match and meets Manmohan Singh.
October 2005: In the aftermath of the earthquake, India provides (and Pakistan reluctantly and hesitantly accepts) relief aid, and the Line of Control is opened at five points.
2005–07: Prime ministerial, foreign minister, and foreign secretary talks continue on the composite dialogue; additional meetings by home and defense secretaries; other negotiations and meetings at several levels.

record for any pair of neighboring countries. There have been intermittent efforts at normalization, however, summarized in box 2-3.The one major agreement between India and Pakistan that has endured is the Indus Waters Treaty, brokered by the World Bank and the United States. Signed in Karachi in 1960, it took five years to negotiate and provided for the division of canal and water systems on which then West Pakistan was vitally dependent. India and Pakistan have also addressed each other with proposals for joint defense, confidence-building measures, no-war pacts, friendship treaties, and other arrangements aimed at achieving peace. Most of this has been diplomatic gamesmanship, some of it sincere perhaps, but peace in South Asia remains as uncertain as war.

Most of the crises and wars described in this chapter have been followed by efforts to find ways to restore trust and normalize relations. For instance, the 1965 India-Pakistan war was punctuated by the signing of the short-lived Tashkent Agreement, and the 1971 war by the Simla Agreement, which provided a framework for peace between the two countries for almost three decades. Following the multiple crises of 1984–85, the countries decided to negotiate a non-attack pact, which eventually led to the Agreement on the Prohibition of Attack against Nuclear Installations and Facilities in 1988. Similarly, the tense Brasstacks (1986–87) and 1990 crises led to the negotiation of the Agreement on Advance Notice of Military Exercises, Maneuvers and Troop Movements (1991) and the Agreement on Prevention of Airspace Violations and for Permitting Overflights and Landings by Military Aircraft (1991).

In sharp contrast, no effort was made to revive normalization at the end of the Kargil conflict. When Pervez Musharraf, the general who planned Kargil, seized power in a coup, India grew deeply distrustful of his military regime. Both sides were still trying to calculate the impact of nuclear weaponization on their relationship, and the uprising in Kashmir continued apace. Further, the new Bush administration had yet to focus on South Asia. All of this contributed to the failed summit in Agra in July 2001, which only worsened relations between the two countries. It took a year after the conclusion of the 2001–02 crisis for a serious period of dialogue and engagement to begin. Since then, apart from a couple of minor lapses, a cease-fire announced in November 2003 has held, and the two sides have conducted numerous rounds of dialogue on a range of issues.

India and Pakistan are now engaged in an extended but still inconclusive attempt to resolve outstanding issues, including Kashmir; they are also moving up (and down) the escalation ladder as they acquire more and more advanced conventional weaponry, improve their nuclear arsenals and delivery systems, and are tempted to toy with ballistic missile defense (BMD) technology. These and other developments might transform what Ashley Tellis, for one, calls "ugly stability" into ugly instability or confusion as to whether stability will ever be achieved.[28] We return to this theme in chapter 7, after reviewing the linkage between crisis, war, and nuclear proliferation in the case studies and the recent efforts to establish a peace process between India and Pakistan.

CHAPTER THREE

The Brasstacks Crisis of 1986–87

Launched in November 1986, Brasstacks was a year-long Indian military exercise that sparked a three-month crisis. Part of the military's triennial program of such exercises, it came hard on the heels of the 1982 and 1983 mini-crises described in chapter 2. Although it did not lead to war, it helped accelerate India's and Pakistan's nuclear programs.[1]

Many Pakistani officials were alarmed by the scale and scope of the Brasstacks exercise, especially in view of its proximity to the India-Pakistan border and positioning of Indian forces in a way that suggested they might be able to bisect Pakistan. During the South Asian Association for Regional Cooperation (SAARC) summit in Bangalore later in November 1986, India's prime minister, Rajiv Gandhi, assured his Pakistani counterpart, Mohammad Khan Junejo, that the exercise would be reviewed, but its scale and contours were not altered.

In December 1986 Islamabad retaliated by moving two strike corps—its Army Reserve South (ARS) and Army Reserve North (ARN), which had just completed their annual training exercise—to a position where they could have threatened India's Punjab, then in internal disarray because of Sikh militancy. This stemmed from the partial destruction of the holy Golden Temple in early 1984 and subsequent attacks on Sikhs, especially in Delhi, after Prime Minister Indira Gandhi was assassinated by her Sikh bodyguards on October 31, 1984. India assessed these moves as defensive and precautionary until the ARS crossed the Sutlej River from its southern to its northern bank in the second week of January 1987 and stationed itself facing the Indian cities of Bhatinda and Ferozpur. Now seriously alarmed itself, India saw that Pakistan could launch a pincer movement to either detach a part of

Punjab or disrupt communications between India and the state of Jammu and Kashmir. The Indian army then mounted Operation Trident, a defensive move to strengthen its borders (this *operation* took place alongside and within the Brasstacks *exercise*, which resumed after Operation Trident).

The tension escalated when the Indian press was briefed on these developments by Minister of State for Defense Arun Singh on January 18, 1987, and by Chief of Army Staff General Krishnaswami Sundarji. The two briefings led many journalists to believe (and to write) that war was, if not imminent, then at least quite possible.

Third parties tried to defuse the crisis. The United States, for one, stepped forward as it was deeply concerned about the prospect of war between an ally (Pakistan) and a newfound friend (India), and about the pace of the region's nuclear programs.

The crisis effectively ended through a negotiated agreement to withdraw forces from the border in February-March 1987 after direct contact between the Indian and Pakistani leadership. Developments within India's inner decisionmaking circle may have helped. From inception to conclusion, the crisis involved no fighting and, as already mentioned, lasted about three months.

The Crisis

The Brasstacks crisis took place in a complicated political and military environment. For two and a half years, the Indian and Pakistani armies had been firing at each other regularly on the Siachen Glacier. Each side suspected the other of trying to grab control of the glacier and its environs and of supporting separatist movements across the border: Pakistan was alleged to be supporting the Sikhs and Kashmiris in India, and India the Sindhis in Pakistan, reviving memories there of the secession of East Pakistan from Pakistan in 1971. The atmosphere was already clouded by several earlier war scares over possible attacks on Pakistan's nuclear facilities. To add to the strain, the Soviet occupation of Afghanistan had produced a massive influx of refugees into Pakistan and transformed Pakistan into a "frontline state," in cold war parlance.

At that point, the United States was deeply involved in South Asia: it was supporting the Afghan mujahiddin forces against the Soviet invaders while delicately trying to manage its relations with India and Pakistan. In attempting to shore up its rediscovered ally in Islamabad, the U.S. government was lending a hand to a fairly brutal military regime that was passing milestone after milestone on the road to acquiring a nuclear weapon; at the same time, New Delhi and Washington were warily trying to build a political relationship that had ranged from cool to hostile for almost two decades.

Initiation

All armed forces need to hold training exercises and maneuvers regularly to ensure combat readiness, develop new tactical concepts, and evaluate the integration of new weaponry and equipment in an operational setting. These exercises are also important for the education of senior military officers: they are one way of demonstrating the realities of logistics management and the use of mobile forces in simulated battle conditions. Furthermore, they showcase the professionalism of the armed forces, their state of military preparedness, and the numbers of formations, tanks, and combat aircraft that could be deployed within certain time frames. Collectively, this could convey warnings and deter adversaries from any contemplated adventurism.

The Indian and Pakistani army establishments routinely hold exercises up to brigade and division level, their ground forces based on British tables of organization laid down several decades ago. An infantry brigade consists of approximately 3,000 troops, a division 12,000, and a corps two or more divisions. Armored units are smaller. Evidently the two sides had a semiformal understanding concerning such large-scale maneuvers and exercises in the early 1980s. According to a very senior military official, General K. M. Arif, appointed vice chief of army staff in 1984, had reached such an understanding with his Indian counterpart, General A. S. Vaidya. Arif in effect ran the Pakistan army for President Zia ul-Haq, its chief, and had total responsibility for army strategy, subject to the approval of Zia and Prime Minister Junejo. At least one very senior Indian general claims, however, that any letters formalizing this agreement were exchanged on a demi-official basis and that the Indian chief of army staff, General Krishnaswami Sundarji, may have been unaware of the agreement. Advance notice of large military exercises near the border was not formalized until 1991, when India and Pakistan signed a related agreement.[2]

In the mid-1980s, senior Indian military officers had mixed opinions about the value of large-scale military exercises, although the majority, including Sundarji, felt they were imperative every few years, especially for "learning to handle large formations and bodies of men. For instance, controlling a three-brigade exercise over a 100-mile front would make clear the problems of war in a realistic setting." Some, however, argued that large corps-level exercises have only limited military value and may simply highlight the problem of coordinating several army formations. In any case, India and Pakistan generally conduct such operations at the divisional level, since corps-level exercises are financially costly and a drain on military equipment, which is often either lost or put out of commission for a period of time.[3] Moreover, such exercises have heightened political tensions between India and Pakistan in the past, reminiscent of the anxiety in Europe during large exercises of the North Atlantic Treaty Organization (NATO) or Warsaw Treaty Organization.

Brasstacks was conceived as one of a series of large-scale exercises designed to test military readiness and new military formations—especially a reduced, but more mobile, infantry division—suitable for warfare in the South Asian plains. It was planned by the innovative Sundarji with the encouragement of Prime Minister Rajiv Gandhi. In Indian army parlance, an exercise is a war game or other training activity conducted with or without troops, near or far from potential enemies. The term "exercise" is sometimes confused with "operation," which many accounts of the Brasstacks crisis, including American and Pakistani government documents, have erroneously used to refer to Brasstacks.

Planners decided to conduct Brasstacks in Rajasthan, in an area east of the Indira Gandhi Canal, thinking it was best suited to the likely course of future India-Pakistan conflicts now that Punjab no longer seemed available to be the chief theater of operations (see map 3-1). Over the years, both sides had constructed a number of obstacles along the Punjab border, making attack both costly and time-consuming. According to officers of both armies, but especially on the Indian side, large-scale exercises were not only expensive but also disruptive to the intensive farming practiced in many areas of the Punjab. Standing crops are often destroyed in the course of such maneuvers, and compensation must be paid to local farmers.

India's leaders also assumed that Jammu and Kashmir would remain the main target for Pakistan's armed forces, especially since their acquisition of Chhamb after the 1971 conflict had brought them nearer to the vital Jammu-Akhnur-Rajouri-Poonch road. Kashmir has a much more rugged terrain, however, which impedes the movement of large military formations. The Rajasthan-Sindh area would therefore be the logical place for a major ground war, should one occur. It also has the desert terrain and the space to accommodate a large-scale exercise and could thus add a dimension of realism to the effort, which probably incorporated actual operational

Map 3-1. *The Brasstacks Exercises*

This map is indicative and not to scale. The disputed areas shown in the map reflect the authors' judgement. The boundaries shown in the map may not confirm to the official boundaries of India. The printer and publisher bear no responsibility on the accuracy or otherwise of this map.

This map is indicative and not to scale. The disputed areas shown in the map reflect the authors' judgement. The boundaries shown in the map may not confirm to the official boundaries of India. The printer and publisher bear no responsibility on the accuracy or otherwise of this map.

plans. Exercise Digvijay, conducted in 1983 (and commanded by then Lieutenant General Sundarji before his promotion to army chief), had been held in roughly the same area.

The Scenario and Its Implementation

Brasstacks' political scenario assumed that the insurgency in Kashmir had reached unmanageable proportions and that Sikh militants had declared Khalistan an independent Sikh nation, encouraging Pakistan to make a "final push" to detach both Kashmir and Khalistan from India. The weight of the Pakistani thrust would make a dent in Indian defenses, requiring an Indian counteroffensive to relieve pressure by carrying the conflict into Pakistan. The scenario was not altogether unrealistic in that it resembled the course of events in 1965, when Pakistan expected an uprising to occur in Kashmir. It also foreshadowed the events of late 1989–90, when a serious insurrection in Kashmir supported from the Pakistani side of the Line of Control was followed by yet another crisis (discussed in chapter 4). General Sundarji later wrote a novel dealing with these events and has developed a fictional version of these scenarios.[4]

The underlying concepts, setting, size, and parameters of Exercise Brasstacks made it comparable to the most massive NATO and Warsaw Pact exercises. By Pakistani estimates, Brasstacks involved a quarter of a million troops and 1,300 tanks and cost a quarter of a billion dollars. The exercise took place in four phases: Brasstacks I, in May-June 1986, was essentially a mapping exercise by the Southern, Western, and Northern Army commands; Brasstacks II, in November 1986, was a computerized war-game-cum-sand-model exercise in which the Indian navy and air force held their exercises separately; Brasstacks III, scheduled for November-December 1986, was envisaged as segmented exercises by different arms and services to support divisional and corps-level offensive operations in a mobile battleground environment; and Brasstacks IV was scheduled for February-March 1987.

One of Brasstacks' central objectives was to evaluate the following new military concepts in field conditions:

—The Reorganized Army Plains Infantry Division (RAPID) formations, consisting of two infantry and one mechanized brigade, designed to be partly mobile but capable of holding territory, which was a uniquely Indian concept suitable for the India-Pakistan theater.

—Plan AREN (Area Radio Engineered Network), an indigenously developed and produced communications grid, which could provide secure links with voice, telex, facsimile, video, and computer terminals.

—The command, control, communications, and information systems (C3I), based on commercially available computer equipment and intended to provide field commanders with real-time information on troop movements, battle situation, logistics, and so on, for effective decisionmaking and control over the developing battlefield.[5]

At the same time, officers and troops were to be evaluated in simulated battle conditions. In the event, several officers were found to be "unfit for modern warfare conditions" and undeserving of further advancement. The Indian air force was instructed to use its frontline combat aircraft in a close air support and strike role. A large number of sorties were to be flown, with tactical routing, to simulate war conditions realistically.

A preliminary evaluation of the first three stages was encouraging, and army commanders strongly opposed a suggestion that the exercise be terminated at that point to save on the wear and tear, costs, and equipment losses inherent in a massive field exercise. They advised the political leadership to continue with Brasstacks IV, which translated the exercise to the ground in an area of about 100 by 150 miles, with the longer axis along the India-Pakistan border. Similar in character to Exercise Digvijay, it designated Blueland (India) the northern force and Redland (Pakistan) the southern force, with Greenland (China) to the west. Since Exercise Brasstacks was seen as an extrapolation of Exercise Digvijay, the military establishment gave no serious thought to the possibility that it might cause serious concern in Pakistan and trigger a major crisis.

In the interviews for this study, respondents familiar with Brasstacks pointed out that the concept of holding a major exercise to mobilize all relevant wings of the government of India—including the railways, airlines, and port authorities—had been articulated by Rajiv Gandhi at a Defense Ministry meeting at the end of 1985. He was then both prime minister and minister of defense. Apparently fascinated by the scale of this exercise, Prime Minister Gandhi wanted it to be larger than any ever held in the subcontinent. He seemingly had no larger political or strategic objective in mind at that time, although some believed that he wished to strike a heroic pose and impress India's neighbors.

At the map exercise stage, Brasstacks was considerably larger than Digvijay, with three army commands, two air force commands (western and southwestern), and a navy component to simulate an amphibious landing.

Apart from the forces available in situ, the Fifty-Fourth Division was allocated to Southern Command, and the Fifty-Seventh and Eighth Mountain Divisions were positioned in the state of Punjab for internal security duties. These moves were a precautionary measure taken in the last week of January 1987, in association with Operation Trident, which had just been initiated. Altogether, the forces available for Brasstacks amounted to two armored divisions, one mechanized division, and six infantry divisions, two of which had been converted, though not fully, into RAPID formations for this exercise.[6]

An early obstacle to this grand design was the strenuous objections of the heads of the Ministry of Railways (Madhav Rao Scindia) and the Ministry of Surface Transport (Jagdish Tytler), who pointed out the consequent disruption of passenger, air, and shipping traffic as well as freight movement, and the considerable loss of revenue this would entail. When news of the impending exercise and its intended scale began appearing in the press and the matter was discussed with Prime Minister Gandhi, he agreed to scale down the mobilization effort but not the size of the projected exercise. Clearly, the authorities had failed to recognize the economic, financial, and political implications of Exercise Brasstacks or the likely reaction of Pakistan, naïvely assuming that it would view Brasstacks as merely an upscaled version of Exercise Digvijay.

The Political Context

One underlying, and perhaps impenetrable, question about the exercise was the degree to which it was intended as a "political" statement. Its chief planners differ on this score: one claims that while no explicit political goals were attached to the exercise, it was plainly designed to counter the support Pakistan had given the Sikh separatist movement in Indian Punjab. A military exercise aimed at Pakistan's own weak point, the province of Sindh, would be a fitting riposte to Pakistan and a threat (with echoes of 1971) that there might be more to come.

Ravi Rikhye, a perceptive but eclectic civilian strategic analyst who had access to senior Indian military officials, contends that Brasstacks was initially intended to lure Pakistan into a first move via deception and misdirection and then unleash a massive attack in response. The Indian leadership, Rikhye concluded, missed the chance of a lifetime, however, because of their timidity.[7] Pakistanis often cite Rikhye's analysis as evidence of malign Indian intentions. Conversations with key Indian participants tend to support this interpretation of Brasstacks.

Brasstacks was supposed to "game" India's use of its superior armor and air assets in seeking major operational gains across Rajasthan into Pakistan. This move might have achieved several politico-military objectives: namely, the detachment of Sindh, the destruction of Pakistan's nuclear program, the improvement of India's military situation in Siachen, the rationalization of the Line of Control (LOC) in Jammu and Kashmir, and the destruction of militant training camps across the border.

The Military Context

As the exercise shaped up, some members of the Indian armed forces were confident that the military balance between India and Pakistan was tilting decisively in India's favor, especially in view of its weapons acquisitions since the early 1980s and the radical restructuring undertaken to enhance the army's mobility and strike capabilities. The restructuring focused on converting two infantry divisions into RAPID formations designed to be partly mobile, yet capable of holding territory. As some military and civilian strategists pointed out, Pakistan's anti-India policies were neither tactical nor temporary; its decades-long hostility toward India stemmed from its inner existential logic and would not cease—therefore Pakistan had to be decisively defeated.[8]

Other members of the armed forces countered that military action without a political objective is meaningless in the classical Clausewitzian sense. This group asked some key questions about the exercise: "What could be the political objective of such adventurism? Would the international community countenance it? Could India hold territory in the teeth of a rebellious population?"

Unintentionally, perhaps, these conflicting attitudes fed into the belief prevalent in Pakistan that the exercise was intended to convey several messages: warn Pakistan not to meddle in Indian Punjab by supporting militancy, test Pakistan's political will and nerve, and habituate it to concentrations of force across the border. The military reality for Pakistan, especially its armed forces, was that with Indian troops on the border, they would have to move the troops and armor from interior locations with greater speed.[9] This was an inherently dangerous situation, demanding some kind of precautionary measures.

Pakistani Concerns

One of the Pakistan military's studies of Brasstacks saw the exercise as "a challenge to [the] Pakistan Army . . . meant to test its credibility as a dynamic and reliable fighting force."[10] Gazing across the border, Pakistan strategists thought they could discern three major strategic motives here: (1) adventurists in the Indian army hoped some incident along the border would create an opportunity to use the assembled forces for an attack on Pakistan; (2) India was acting at the behest of the Soviet Union, then engaged in a conflict in Afghanistan; and (3) at a minimum, India wanted to cut Sindh off from Punjab.[11] Others believed the exercise was intended to intimidate Pakistan by its sheer scale and to test new concepts of enhanced mobility by the mechanization of infantry.

None of the Pakistani officers interviewed for this project criticized the exercise from a purely military perspective; indeed, many saw it as something they would have done themselves. Pakistani army officers also considered the Indian exercise a useful way to train commanders and gain experience in coping with multicorps exercises, especially in the light of the Indian army's rapid expansion. The shift from a simple plains infantry division to a mechanized formation was believed to be a sensible move in purely military terms, even if it did create new problems for Pakistani planners. A former Pakistani army chief agreed that the exercise was merely meant to introduce new ideas and concepts, whereas the head of Pakistan's air force at the time characterized Brasstacks as an exercise in military intimidation.

The first three phases of Brasstacks were more or less paper exercises and did not cause much concern. The fourth phase, however, made the Pakistanis apprehensive—in part because the memory of 1971 was still fresh in their minds. In 1986–87 Sindh was Pakistan's Achilles' heel.

To add to the Pakistan army's concerns, there was little communication between relevant officials on both sides, and it was not clear whether this was deliberate or not. Although a hotline had been set up between the directors-general of military operations (DGMOs) of both countries, it was relaying little information to Pakistan. "If I were a chief of the Indian army and planning to hold an exercise of this scale," commented one Pakistan general, "I would immediately ask the concerned people to get in touch with Pakistani authorities and inform them." Instead, it was the Pakistani authorities who asked their army attaché in New Delhi to contact Indian army headquarters for information as soon as they learned about the projected troop movements, in September 1986. India's evasive response failed to reassure the Pakistanis, and in October 1986 they again sought information about the exercise. They received another sketchy and somewhat curt reply, stressing that holding an exercise was India's own business. Nonetheless, Pakistan's vice chief of army staff, General K. M. Arif, pressed for more information.[12]

Before he could set his own timetable for collective training, Arif needed to brief Pakistan's new civilian prime minister, Mohammed Khan Junejo, who was about to depart for India to attend the second SAARC summit in Bangalore in November 1986. Since little information was available from the Indian DGMO, the authorities decided to rely more on their own Directorate of Inter-Services Intelligence (ISI) for information, as well as other countries.[13]

Pakistan was also alarmed by the unprecedented scale and length of the exercise, which made its authorities deeply suspicious of Indian intentions and designs. Furthermore, the exercise was being staged very close to the India-Pakistan border (some 60 to 80 kilometers away from Pakistan). The massive logistics operation in Rajasthan, in particular, set off alarm bells at Army Headquarters in Rawalpindi. Pakistan intelligence discovered many civilian trains in Rajasthan had been canceled upon reading numerous letters in the Indian press protesting the cancellations and the rerouting of trains in the exercise area. According to one report, train services to Punjab, Kashmir, and Himachal Pradesh were suspended to facilitate the movement of troops and military equipment. Rail traffic was indeed badly affected by military movements in the northwest Indian states.

Further reports stated that the troops involved in the exercise were carrying live ammunition, which was unusual in military exercises. When a senior Pakistani military official specifically asked, through the DGMO channel, why the Indian troops were carrying first- and second-line ammunition, the Indian DGMO professed complete ignorance about this information.[14] As Lieutenant General P. N. Hoon, the then Western Army commander, later explained, "If Pakistan were to attack my troops, tanks and vehicles which were out in the open, I would not want to go down in history as the General who destroyed the entire army, and, as such, ammunition was being carried."[15]

Rajiv Gandhi's weak reassurances about the exercise also heightened Pakistani suspicions. As Humayun Khan, former ambassador to India, notes, Prime Minister Junejo mentioned the exercise to Gandhi at the Bangalore SAARC summit in November 1986 since "Pakistan was apprehensive about the scale of these manoeuvres and the purpose behind them. Rajiv replied that his army wanted a 'big tamasha' (a grand show) but that he himself was not in favour of spending so much money and wanted to cut down on the expenditure. He assured Junejo that it was nothing more than a training exercise and he hoped the hotline between the two military headquarters would be used to remove any doubts or suspicions."[16] In further discussions about the size and location of Brasstacks, Gandhi apparently assured Junejo that the Brasstacks exercise would be scaled down, cautioning that intelligence people everywhere tend to read too much into such situations. However, Gandhi's assurances appear to have been vague (he was known to be inattentive to details at times and might even have forgotten to inform others of his comments to Junejo). Nor did anyone suggest how the exercise should be scaled down. More disconcerting was the fact that the Indian Ministry of Defense and Service Headquarters were not, as far as can be determined, informed of this assurance. Thus the exercise proceeded on its original scale.

One may well ask why the two military operations directorates ignored the hotline as the crisis unfolded and tension mounted, especially when ARN and ARS moved closer to the border. After all, this form of instant communication was meant precisely to forestall a crisis. India's reluctance in this regard provided grist to the theory that it had a "hidden agenda." In this case, as in other crises, the need to communicate was the first casualty. The explanation goes to the heart of confidence-building measures between adversarial states. In the Brasstacks case, both sides considered information shared through the hotline to be unreliable. Pakistan might in any case have been suspicious and slow to act on information supplied at its request. Similarly, India believed Pakistan would use the hotline for purposes of deception and thought it an unreliable tool. Was this perception realistic? Some evidence suggests that Pakistan did use the hotline in this manner, but that India in turn fed it inaccurate information over the hotline. What is certain is that mutual suspicions eroded the value of this confidence-building measure. This particular problem occurred in earlier crises as well and was especially evident during the buildup to the 1971 war—a fact that those holding key positions in both countries might have remembered.

Could information obtained from a third source, such as a U.S. satellite, have filled the intelligence gap? It might have, but the United States saw no crisis brewing. Of course, a formal "open skies" agreement between the two countries would have provided timely and accurate information, but then such an agreement required a level of cooperation and trust that had not developed between the two countries.

Pakistan's Reaction

In their briefing to the UN National Assembly after the November SAARC meeting, President Zia and Prime Minister Junejo stated that the exercises being held by India and Pakistan were of a routine nature and that there was no immediate threat from India, but that these developments were being watched closely. The Pakistani embassy in New Delhi, as Humayun Khan writes, was also of this opinion: "My Defence Attaché was convinced that no war-like preparations like cancellation of leave, call-up of reserves or movement of back-up forces to other border areas were being undertaken."[17] It is difficult to tell whether this statement reflects successful camouflaging by the Indian forces or miscalculation on the part of the Pakistani attaché.

Following Rajiv's assurance, the Pakistanis waited for the anticipated contact. When India's DGMO did make contact, the data provided seemed sketchy and did not comport with the information Generals Arif and Zia had received from Pakistan's own intelligence services. They felt compelled to take appropriate steps, including a countermovement by their own forces and further consultations with the United States.

In retrospect, the significance of the Gandhi-Junejo dialogue was its thinness. It was another instance of a breakdown in normal diplomatic discourse and further suggested that the word of the highest officials could not be trusted, a view prevalent in all the subsequent regional crises. When coupled with the inability of outsiders to serve as timely and effective channels of communication, this lack of trust increases the risk of an inadvertent crisis.

The Crisis Evolves

The military logic for conducting the exercise east of the Indira Gandhi Canal was impeccable. India's military assumed that Pakistan would have no cause for alarm because a massive engineering effort would have been required to first transport bridges to the canal area and then move armor across this huge waterway to reach Pakistani territory. Pakistan nevertheless believed that an Indian offensive launched from this general area and conceivably from south of the canal posed serious risks, especially if the exercise had an east-west configuration. Islamabad had apparently conveyed these concerns to several countries, including the United States.

Segments of India's military establishment interpreted these objections as a pro forma attempt to create a crisis atmosphere in South Asia before U.S.

Secretary of Defense Caspar Weinberger's visit to the region in October. According to an American official familiar with the visit, when Weinberger visited Pakistan, Prime Minister Junejo asked him to let Pakistan know "if the balloon is going up" during Exercise Brasstacks. Some felt Pakistan's complaints were aimed more at garnering favor in the ongoing U.S.-Pakistan negotiations for a second aid package than at voicing genuine concern about the Indian maneuvers. Pakistan's anxiety was obviously feigned, they argued, since its authorities had not shown any concern over the similar Digvijay exercise.

Uneasy with Gandhi's somewhat unsatisfactory response to Junejo and apprehensive about Indian designs, Pakistan began to take precautionary measures, increasing the vigilance along the border, especially in the Brasstacks exercise area. According to a serving officer, the intelligence agencies had already communicated in their usual guarded manner that war could come.

As the various phases of Exercise Brasstacks unfolded, Pakistan was conducting two military exercises of its own. The first, code-named Saf-e-Shikan, involved Pakistan's Army Reserve South, consisting of the First Armored Division and the Thirty-Seventh Infantry Division, which was exercising in the Bahawalpur–Marot area across the Rajasthan border. The second, code-named Flying Horse, was undertaken by the Army Reserve North, consisting of the Sixth Armored Division and the Seventeenth Infantry Division, which was exercising in the Ravi-Chenab corridor. The ARS exercise was completed by the first week of November and the ARN exercise by the middle of December. Because of their growing apprehension, however, commanders warned their formations that collective training might have to be prolonged and instructed them to remain in their exercise area.[18] This warning was accompanied by the necessary administrative measures, such as canceling leave that had been granted, keeping the Americans informed, and relying more on their own intelligence. One tactic that the Zia regime used was to have the opposition political leader, Benazir Bhutto, convey her concern about Indian intentions to the Americans. She told American officials in December 1986 that "Brasstacks was serious," that the Indians were up to something, and that Kahuta was only two minutes' flying time from Srinagar.[19] Reacting to what it saw as the Indian DGMO's unexpectedly uncooperative and evasive attitude, Pakistan also began to withhold relevant information and give sketchy information regarding its own regular exercise, particularly the movements of its Northern Reserve.[20]

India took these to be normal precautionary steps in case the Brasstacks exercise should turn into an offensive thrust against Pakistan. In December, however, ARN changed its exercise venue to the Shakargarh salient, and the exercise was renamed "Sledgehammer." India saw this, too, as a defensive disposition of forces, since the geography of the Shakargarh "bulge" makes it difficult to defend and therefore an obvious military objective for India in any conflict.

These developments failed to concern India's service chiefs or Minister of State for Defence Arun Singh. Even when it became clear that the ARN and ARS were staying on in their exercise areas, with ARS remaining south of the river, they had collectively decided not to relay the information to Rajiv Gandhi while he was away on a well-publicized holiday in the Andamans. If the prime minister interrupted his holiday, they reasoned, it would merely convey the unnecessary impression that an India-Pakistan crisis had occurred. In light of subsequent events, especially the contingent moves of the ARN and ARS opposite the Punjab border, this could have been an error of judgment.

India felt it could remain sanguine because Pakistan's air force (PAF) and navy were not on high alert. Although some satellite airfields were being kept activated following the Highmark exercise (which had taken place about the same time that Pakistan had held army exercises) and the majority of the PAF units involved in the exercise had continued to remain active, some squadrons had returned to their respective bases. According to a very senior military official, the Pakistanis deliberately prolonged the stay of certain army formations, particularly in the areas of strategic importance, but this was primarily a precautionary move. The collective weight of this evidence suggested a defensive deployment of forces by Pakistan.

More worrisome from India's perspective was a shift in the position of ARS as it moved across the Lodhran Bridge over the Sutlej River near Bahawalpur, apparently heading for its peacetime location in Multan. As nearly as can be surmised, the ARS move took place in the second week of January. Specifying a precise date is difficult, since the movement across the bridge itself took several days. The corps did not stop at Multan, however, but continued marching until it occupied positions opposite Bhatinda and Ferozpur. According to a high military official, the First Armored Division, which was located at Tamewali (between Bahawalpur and Bahawalnagar) at that time, was withdrawn to a location north of the Sutlej River, and the Sixth Armored Division was moved closer to the Gujranwala area. While making these moves, Pakistani officials stressed that they were being extremely careful to avoid any appearance of being provocative or threatening to the Indians.

In sending its troops across the Sutlej, Pakistan exposed its entire flank to Indian armor in the Rajasthan sector. Furthermore, this action committed Pakistan's armor to achieving definite military objectives in a possible conflict. This was a somewhat premature action since India's contingency plans, if any, had not been evident. In previous India-Pakistan conflicts, a good deal of feint and maneuver had preceded any irrevocable commitment of armor. This move has been interpreted as either a defensive measure to avoid being caught on the eastern (wrong) side of the river, and having to face the Indian forces there, or as a defensive-offensive measure since it would allow ARS to threaten the rear of the Indian forces or excise Indian territory in Punjab by a pincer movement in conjunction with the ARN. In a calculated risk, Pakistan left Sindh exposed to "slicing" by India's Brasstacks strike corps, hoping that the Indian army would divert the exercise from its original purposes.

Despite Pakistan's reassurances, notes a senior Indian official, the positioning of the reserves painted the picture of an enemy that could now strike at two targets simultaneously: one in Kashmir and the other in the Punjab, where it could cut off Amritsar and Ferozpur and thus deny India access to Kashmir.[21] The positioning also posed two other large problems for India: militarily, Pakistan could isolate its troops in strategic areas; and a show of force on the border could generate confidence for the supporters of Khalistan. Furthermore, Pakistan's reserves were now well situated for a pincer movement to capture a salient post in Punjab or attack it and Jammu and Kashmir simultaneously to disrupt communications between India and Jammu and Kashmir. These developments seemed all the more ominous because they coincided with a meeting of a politicized group of religious leaders known as the Sarbat Khalsa. The Sikh community had organized the meeting to endorse an earlier call for an independent Khalistan by the five-member Panthic ("Holy Book") committee. One of India's fears was that Pakistan might indeed help the Sikh militants establish an independent state outside India or assist them militarily in a general insurrection.

Indian authorities now moved to corroborate their human intelligence through electronic means.[22] In mid-January 1987 they were able to confirm the location of the Pakistani armored divisions. The most likely explanation for India's inactivity from the time it detected the ARS move to when it reacted is that since it only had information on the movements from one source, it was waiting for corroborating evidence. Others believe that adequate troops were available locally and that this deliberate inactivity was the result of a hidden agenda. However, this assessment remains purely speculative. India next informed the press that after Pakistan's forces had completed their exercise and returned to their peace stations, they began moving toward Kashmir and Punjab.[23] Alarmed by Pakistan's "cautious defensive moves," India immediately ordered some counterdefensive measures.

It remains unclear why India precipitously moved its troops into forward defensive positions along the border, reinforcing them through a massive airlift, but all the while seeking a highly publicized modus vivendi with Pakistan. In all likelihood, Pakistan's military movements were intended to disrupt the Brasstacks exercise. Pakistan would have been far less anxious about the exercise had its scale and scope been reduced or the whole maneuver deflected. Incidentally, India's army had ensured that adequate defensive forces were available in Punjab to meet any contingencies arising out of the moves by ARN and ARS because it could have deployed additional forces from the Central/Eastern Command and training establishments. Indeed, it was confident that any Pakistani offensive could be blunted after comparing the forces available with those needed for an offensive operation in the heavily fortified Punjab sector. Besides, the canal system in Punjab strengthened the prepared defenses, making any armored thrust very difficult. Troops were not moved into their defensive positions initially because these movements would have sent out the wrong signals and heightened tensions. Therefore no crisis need have occurred, and the Brasstacks exercise could have continued on course as scheduled.

India's contradictory actions can be explained in several ways. India may have wanted to strengthen its borders even as it intended a troop disengagement. While hoping to allay Pakistan's fears about the exercise, it might have also felt the need to assure the Indian public that it would proceed without change. By January 23, however, both sides had been overtaken by suspicion of what they saw as the other's offensive moves and seemed poised for confrontation.

As war hysteria began to spread, the senior Pakistani military and civilian strategic communities (the latter both within and outside the government) were divided in their assessment of the crisis. Two of the most senior Pakistani military officials of that time remember thinking war was unlikely, despite the ominous ground positions and associated preparations. As one of them pointed out, war was far from certain for many reasons. For one thing, most India-Pakistan wars in the past had been fought because of

Kashmir, but Jammu and Kashmir was enjoying a period of relative calm just then. With the Afghanistan crisis still in progress and the Americans deeply involved, the possibility of Soviet instigation was discounted, especially after India's prime minister, Morarji Desai, had earlier refused to initiate trouble on Pakistan's eastern border when pressed to do so by the Soviet Union. A senior Pakistani military official stressed that there was no political reason so overwhelming as to go to war and no military provocation strong enough to initiate one. Because India is a cautious country, he added, it tends to button up its entire border in a war, although at that time the border was not closed. Similarly, Indian analysts could not see Pakistan starting a war because of India's military edge. Even Rajiv Gandhi, in his press conference of January 20, stressed that India had not reciprocated in a manner that could heighten tension. Some Indian officials and soldiers believed that the government had deliberately concocted the entire border scenario in order to facilitate the army's entry into Punjab without having to declare an internal emergency.

Crisis Concluded

January 24 brought a flurry of regional diplomatic activity that matched the military maneuvers in intensity and seriousness. The various meetings that took place were followed by a Pakistani proposal for urgent talks with India to resolve the problem. There were two other conciliatory events: in a widely reported remark to the Pakistani ambassador at New Delhi airport (in advance of a meeting to set up an Africa Fund), Rajiv Gandhi indicated that the border situation needed to be deescalated expeditiously; and Arun Singh was removed from the Ministry of Defense and replaced by V. P. Singh, who was shifted from the Finance Ministry. This move possibly sprang from mixed motives, but it did convey a conciliatory message to Pakistan in a supercharged atmosphere. A press conference by Humayun Khan in New Delhi also had a calming effect, as he publicly discussed the assurances he had received from Rajiv Gandhi.[24]

The next day, Prime Minister Junejo announced that Pakistan was willing to hold consultations with the Indians for the return of normalcy, and the two prime ministers spoke with each other, reaffirming their desire for deescalation. Subsequently, India accepted the request for immediate talks on deescalating the border crisis. The telephone hotline between the two militaries was at last activated, with discussions between military officials of the two operations directorates.

On India's Republic Day (January 26), Pakistan announced that Foreign Secretary Abdul Sattar would visit India for talks to defuse the border tensions and would meet with the Secretary (East), Alfred Gonsalves. Clarifying India's position, a government spokesman noted that although its army and air force would remain on alert, there would be no new deployments. Both President Zia and Prime Minister Junejo conveyed greetings to Rajiv Gandhi on the occasion of India's Republic Day. President Zia, who had left a day earlier for Kuwait to attend a summit conference of Islamic nations, commented that for the past decade Pakistan had been attempting to convince India that it did not present any security threat to its neighbor, before adding gratuitously, "Pakistan has never felt any threat from India during the last ten years and, as such, it never asked New Delhi why it had been buying large quantities of weapons from several countries." Zia's willingness to leave Pakistan at this juncture indicated a degree of confidence that the crisis was under control. It had, indeed, definitely passed by this date, although with the Indian and Pakistani armed forces still in close proximity, there was always the possibility of a miscalculation and actual conflict.

Pakistan then decided to enter into negotiations with India to end the confrontation and relieve the tension, announcing its decision through the country's still-censored press.[25] On January 30 a delegation of Pakistani officials headed by Foreign Secretary Sattar proceeded to India and began negotiations to deescalate the tensions. As the Pakistan delegation arrived, pro forma saber rattling continued on both sides. Meanwhile, India's Cricket Control Board invited President Zia to watch the India-Pakistan cricket match to be held in Nagpur or Pune in March, and he promptly accepted in principle. The match in Jaipur on February 21, he suggested, might be more convenient since March 23 was Pakistan Day.

The secretary-level talks from January 31 to February 4 started on a positive note, with the two sides agreeing on the need for greater transparency and for more frequent talks between their respective DGMOs. India's delegates agreed to study Pakistan's twelve-point proposal for reducing tension, which aimed among other things to halt any further forward movement of troops, prohibit the laying of minefields and digging of trenches, pull forces back to a distance of 10 miles from the border, and bring the air forces to a lower state of alert, with subsequent disengagement and measures to prevent a recurrence of such crises.[26] Pakistan did not urge the cancellation of Brasstacks, which was to continue into March.

In response, India suggested an eight-point proposal. It sought the withdrawal of Pakistani armored divisions but offered no withdrawal on its side.

Negotiations on February 2 and 3 injected a degree of balance, whereupon the talks were extended by a day and an agreement was signed on February 4 providing for a sector-by-sector disengagement, starting with the Ravi-Chenab area. Pakistan was to withdraw an armored division and an infantry division, and India was to withdraw a mountain division to peacetime locations. Both sides also agreed not to make any offensive movement to the border in any sector. All mines were to be lifted and satellite airfields deactivated. However, Pakistan was to retain one independent armored brigade and an infantry brigade in the Ravi-Chenab corridor. The other precautionary placements, including that of the Pakistani armored division in the south and the Indian forces, were not affected.

The key clause in the Sattar-Gonsalves Accord was not just the provision for a step-by-step withdrawal but a firm commitment by both sides not to attack each other.[27] Admittedly, this clause was specifically related to the crisis under discussion, but it did certainly raise hopes that it might become permanent. The accord initiated a gradual withdrawal of forces to peacetime locations, starting with the Ravi-Chenab corridor. While welcoming the accord as a first step toward peace, many in Pakistan felt that it mainly helped to allay Indian anxieties as it concentrated on withdrawals from the Ravi-Chenab sector and not on the Rajasthan area. The Indian deployment in Rajasthan, especially in the light of the troubled situation in Sindh, was viewed with some concern because the Indian government had conceded nothing in this sector.

The pledges not to attack each other, to exercise maximum restraint, and to avoid all provocative actions along the border indicated that deescalation was well under way. After the two countries completed the partial and phased fifteen-day withdrawal from the Ravi-Chenab salient, President Zia ul-Haq visited India, ostensibly to watch the cricket match at Jaipur. This cricket diplomacy had nothing to do with defusing the Brasstacks crisis, but it certainly helped consolidate the tenuous peace just established. Cricket diplomacy also provided an opportunity for informal talks between Zia and Rajiv, covering the whole range of contentious issues, and they, too, accelerated the process of normalization.

In purely military terms, the Brasstacks exercise achieved its essential objectives of providing ground experience in using the newly raised RAPIDs and mechanized infantry divisions, operating signals and communication equipment in desert conditions, and implementing real-time computerized command and control arrangements. The Indian military learned important lessons from this exercise, especially in the area of logistics management. The significant shift in Indian military doctrine announced in 2005 (see chapter 7) is directly traceable to innovations developed by the Brasstacks exercise. Brasstacks also raised questions about the wisdom of holding a large-scale military exercise in border areas, a point that was emphasized again in 1990 during the crisis following Pakistan's large-scale Zarb-e-Momin exercise.

Policymaking

The Brasstacks crisis revealed important policymaking lapses in India. The most notable was the breakdown of communications. In New Delhi, the prime minister (who also held the defense portfolio at that time), his minister of state for defense, and the service chiefs seemed to have had few exchanges as the crisis unfolded. There was a serious lack of communication between the prime minister's office (PMO) and the Ministry of Defense over the nature and implications of Pakistani force movements (particularly with regard to the Army Reserve South), and perhaps even over the scope, nature, and intent of Brasstacks. The late intelligence on the Pakistani movements certainly did not help matters. At one crucial moment, the PMO clearly had serious doubts about the capacity of the services to handle the situation.

No less problematic, the Ministry of External Affairs had not been included in the strategic planning and management of Brasstacks. Much to its embarrassment, the ministry was caught by surprise when news of the maneuver was released at press briefings by General Sundarji and Arun Singh on January 18. It was most unusual for the army chief to brief the press—a function typically handled by the Directorate of Public Relations in the Ministry of Defense and the civilian bureaucracy. Subsequently, at a press conference on January 20, the prime minister offered something of an explanation for the exercise by drawing pointed attention to the concentration of Pakistan's troops along the India-Pakistan border, which was heightening the tension between the two countries. A casualty of this conference was Foreign Secretary A. P. Venkateswaran, who submitted his resignation after Rajiv Gandhi announced that he would be removed from office for suggesting that the prime minister would be visiting Pakistan as the current president of SAARC. This created a gap in the higher decisionmaking apparatus at a critical juncture, as did the removal of Arun Singh as minister of state for defense. A theory expounded by some knowledgeable officials is that Rajiv Gandhi saw the Brasstacks crisis as an opportunity to move some of his key advisers to new positions. As already mentioned, V. P. Singh was moved out of his post as minister of finance and shifted to the politically less important Ministry of Defense; others claim that this shift was made for entirely different reasons—V. P. Singh's campaign against tax evaders had begun to make Rajiv Gandhi uneasy, especially since it was targeting the actor Amitabh Bachhan, a close friend of Rajiv's at the time. In terms of strategy, replacing Arun Singh with V. P. Singh could have shifted the blame to the latter if the Brasstacks gambit turned out badly for India; there was also some suspicion that V. P. Singh had his eye on the prime ministership himself. The prime minister might have also lost confidence in Arun Singh, who, as de facto defense minister, had not kept him informed of Pakistan's troop movements.

The crisis also raises questions about the configuration of power within India. Did the military and civilian participants in these events see opportunities or threats in the crisis with respect to the balance of power between them? While the move of V. P. Singh from the Finance to the Defense Ministry may have reflected domestic political exigencies, there is evidence that Rajiv Gandhi also wanted to achieve greater control over the military during the crisis. The *Hindu's* well-informed correspondent G. K. Reddy reported on January 30: "There is now firm assertion of political control over the formulation of policy on such matters without letting the defence establishment influence such decisions on purely tactical considerations."[28]

Channels of communication between the Defense and Foreign Ministries must have been equally poor, since the latter did not seem to have joined the discussions at the planning stage of the exercise or during the evolving crisis. Explanations for this differ. Some blamed the Ministry of External Affairs (MEA) for a lack of interest, while some in the ministry itself believed that Brasstacks would only create trouble and that it was best, bureaucratically, to stay away from the exercise. Others, including a senior Indian army general, have asserted that the MEA was deliberately kept uninformed about key elements of Brasstacks because it "could not be trusted to keep a secret." Apparently, the ministry got its first inkling of the crisis from the Sundarji-Arun press briefing. In response, several diplomatic missions showed up seeking clarifications from the MEA, which had no answers. For that matter, even the Ministry of Defense was kept on the periphery, since all Brasstacks-related decisions were being made by the minister of state and the Chiefs of Staff Committee. The defense secretary was only called upon for help with administrative matters.

This situation highlighted the lack of institutional decisionmaking during the Rajiv Gandhi years. Rajiv made major decisions himself or in consultation with his personal staff, without having the concerned bureaucracy properly examine the issues involved. For instance, it remains unclear whether MEA was ever asked to ascertain Pakistan's reactions to Brasstacks or to convey its peaceful intent. The general criticism of the way the Brasstacks exercise and resulting crisis was handled is that nobody except a small group in the prime minister's office and a few officers close to the army chief was aware of the crisis, ostensibly because of the need for secrecy. With wider consultations, there would have been greater appreciation of the disruption to rail, air, and ship movements and hence to the national economy, and greater awareness of the political dimensions of the exercise.

Personalized decisionmaking without structural ties can have another disconcerting effect: decisions will not have the benefit of the institutional memory of the concerned bureaucracies. In this instance, some might have pointed out that past experience with large-scale exercises such as Digvijay indicated that questions were likely to arise on the Pakistani side. The authorities might then have exercised more caution in deciding whether to proceed with Brasstacks. At least more effective confidence-building measures could have been put in place before India embarked on this exercise.

Jaswant Singh, a leading opposition figure, who would later be close to the center of the crises in both 1999 and 2001–02, found this approach to decisionmaking very troubling: "We are left with an overriding and unfortunate impression, [that] our Prime Minister is unable to command his own brief and, what is even more distressing, he is no longer able to conceal his incomprehension of it either."[29] It is possible that Rajiv's interest in Brasstacks started off as an adventure, but that he got cold feet when it blew up into a crisis. Compared with his mother's masterful preparation before the 1971 war that broke Pakistan in half, Rajiv's efforts at high strategy seem amateurish. Yet it is possible that Rajiv was not fully informed. As already mentioned, he certainly was not told that Pakistan's Army Reserve South had crossed the Sutlej—he was holidaying in the Andamans, hardly an indication of a leader bent on fomenting a crisis. Perhaps the crisis was simply due to an error in judgment on the part of Rajiv and several of his advisers.

On the Pakistani side, the military establishment dominated the policy process, and those largely responsible for defusing the crisis were President Zia ul-Haq and General Arif, the virtual head of the Pakistan army. During January 1987, the Defense Committee of the Cabinet (DCC) and Joint Chiefs of Staff Committee (JCSC) held innumerable meetings to address the crisis, and the pace stepped up as the threat from India seemed to grow.

Pakistan's air chief said he had never seen so many meetings in such a short time. The physical presence of large Indian forces so close to the border was in itself enough to worry the Pakistanis, but, added to Islamabad's intelligence information, it created an alarming sense of Indian intentions and capabilities. At the height of the crisis, President Zia was supposed to go to Kuwait to attend a meeting related to the Organization of the Islamic Conference (OIC). Many in the DCC urged him not to go because they thought a war was imminent. But Zia said that going to Kuwait would generate positive signals for the Indians, and Kuwait was after all only one hour (flying time) away. Zia appeared to be the calmest of the DCC members and had recommended caution.[30] If he did not go to Kuwait, Zia thought, it would intensify an already palpable war hysteria. Besides, he also advised Prime Minister Junejo to talk to Rajiv Gandhi on the telephone.

At the same time, there is strong evidence of a wide civil-military gap in communication. For instance, Junejo and Ambassador Humayun Khan appear to have been kept outside the decisionmaking chain of command at various times and with respect to various issues.[31]

What general conclusions, then, can be drawn about security decisionmaking up to and during the crisis? Governments obviously cannot be held to abstract standards of perfection. A degree of error, miscalculation, and misjudgment enters into all decisionmaking, particularly under conditions of stress. Therefore policymakers need to take advantage of internal checks and balances and be ready to review a decision to make sure it is not wrong or counterproductive. The history of South Asia is replete with examples of policymakers who, confident in their ability to manipulate a fast-changing situation, led their countries into extreme danger. This seems to be an accurate description of the way in which India's policy process operated in this particular crisis.

Perceptions, Misperceptions, and the Press

As the crisis progressed, both sides quickly assumed the worst about each other's intentions. Perhaps officialdom's most serious and enduring misperception in this regard occurred on the Indian side. India's decisionmakers appear to have consistently misjudged Pakistan's potential reaction to their military exercises. Drawing on their memory of Exercise Digvijay and the relatively sanguine Pakistani reactions in 1983–84, they seemed persuaded that Islamabad would not be troubled by the considerably expanded dimensions of Brasstacks. Although Pakistan made several attempts in the latter half of 1986 to express its concern, the Indians repeatedly discounted the messages they received, insisting that Pakistan was only "beating the drum" (*dhol bajana*) to attract Washington's attention in order to remind it that India was "dangerous" and duplicitous. Others saw Pakistani messages as more or less pro forma diplomatic and political statements.

The Junejo-Gandhi meeting during the Bangalore SAARC summit provided further evidence of misguided thinking. From their conversation, Junejo concluded that Gandhi knew little about the exercise, but that in any case he would scale it back upon his return to New Delhi. When signs of a downsizing did not appear by early December, Pakistan decided to extend its own exercises and stopped operating the hotline. On the Indian side, the Junejo meeting was quickly forgotten or ignored. Gandhi may have viewed Junejo's request to scale back Brasstacks in the light of modifications already made to the original "full mobilization" exercise for cost and administrative reasons. In mentioning a scaling down, Gandhi may have been referring to these changes. The Indian side therefore interpreted continuing Pakistani expressions of concern as ingenuous and obstructive. It should be noted that Washington also became more and more worried about the lack of Indian action after Gandhi's apparent commitment to scale back the exercise.

To add to the confusion, intelligence reports reaching Pakistan about Brasstacks seem to have been exaggerated and alarmist, viewing the intentions behind the exercise and the capabilities deployed as indicating sure signs of a likely war. In retrospect, that assessment seems to have been correct, although Pakistan may have been unaware of changes in Indian planning. It assumed from intelligence reports, for instance, that the Brasstacks exercise would be held along an east-west axis and could therefore conceal a thrust into Sindh, whereas Indian decisionmakers had eventually settled on a south-north axis on the eastern side of a major obstacle, the Rajasthan canal, and therefore the exercise could not have been converted into a surprise attack. In truth, as noted earlier, the exercise originally had an east-west configuration, but this was changed to a south-north configuration after the crisis erupted.[32]

Pakistan's faulty ideas about Indian intentions may have sprung in part from an inaccurate story filed during the crisis by the widely read and respected Indian journalist G. K. Reddy, who referred to an east-west axis. As mentioned earlier, Pakistani intelligence also suggested that Indian troops were carrying first-line ammunition, which to them signified an "operation" rather than an "exercise." However, this ammunition was apparently dumped into divisional storage areas rather than carried by the troops.

Again, as noted, this was true and ostensibly designed to provide greater realism to the exercise, as well as enable India to be prepared should Pakistan react militarily.[33] Intelligence also reported that India's Sixth Mountain Division from Uttar Pradesh had been moved into Kashmir. The military rationale for this move was probably to relieve border security force units in the state but, as part of a larger picture of Indian actions and seeming obfuscation, it was viewed with trepidation in Islamabad.

While senior army commanders and Generals Zia and Arif were inclined to discount these reports, they were not without effect. Arif, although doubtful about their authenticity and implications in certain respects, could not afford to ignore them. He promised Junejo that he would take necessary precautions, which turned out to be the ARN and ARS movements that were to alarm India.

Despite their own misperceptions and misinterpretations, both sides were at times sensitive to the possibility of misperceptions in the other, and this may have helped them to make stabilizing decisions as well. Pakistan's uneasiness about India's decision to man defensive positions along the Punjab border appears to have quickly dissipated after Arif's precautionary moves, and to have prompted the two sides to negotiate. In making their ostensibly defensive move, the Indians had calculated that it might be misread as a "buttoning up" of the Punjab border before launching an offensive into Sindh through Rajasthan, which was the Brasstacks exercise area. Therefore they simultaneously announced their readiness to negotiate a joint withdrawal of forces from forward positions. This was perhaps the most serious moment of the crisis for both sides; indeed this reassuring move itself could have been misinterpreted, but it seems that Islamabad eventually recognized India's defensive intent, and the danger passed.

The Press

Brasstacks was South Asia's last crisis in a nonelectronic media environment. As far as the rest of the world was concerned, it did not merit the attention of Afghanistan, South Asia's ongoing crisis of that era, which was far more newsworthy. Of the four crises considered here, Brasstacks received the least intense and briefest coverage in the elite print media of India, Pakistan, and the United States.[34]

Pakistan's coverage began in early December, when Indian troops were massing on the Indo-Pakistani border. This beat the first Indian coverage by two weeks and U.S. mention by three weeks. It was also more intense than

Figure 3-1. *Press Coverage of the Brasstacks Crisis, December 1986–February 1987*

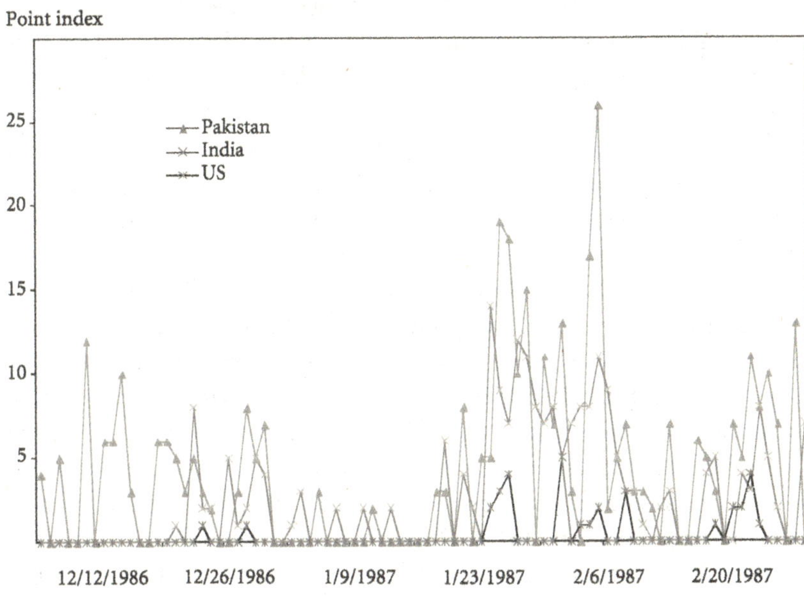

in either India or the United States and reached its peak in early February, as the crisis was deescalating and peace accords were being signed. Indian coverage got off to a very slow start, but a peak came in the last week of January, when the Indian military was put on alert.

Of the three countries, the United States had the least intense press coverage (figure 3-1). In the first seven weeks of the crisis, it merited only two passing references in the *Washington Post* and the *New York Times.* Neither American paper covered the very important briefing given to Indian editors on January 18 by Arun Singh and General Sundarji, where the imminence of war was discussed. Certainly, American officials were trying to downplay the seriousness of the crisis, and the press never zeroed in on Brasstacks as it was escalating.

These references in the press indicate delayed, and then muted, coverage by the state that by and large initiated the crisis. The American press came to the story only after it was fully aired in the regional press.

The press clearly contributed to the general misunderstanding and may have affected policy perceptions. The media in both India and Pakistan not only saw the troop concentration differently but also read too much into each other's actions. The Indian newspapers were of the opinion that Pakistan was poised to initiate armed action at very short notice.[35] Some speculated that Pakistan wanted to acquire territory for the Khalistanis, which would enable them to declare their independence; Islamabad would then concentrate on seizing its own main objective, the Kashmir Valley. The Pakistani press read the same motives in the Indian troop concentration close to their border, which they saw as an imminent, highly visible threat, with an implicit target in Sindh. The exercise resembled India's successful 1971 operation, which resulted in the detachment of a province (East Pakistan) from Pakistan and the creation of Bangladesh.[36]

What stands out in the Brasstacks crisis is the Indian media's unquestioning attitude toward Indian policy. During the crisis, as noted earlier, General Sundarji briefed the editors of major newspapers about the belligerent moves of the Pakistan army on January 18. Despite their skepticism, the newspapers dutifully generated headlines the next day about the security threat posed by Pakistan, underplaying the Indian role in fomenting the crisis. The lead was provided by the official television channel Doordarshan. According to the Pakistani high commissioner in India at the time, Doordarshan changed its tone on January 25 when the prime minister's office directed it to claim that India took the initiative to defuse the situation.[37]

American press coverage of Brasstacks was reasonably well informed because a number of reporters were based in India and Pakistan, covering primarily the war in Afghanistan. They accurately presented both countries' claims and counterclaims concerning the responsibility for escalation. However, most of these reports missed the deeper story of Brasstacks, namely, the great distrust between the two countries. Also, few American reporters were aware of the nuclear implications of Brasstacks, because developments within the Pakistani program were being withheld by American officials. Those who may have known had not publicly made the connection between the crisis and the state of Pakistan's (and India's) nuclear weapons programs. By the time the American press realized the severity of the crisis, it was over, and the media had moved on to other issues.

Nuclear Developments

The crisis itself was not overtly a nuclear crisis, but shortly afterward a key figure in the Pakistani nuclear program, Abdul Qadeer Khan, fired a nuclear warning across India's bow. A sensational press report by Indian journalist

Kuldip Nayar appeared in the London *Observer* on March 1, 1987, based on a January 28 interview with A. Q. Khan suggesting that Pakistan, if pressed, would develop a nuclear weapon. A close study of the story indicates that much of the material may have been drawn from earlier public statements of A. Q. Khan. It did not affect the course of the crisis because it did not appear until after the crisis had subsided and therefore was not received in time to affect key decisions. When it was received, according to Indian decisionmakers, it was not taken seriously because of the source of this nuclear signaling and the means by which it was conveyed.

Still, this event remains one of the puzzles of 1987. The A. Q. Khan interview has been discussed with most of the key individuals involved, but some questions surrounding it remain unanswered. For one thing, Pakistan had begun nuclear signaling of one sort or another as early as 1984 (and India perhaps as early as 1974 with the Pokhran test, although the audience was domestic rather than foreign). If Pakistan was sending a signal, its intended audience is unclear: Indian decisionmakers, the Americans, or the Pakistani public? Or was it an instance of individual self-publicity? If the interview had been made public somewhat earlier, it might have had a direct impact on the course of the Brasstacks crisis itself. In any case, the crisis did evidently accelerate the nuclear programs of both India and Pakistan.

Certainly, 1987 was colored by a nuclear crisis in the mind of one key participant, General Sundarji, who afterward remarked that this was India's last chance to defeat Pakistan by conventional arms before the latter acquired a nuclear deterrent that would make all-out war impossibly dangerous for both sides.[38] Sundarji's views about Pakistan's nuclear ambitions gained added strength shortly after the crisis when, in an interview with *Time* magazine, President Zia declared: "Pakistan has the capability of building the Bomb. You can write today that Pakistan can build a bomb whenever it wishes. Once you have acquired the technology, which Pakistan has, you can do whatever you like," adding that "Pakistan still has no actual plan to make nuclear weapons."[39]

The American Role

When the Brasstacks crisis erupted, as mentioned earlier, the United States was in the midst of a major effort to expel the Soviet Union from Afghanistan. While the United States played a modest role in the crisis and in bringing about a peaceful outcome, the Soviet Union was unhelpful and China played no role. Moscow appears to have felt that an India-Pakistan conflict would help its forces in the war in Afghanistan. The Chinese were observers, but the episode may have strengthened their view of what they regarded as Indian adventurism. Washington had entered into a close military, intelligence, and political relationship with Pakistan and had also initiated a new relationship with India, highlighted by the 1985 visit of Prime Minister Rajiv Gandhi to the United States. Washington wanted not only to wean India away from its long-term alliance with the Soviet Union but also to expand influence in New Delhi, to avert Indian pressure on Pakistan's eastern front. For its part, New Delhi thought it could use the new relationship with Washington to acquire military and dual-use technology as well as to wean the United States away from Pakistan. These calculations appeared again in both the Kargil and 2002 crises in different guises.

Initially, Washington saw the Brasstacks exercise as a non-event, and American policy concentrated on hoping for the best, wishing that two "friends" would not go to war. Privately, White House officials denigrated the Indian relationship and believed that, if they had to choose one side over the other, they would certainly pick Pakistan, not India, a Soviet ally.[40]

The American assessment of the Brasstacks crisis might appear to be rooted in a quintessential cold war attitude: the enemy of a friend, who is also a friend, threatens war, which in turn threatens a larger cold war objective (in this case defeating the Soviet Union in Afghanistan). The response, urging India to exercise restraint and Pakistan to exercise caution, was unexceptional.[41] There was, however, a nuclear undercurrent to the crisis that was not publicly evident at the time.

American policy toward South Asia at the time of the Brasstacks crisis was embodied in two National Security Decision Directives (NSDDs). NSDD 99, issued in 1983, urged strategic support for Pakistan but was ambiguous about whether this support should be extended in the case of an India-Pakistan war, and not just against Soviet-related threats. The directive did acknowledge that another India-Pakistan war would pose a grave danger to American interests. NSDD 147, issued in October 1984, claimed that American aid gave Pakistan a sense of security and an incentive to forgo a nuclear weapons program; in retrospect, neither assertion seems to have been true. This document also repeated the Pakistani claim, not based on any substantial new intelligence, that there was still a possibility of an Indian preemptive strike on Pakistani nuclear facilities, which would probably lead to an all-out war. The directive urged that contingency plans be developed in the event of such a strike on Pakistani nuclear facilities or a general war (it is not clear if any such plans were formulated). It also suggested enhanced dialogue with India, a recommendation that led to Prime Minister Rajiv Gandhi's successful visit to the United States in June 1985.

The three near-crises that took place just before Brasstacks sensitized American officials to Pakistan's evident strategic and military vulnerability. Collectively, they created an atmosphere in which Pakistan's 1986 request for Airborne Warning and Control Systems (AWACS) planes was treated very seriously. Indian officials' statements that the AWACS was a "force multiplier" and would somehow destabilize India-Pakistan relations or unnecessarily threaten India were greeted with astonishment by American officials, who had come to believe that Pakistan, a frontline state, was indeed under direct threat from both the Soviet Union and India. Much as American officials, especially the core group that was aware of the discrepancy between Pakistani pledges and the reality of its nuclear program's steady progress toward a weapon, hesitated to trust Pakistan, the three crises, even if imaginary, boosted Pakistani credibility with regard to its conventional vulnerability.

On the nuclear front, it is certain that in this period Pakistan crossed one or more "redlines," drawn by the U.S. administration in its effort to contain Islamabad's nuclear program. These included the enrichment of uranium to the level required for making a nuclear weapon. While senior Pakistani officials provided assurances that these lines had not been breached, the inner core of American policymakers was desperately trying to work out a formula that would return Pakistan to compliance with the redlines without damaging the war effort in Afghanistan.

Therefore American policy before and during the Brasstacks crisis was guided by the following assumptions about Pakistan, India, their relationship, and the role that the United States might play in South Asia:

—Pakistan was vulnerable to Soviet pressure, and only consistent U.S. support would keep it in the conflict in Afghanistan, since there was strong domestic Pakistani opposition to the war.

—Pakistan could not end its nuclear program for domestic political reasons, but official reassurances that "we will not embarrass you" could be taken at face value.

—The U.S. military aid program had to remain at a level high enough to keep Pakistan in the war, a level of support that would, it was hoped, keep Pakistan from advancing its nuclear program beyond various redlines agreed upon by the two states but not exaggerate Pakistan's own judgment about its ability to take on India's superior numbers.

—In the meantime, various regional efforts at furthering India-Pakistan normalization would be pursued. These efforts included new confidence-building measures (CBMs), support for India-Pakistan dialogue, an elaborate public information and education program on conflict resolution, and the "opening" to India, so that the United States could better serve as a channel of communication between Islamabad and New Delhi. Such measures, if they succeeded, would presumably make it easier for Pakistan to slow the pace of its nuclear program, because the Indian threat would be reduced. If they failed, however, then the administration would find it easier to explain away Pakistan's nuclear program to Congress, where most of the nonproliferation pressure came from.

It was in this political environment—with the United States attempting to control the Pakistani nuclear program, jointly pursue a critical struggle against the Soviet Union in Afghanistan, and normalize relations with New Delhi—that Exercise Brasstacks took place. In retrospect, it had the potential to create a crisis in all three areas of U.S. concern but in fact affected none of them, at least not immediately.

Washington's Assessment

In the U.S. assessment, Brasstacks was a military exercise planned by an American-trained general (Sundarji had attended the U.S. Command and General Staff College, Fort Leavenworth, as had President Zia), using British military doctrine and formations, with Soviet-designed equipment. The U.S. intelligence community was impressed by the scope and complexity of Brasstacks and initially regarded it as a powerful indicator of the sophistication of India's armed forces (Brasstacks was to include an interservice component). It did not treat the exercise as anything other than routine until December 1986. At that time, intelligence analysts cautioned policymakers that Washington and Islamabad would have little or no prior warning if India decided to change direction and advance across the international border. If this were to happen, the Americans believed that Pakistan could last no more than a month unless India committed a major military blunder or unilaterally halted fighting.

The crisis, according to the American consensus, evolved out of India's decision to extend its maneuvers beyond December. After the subsequent Pakistani maneuvers, the Indians became erroneously alarmed and moved their reserves (a total of fifteen divisions) to the border. American officials believed that the actual military balance along the India-Pakistan border was closer than the overall balance, which was clearly in India's favor. The corps-level balance was thought to be even (5:5), as was the divisional balance

(16:16), but the Indians had a substantial eight-brigade advantage in maneuver brigades, with six regular divisions in reserve, to Pakistan's none. Beyond this military assessment, there were also a number of political interpretations of the crisis, although none altered the belief that the core problem was misjudgment or misperceptions on both sides of the India-Pakistan border. American officials discounted arguments emanating from both India and Pakistan concerning the crisis. There was no doubt, they told the Indians, that Brasstacks was a provocative exercise, even if the United States took Indian explanations at face value. They also rejected the Pakistani claim that Brasstacks was being conducted at the behest of the Soviet Union to "soften up" Pakistan before another round of negotiations at Geneva. Those officials who had dealt with Pakistan over the years had often heard the argument of India-Soviet complicity, as Pakistan tried to stretch the 1959 U.S.-Pakistan agreement to cover India as a "communist" power. With the exception of some strongly anti-communist conservatives (but not all), few took the argument of an Indian-Soviet linkage seriously. For some, especially the Reagan conservatives, a Soviet hand was thought to be behind Indian actions.

The idea of Soviet inspiration was generally rejected, as Rajiv Gandhi was thought to be one of the least pro-Soviet of Indian leaders. While an important American goal was to reduce the Indian pressure on Pakistan, there was also an interest in reducing Soviet influence on India. However, American policymakers found it hard to reverse their assessment of the Indian-Soviet connection so soon after they had concluded that India could be lured away from the USSR. Yet while some of India's greatest critics were on the right, so were some of its strongest supporters. Many Reagan conservatives saw India as a noncommunist counter to China; others saw the importance of "weaning" India away from the Soviet Union, weakening the latter further. With conservative opinion on India divided, it was possible for the State Department bureaucracy and White House staffers to construct a middle-of-the-road policy toward New Delhi.

Some American officials felt there might have been domestic reasons for the provocative nature of Brasstacks: perhaps Rajiv Gandhi wanted to demonstrate his anger at the Pakistanis for their support of Sikh separatists and his resolve at home in preparation for elections scheduled for 1989. Others suggested that Rajiv wanted to stake a claim in any Afghan settlement by displaying Indian military power. Pressuring Pakistan was one of the few cards New Delhi could play to win a place at the negotiating table. Furthermore, such military exercises were thought to be one way that India could actually keep itself in the regional strategic game: if India created an atmosphere of uncertainty and crisis, the United States, the Soviet Union, and China, as well as Pakistan, would have to pay more attention to New Delhi.

Without exception, *no* American analyst or policymaker at this time predicted war. While American officials did note that the timing of the crisis phase of Brasstacks was advantageous to India (the Himalayan passes would be snowbound, and China could not intervene), the assessment at the highest level of the Department of State was that a war with Pakistan would be costly and risky and could uncork the nuclear genie in an unpredictable way. Furthermore, a war in 1987 would not, as a war in 1984 might have, stop a Pakistani nuclear weapon from being developed, and this was probably also India's estimate.

The day-to-day American response to the Brasstacks crisis was largely shaped within the Department of State, which viewed Brasstacks as a minor crisis, one that did not need high-level attention or presidential intervention. Yet, with its cold war and containment overtones, this crisis had become, from an American perspective, the most important dispute in the region since the 1971 war. However, the crisis took place at the time of the Iran-Iraq war and heightened tension in Arab-Israeli relations. This meant that the relevant assistant secretary of state (for the Near East and South Asia) was usually deeply engaged in the bureau's other two crisis areas (this was a factor that eventually led to the creation of a free-standing Bureau of South Asian Affairs).

In the case of Brasstacks, institutional and personal memory was good.[42] Important ideological differences within the American policy community affected the response to events in South Asia. As noted, while most senior policymakers, especially political appointees, considered Pakistan a frontline state and one worthy of strong American support in its struggle against the Soviet Union, many conservatives in the administration thought there was an opportunity to lure India away from the Soviet Union; for others, India was a democratic counter to Communist China. None of this dampened their enthusiasm for Pakistan, but the idea of supporting Pakistan and India led, inexorably, to a strategy of encouraging them to normalize their relations. This strategy, embedded in at least one National Security Decision Directive, was to be severely tested during Exercise Brasstacks.

Congress played a marginal role in this crisis. It showed overwhelming and bipartisan support for Pakistan and voted several billion dollars in economic and military aid for Islamabad between 1981 and 1988. However, Congress was deeply concerned about regional nuclear proliferation.[43] The administration had presented the military aid package as an arms control measure: if Pakistan were to be adequately armed and equipped, it would not need American security guarantees against India, nor would it have any incentive to acquire a nuclear weapon.

Congressional critics of Pakistan's nuclear program failed to come up with a policy that would have protected Pakistan's role as the chief arms supplier to the Afghan mujahiddin while constraining its nuclear program. The most vehement critics, such as Senators Alan Cranston and John Glenn, were outflanked by the argument that any tampering with the aid package would endanger the war effort in Afghanistan; they were also not given a complete picture of the Pakistani nuclear program because administration officials were secretive, if not deceptive, in their briefings to members of Congress and their staff. Senator Larry Pressler was chosen to offer a crucial amendment to the Foreign Assistance Bill (the Pressler Amendment) because he was unaware of, or uninterested in, the rate of expansion of Pakistan's clandestine program. He was told, and he believed, that the threat of a complete cutoff was enough to contain this program. Privately, American officials at the core of the policy process acknowledged that this was not true, and that the Pressler Amendment had merely bought time, both for the war in Afghanistan and for a comprehensive approach to regional peacemaking that would, they hoped, make a Pakistani nuclear weapon unnecessary.

Crisis Management

The Brasstacks crisis forced U.S. decisionmakers to confront directly the risks and opportunities of being the go-between. Theoretically, the United States could do nothing and still be blamed by one or both sides. It could get involved and risk making an error. It could help an old friend, Pakistan, possibly risking a relationship with a new friend, India. It could help the bigger power, India, but that could have had an impact on American relations with an important ally, Pakistan (and, later, a strategically significant China). In fact, these alternatives were not discussed at length in American policy documents because there was a benign assumption that neither side intended a provocation. For the most part, American officials played the Brasstacks crisis "down the middle," treating it as if no real crisis were at hand. The basic U.S. assessment at this time was that both sides were guilty of not communicating adequately with the other and that each one misperceived the moves of the other side. Thus the American role was narrowed down to that of providing its good offices to both sides, reassuring each that the actions of the other were well-intentioned, and that mistakes or misjudgment had to be avoided. In the words of one American policymaker involved in shaping the American response to the Brasstacks crisis: "We said to both sides: 'We don't think they are doing what you think they are doing.'" On the basis of information available to Washington, this was reasonable, although in retrospect the chances of war were considerably greater than the American intelligence and policy communities thought.

The closest the United States came to crisis management during Brasstacks was toward the end of January 1987, when American officials began to talk to both sides about the location of their respective armored forces and were asked to confirm these locations. On January 23, Washington came as close as it could to playing the role of intermediary when Ambassador John Gunther Dean had a crucial conversation with Minister of State for Defense Arun Singh. The latter complained that the movement of Pakistan's Army Reserve South from Bahawalpur to Sahiwal was threatening and asked for specifics. In turn, American officials told the Pakistanis of this request and suggested that Pakistan talk directly to the Indians about the ARS movement. The United States also told both sides that it accepted the assurances of each "as sincere" that nothing more than normal (if excessively large) military maneuvers were taking place, but that there was a danger of misperception and a need to consult on the hotline. No information about troop deployment or movements was offered to either side at this moment or at any other time during the crisis. The statement itself, however, was a form of intelligence sharing as India and Pakistan could have read into it that American intelligence had seen nothing out of the ordinary. This engagement continued when, on January 30, officials in Washington reminded both embassies that troops had not been withdrawn according to plan.

A Hidden Nuclear Crisis

From an American point of view, the deeper regional crisis was not Brasstacks but Pakistan's move to acquire nuclear weapons. As piece after piece of the program became known (in many cases through the discovery of illegal Pakistani purchases in the West and in the United States itself), senior American officials began to discuss how the Pakistani nuclear program could be contained without damaging U.S. strategy in Afghanistan. There was not so much a fear that India and Pakistan would eventually acquire nuclear weapons (there were good reasons, it was argued, why neither would want to actually build and deploy them), but that Pakistan would move across several redlines that had been mutually agreed upon. It was these agreements that made it possible to launch a major conventional military assistance program, which in turn was thought to be important in restraining Pakistan's nuclear ambitions. Here there was a fundamental contradiction in U.S. policy, a contradiction that could be exposed in a crisis. Brasstacks was one of a series of such crises, and American officials were less concerned about the actual outbreak of war (indeed, they downplayed its likelihood then) than about changes in Pakistan's nuclear status that would lead to termination of American military sales and other forms of aid, directly endangering the war effort in Afghanistan.

One reason for heightened American concern on the nuclear front was an apparent change in India's policy. Following General Sundarji's appointment as the new army chief, Arun Singh (the de facto minister of defense) left the impression that not only were the Indian armed forces going to develop new strategies and induct new weapons, but that the nuclear option was being reconsidered at the highest level.[44] American officials recognized that they were faced with a dilemma: by strengthening Pakistan against the Soviet Union, they had inadvertently challenged India.

The American response to Brasstacks reveals both the strengths and weaknesses of U.S. policy focused on the cold war competition. Its strength was that it lavished high-level attention on Pakistan, the cold war ally vital to the American effort to evict Soviet forces from Afghanistan. Also, India was newly important, more because of an interest in weaning it away from Soviet influence than for its own sake. The Department of State, the National Security Council, and the Central Intelligence Agency, as well as a number of important members of Congress in both political parties, were eager to fight on what many thought to be the most important battlefield of the cold war. Just as Brasstacks was taking place, the Afghan crisis reached a military and political turning point of its own, with heightened Soviet pressure on the mujahiddin and Pakistan, the introduction of Stinger surface-to-air missiles, and the expansion of the political dialogue held at Geneva under the auspices of the United Nations.

The weakness of the cold war–first attitude was that, since American priorities and interests were not necessarily those of the regional states, the United States could be, and often was, manipulated by a regional power that best knew how to address those priorities. In South Asia, this regional power was Pakistan, which effectively appealed to American cold war concerns to elicit benefit in many ways, including through the supply of significant quantities of conventional weapons and economic assistance, support for the military regime, and a tolerant attitude toward its covert nuclear weapons program. This is not to say that the two countries did not share important interests, but Pakistan's overriding goal was to strengthen itself in relation to India, and the Afghan war provided it with the means to do so through an upgrading of its conventional weapons and continuation of its nuclear program.

Brasstacks was a "typical" cold war crisis for the United States. While no vital American interests were engaged, larger, global concerns were present: containment and nonproliferation. These had led the United States to pursue seemingly contradictory policies, although they were intended to be complementary, supporting Pakistan with conventional arms while opposing its nuclear program. Brasstacks illuminated the risks involved in this policy: the crisis indicated Pakistan's vulnerability and America's need to help an ally, but this also meant that it would be more difficult to pursue a tough nonproliferation policy toward Islamabad—inadvertently, India's Brasstacks exercise strengthened Pakistan's nuclear program.

A major mid-crisis policy assessment concluded that Brasstacks would not lead to war, but that American regional policy in South Asia would have to be cast in terms broader than mere anti-Sovietism. While accepting the value of the earlier "weaning" policy, luring India away from the Soviet Union, it concluded (reflecting the views of both the India and Pakistan desks), that India's view of itself as the regional dominant power had to be factored into American policy. In particular, a strategy of encouraging India-Pakistan regional talks, CBMs, and possibly conventional arms control measures was seen as being in U.S. interests, though India might well have to be persuaded to enter into such a dialogue. There was widespread agreement within the policy community that this strategy need not compromise America's close relationship with Pakistan, but would strengthen its southern flank and might eventually lead to a more active Indian role in bringing about a Soviet withdrawal from Afghanistan.

Brasstacks had no immediate impact on U.S.-Pakistan relations because the two countries were so closely intertwined in Afghanistan. It generated considerable skepticism within the Reagan administration about India's intentions toward Pakistan, and for several years at least, the U.S.-Pakistan connection was to remain inviolable. However, if the crisis precipitated the production of a Pakistani nuclear device, as some have alleged, then it indirectly transformed U.S.-Pakistan relations and led to the rupture of 1990, when the Pressler Amendment was invoked. Indeed, this may have been one of the goals of Brasstacks (from the Indian perspective), but by that time some senior Pakistani officials also wanted a break with the Americans and saw the nuclear program as the way to achieve this break and ensure Pakistani security once it occurred.

Brasstacks certainly delayed the normalization of India-U.S. relations. The opening to India had been achieved in 1985 but had not gone smoothly. For India, a test of the relationship was gaining access to increased dual-use technology, but Brasstacks was a military crisis and forced the United States to think about its overall relationship with New Delhi. In January 1987, American officials told visiting Foreign Secretary A. P. Venkateswaran (soon to be fired by Rajiv Gandhi) that Exercise Brasstacks made it easier for Pakistan to obtain advanced weapons; thus while Brasstacks might have improved the operational readiness of the Indian military, it had the ironic effect of strengthening Pakistan's case in Washington. After Brasstacks, India had more difficulty getting access to dual-use technology items because it was seen as reckless and provocative, especially when its July 1987 Checkerboard military exercise along the border with China was factored in.

In the end, the American effort to walk down several roads at the same time failed. Inadvertently, what might have been an Indian attempt to drive a wedge between the United States and Pakistan may have succeeded in providing the strategic justification and political cover for continued work on the Pakistani bomb, with tacit American support. If, and one can only conjecture, this was the Indian goal, then it played directly into Pakistani hands by demonstrating, in such exercises as Brasstacks, that previous Pakistani alarms over Indian aggressiveness were well grounded. If the United States was unwilling to come to Pakistan's aid against such tangible threats, then it could not keep Pakistan from acquiring the kind of weapons that would, once and for all, deter a major Indian attack.

Thus, at least from the vantage point of Washington, (1) Brasstacks pushed Pakistan down a path that led it away from the United States and toward an unknown region of weak nuclear deterrence; (2) the exercise conveyed the impression of an unpredictable and possibly irresponsible Indian leadership, making it more difficult to expand U.S.-Indian ties; and (3) as for India's own decisionmaking system, the crisis demonstrated that, with the best of people and the best of information, it was possible to misjudge events in a region of considerable importance to the United States. Finally, from an American perspective, one of the most important elements of the Brasstacks crisis was the opportunity it provided to urge both India and Pakistan to consider CBMs. In retrospect, American officials believe that regional understanding of the importance of CBMs really increased during 1986–87, with both countries welcoming and appreciating the American role in providing information about such measures.

In late October 1986, as a result of conversations during Secretary of Defense Caspar Weinberger's visit earlier that month, talking points were sent out to both New Delhi and Islamabad on the recently negotiated Conference on Security and Cooperation in Europe (CSCE) Stockholm agreement. Drawing on the U.S.-Soviet experience in Europe, the United States also presented a non-paper to India and Pakistan on prenotification of major military exercises. In various démarches concerning the Brasstacks exercise, in late January and mid-February 1987, the United States reminded both countries of the earlier discussions on the Stockholm procedures. On February 14, 1987, a follow-up paper, complete with a list of CBMs, was provided to both countries, with the suggestion that the United States would be prepared to send an "appropriate expert in CBMs" to Islamabad and Delhi. These CBM proposals originated with a staff member in the National Security Council but were turned into "talking points" by the relevant country desks in the Department of State.

Observations and Lessons Learned

This overview of the Brasstacks crisis suggests several lessons. First, states in an asymmetrical situation to each other run an obvious risk in conducting large military exercises near their borders. Naturally, such exercises are most realistic if they are conducted in the actual areas where hostilities might take place, but this, equally naturally, also heightens the danger that the other state might assume the military exercises are a ploy to initiate military operations against them. These fears need to be allayed by conducting such exercises in an area somewhat removed from the border, all the while ensuring full transparency about their details, such as troops to be employed, armor involved, and so on. Inviting observers from the other state to attend could also go a long way in allaying suspicions.

Second, it is crucial for the highest level of leadership of adversarial countries to maintain communication at all times. If this does not happen, control of the crisis may pass into the hands of the armed forces and intelligence agencies. Being professional pessimists, these organizations could readily function on the basis of worst-case scenarios that could thereafter become self-fulfilling prophecies.

Third, it is important to establish confidence-building measures between adversarial countries. The highest priority should be accorded to hotlines and similar communications and transparency measures. The need for greater transparency is obvious to avoid the kinds of misperceptions that led to the Brasstacks crisis, given that both sides were proceeding on the basis of worst-case scenarios to plan their countermeasures. Brasstacks, as a crisis, did suggest that both sides invite military observers from the other country to watch military exercises as they unfolded; it also suggests the importance of establishing crisis management centers in suitable administrative sites in both countries, perhaps in their respective cabinet secretariats or prime minister's offices. Partial steps along these lines were taken subsequently but did not prevent the major crisis of 2002, let alone the Kargil conflict of 1999.

Fourth, a likely intermediary, such as the United States, failed to see that a crisis was building and therefore did not intervene either early or effectively enough—and may have offered both sides misleading information to the effect that there was no genuine need for alarm. Washington had a very benign view of Indian intentions, and its perceptions were shaped by wishful thinking and concerns over the war in Afghanistan rather than by an objective assessment of the situation at hand. It was also unable to see how quickly misperceptions could lead to a crisis situation.

In retrospect, Brasstacks still remains a puzzling event. It did *not* directly involve Kashmir; in 1986–87 the Valley was quiet, with no hint of the brewing storm that began in 1989 and continues to smolder. Internal politics did not cause any special anxiety, although the militancy in the Punjab was still a challenge. India was well aware that Pakistan was steadily proceeding toward gaining nuclear capabilities, but the earlier crises in 1984–86 (mentioned in chapter 2) had underlined the reality that no military solution would reverse Pakistan's nuclear quest. Finally, Rajiv Gandhi had a three-fourths majority in parliament, and there was no reason for him to divert attention from domestic problems and liabilities by seeking a foreign adventure.

Still, the Brasstacks crisis did occur and had the dangerous potential to trigger a conflict as much by accident and misperception as by design. It revealed what a "Guns of August" scenario might look like in South Asia. That this lesson was not learned is evident from the Kashmir-focused crisis of the spring of 1990, which exacerbated India-Pakistan relations a scarce three years later.

CHAPTER FOUR

The Compound Crisis of 1990

Only three years after Brasstacks, India and Pakistan were once again at odds, this time in a rapidly changing and complex environment. The cold war had just ended, the Soviet Union and the Warsaw Pact were disintegrating, and the Persian Gulf was on the verge of instability. Closer to home, Indian-administered Kashmir was in ferment following a crackdown on militants and kidnappers of the daughter of India's home minister (she was later freed in exchange for the release of jailed separatists). Equally significant, both countries had new and untested governments, each faced with an assortment of escalating domestic problems. Not surprisingly, the 1990 impasse was not the product of a single event or idea but of a confluence of actions, statements, and perceptions. Toward the end, it also acquired a nuclear dimension.

Trading accusations and threats, India and Pakistan spent February, March, and April of 1990 seemingly preparing for war. India accused Pakistan of supporting the Kashmiri militant separatist groups, while Pakistan criticized India for the crackdown in Indian-administered Kashmir and called for a plebiscite there. Both countries moved significant forces to the international border and placed their air forces on higher alert. There was also a spurt of intense diplomacy, with a visit to India by a high-level Pakistani emissary, Yaqub Khan (which may have heightened rather than eased the tension), and a meeting between the Indian and Pakistani foreign ministers in New York. The U.S. ambassadors to Islamabad and New Delhi and their staffs also became deeply involved in crisis prevention (going so far as to informally monitor the movement of Indian and Pakistani forces in the field), and in mid-May Washington sent a high-level mission headed by Deputy National Security Adviser Robert Gates.

By the first week of June, the crisis had subsided. Both countries agreed to withdraw their additional troops from the border and to hold talks. This crisis had been briefer than others in the region and left observers debating whether war had been likely or might have evolved into a nuclear confrontation. Many also wondered whether outside intervention had helped defuse the tensions.

The Strategic Context

The eighteen months preceding the 1990 crisis were an astonishingly dramatic era in contemporary history. The period saw the further enfeeblement of the Soviet Union, which was loosening its grip both internally and in countries of the Warsaw Pact. Mikhail Gorbachev's announcement on December 7, 1988, that Soviet troops would withdraw from Europe gave the Warsaw Pact countries added incentive to overthrow their communist governments. Throughout 1989, Soviet forces had exited in whole or in part from Mongolia, Hungary, Czechoslovakia, and East Germany. In November 1989, the Warsaw Pact foreign ministers formally abandoned the Brezhnev doctrine. By October 1990 the Berlin Wall was dismantled and Germany reunified. Perhaps most significant for South Asia was the Soviet withdrawal from Afghanistan in mid-February 1989. By 1990 the Soviet Union was requesting Pakistan's support to secure the release of Soviet prisoners of war being held by the Afghan mujahiddin.

The disintegration of the Soviet Union coincided with Beijing's emergence as a global power. Despite the 1989 uprising in Tibet and the brutal treatment accorded to students and workers who had occupied Tiananmen Square, China had been trying to normalize relations with the United States and the faltering Soviet Union. Earlier, in 1988, it had hosted a visit by Rajiv Gandhi, the first visit of an Indian premier to China in thirty-four years. By 1990 the two countries were moving toward a dialogue to resolve their border disputes. At the same time, China continued to regard its relationship with Pakistan as important, not least out of concern about the spread of Islamic fundamentalism into its Muslim minority provinces.

Elsewhere, events had also been moving very rapidly. The Yugoslav federation was crumbling, Vietnam had withdrawn its troops from Cambodia in April 1989, and in South Africa President F. W. de Klerk had begun negotiations with the still-imprisoned Nelson Mandela. In addition, the mounting Palestinian Intifada was eliciting strong sympathy on both sides of the Line of Control (LOC) in Kashmir.

The United States, from the time George H. W. Bush became president on January 20, 1989, had been trying to adjust to these major events. With the Soviet Union posing less of a nuclear threat, the U.S. Congress focused its attention on the issue of proliferation. The growing nuclear capability of South Asia was of particular concern, despite the Rajiv Gandhi–Benazir Bhutto agreement of 1988 not to attack each other's nuclear facilities.

Even so, the world's press seldom discussed the region except insofar as it was affected by the Geneva agreement of April 1988, which paved the way for the Soviet withdrawal from Afghanistan. The earlier Brasstacks crisis (1986–87) had ended peacefully, even on a note of hope—it had been followed by Zia ul-Haq's "cricket diplomacy" trip to India and regional consideration of confidence-building measures (CBMs), earlier proposed by the United States. Many outsiders viewed the Indian military interventions of late 1987 and 1988 (in Sri Lanka and the Maldives) as benign at worst and helpful at best (the full, tragic costs of the former intervention would soon become all too apparent). The general assumption was that South Asia was returning to "business as usual." General Zia's death in August 1988 and the move toward democratization in Pakistan seemed to mark the end of the region's greatest crisis.

Both India and Pakistan began focusing on a search for new policies. For India, the principle of nonalignment in a bipolar world, on which it had built a stable and consistent policy in previous decades, no longer seemed relevant, and the support traditionally provided by the Soviet Union was growing uncertain. While praising *perestroika,* New Delhi was nervous about the rapidly changing global order. Earlier, the Soviet veto had shielded India from international censure on the Kashmir issue—but how could that support continue when the Soviet empire was losing its allies and coming apart? New Delhi's learning curve regarding the new international system was very steep, indeed.

This was no less true of Pakistan, which was becoming strategically marginalized. Its value to the United States and China was declining, and the possible spread of its influence from Afghanistan into the Muslim Central Asian republics was an irritant to U.S.-Pakistan relations. Pakistan's covert nuclear weapons program was another large concern, which by 1990 had replaced the Afghan war as the primary focus of America's South Asia policy.

A Region in Turmoil on the Eve of Crisis

In 1989–90 both India and Pakistan found themselves grappling with political instability, the strong governments of Rajiv Gandhi and General Zia by then a thing of the past. Their respective prime ministers, V. P. Singh, elected in late 1989, and Benazir Bhutto, in late 1988, had both failed to obtain a majority in their parliaments. To add to their political insecurity, both governments faced powerful opposition groups, waiting to topple them.

The separatist Sikh movement in Punjab was still creating problems for India just as it was on the verge of economic collapse. With foreign exchange reserves down to barely two weeks' requirements, V. P. Singh's minority National Front government blamed the preceding administration for overextending itself under Rajiv Gandhi, pointing to the effects of the Brasstacks crisis, the intervention in Sri Lanka, and threatened confrontation with China, not to mention the current insurgencies in Punjab and Kashmir. The government believed this was a time for consolidation and domestic healing, not foreign adventure and brinkmanship. India's most pressing threats, it argued, came from within, not from abroad, although it continued to condemn Pakistan's support of Khalistani Sikh separatists and terrorist elements in Kashmir. The central government thus felt it needed to pursue a conciliatory policy toward dissidents and separatists and reach an accommodation with these groups. However, the permanent bureaucracy felt hawkish toward Pakistan. This was especially true of the Ministry of External Affairs, despite the dovish views of its minister, Inder K. Gujral. S. K. Singh, the foreign secretary, and J. N. Dixit, India's high commissioner in Islamabad, considered Gujral's conciliatory policy toward Pakistan naïve. Many of India's politicians and bureaucrats also distrusted the United States because it had armed Pakistan, tolerated Islamabad's covert nuclear bomb program, and was still very close to China.

Pakistan's domestic political situation was even more tumultuous. Once elected, Benazir Bhutto shared power with President Ghulam Ishaq Khan and the army chief, General Mirza Aslam Beg, as part of a "troika," although this was not a partnership of three equals. Bhutto felt particularly insecure despite the fact that the military saw her as an asset in relations with the United States: Pakistan needed U.S. arms and economic assistance for its Afghan policy, and Bhutto was widely liked by the Americans and had a number of influential American friends.

However, Bhutto chafed under the army's continued dominance over vital national security issues, such as the nuclear program and relations with India.

She has claimed that she was not fully informed about key elements of Pakistan's foreign and security policy, especially the nuclear program.[1] Others disagree, speculating that she was indeed informed about these programs but was hemmed in by the powerful security establishment and faced a strong center-right opposition coalition assembled by a protégé of Zia ul-Haq, Mian Nawaz Sharif, who was popular in the dominant province of Punjab.

Pakistan's policy toward India now displayed even more hawkishness than under Zia. Many Pakistani strategists had concluded that Islamabad had "won" the 1987 Brasstacks crisis and that Pakistan's countermove in the direction of Indian Punjab had deterred New Delhi from attacking across the Rajasthan border. According to some in the military, Pakistan's near-possession of a nuclear program had induced India to withdraw. At the same time, Pakistan's civilian foreign policy establishment, though equally persuaded of India's hegemonic ambitions, was less certain that they could be countered merely by the acquisition of more firepower or even nuclear weapons. In short, its members understood Pakistan's vulnerabilities better than the military.

Separatist Sentiments in Kashmir

By early 1990, the tension between India and Pakistan was alarmingly high, primarily because of the intensifying separatist movement in Indian-administered Kashmir. New Delhi saw this as a Pakistan-inspired, funded, and led terrorist campaign, whereas Pakistan considered it a push for Kashmiri independence to secure the right of self-determination. Traditionally, the Muslims of the Kashmir Valley and their Hindu Pandit neighbors shared a special Kashmiri culture, often referred to as Kashmiriyat, which for many years meant more than ties of religion. Kashmiri Muslims had valued the high degree of autonomy they (and indeed the state of Jammu and Kashmir) had been given under Article 370 of India's constitution.

Following its first truly free election in 1977, Indian-administered Kashmir had enjoyed five years of relative calm under Chief Minister Sheikh Abdullah (who had previously been under arrest). Presiding over the social and economic transformation of the region, he helped guide educational and training institutions on a path of rapid growth. Eventually, these establishments turned out a new generation of educated Kashmiris who went on to form the separatist movement's core.

Upon Sheikh Abdullah's death, his son Farooq overcame a challenge by his brother-in-law, Ghulam Mohammad Shah, and succeeded his father in office.

In the state assembly elections of 1983, his National Conference (NC) party faced off against Prime Minister Indira Gandhi's Congress party. In the wake of a campaign marred by violence and communal appeals, the elections polarized the population along communal lines, with Farooq Abdullah winning in predominantly Muslim areas and the Congress in Hindu ones.

As chief minister, Farooq Abdullah aligned himself with other Indian opposition parties on the question of center-state relations. In retaliation, Indira Gandhi dismissed the governor of Jammu and Kashmir—B. K. Nehru, her own cousin—for failing to remove Farooq Abdullah as head of the Jammu and Kashmir government. She replaced Nehru with Jagmohan Malhotra, who obligingly dismissed Farooq, branding him pro-Pakistani and anti-Indian. Ghulam Mohammad Shah, who by then had joined the Congress, replaced him. The move was extremely unpopular and unwise, as pointed out by the eminent British scholar W. H. Morris-Jones: "It seemed an act of gratuitous folly not to accept the electoral verdict of 1983 which saw Congress defeated."[2]

Shah ruled ineffectively for two years. The next election, in 1987, pitted Farooq Abdullah's National Conference, which had aligned itself with Congress, by then headed by Indira Gandhi's son, Rajiv, against a coalition of smaller parties under the banner of the Muslim United Front (UF). The results put Abdullah back in office, but not without large-scale ballot rigging. Disillusioned young Kashmiris, even well-educated ones, headed into the arms of extremists, alienated by the persistent lack of good jobs as well as the increasing inefficiency and corruption of the Abdullah government.

Things came to a head just before the respective Pakistan and Indian Independence Days of August 14 and 15, 1988, when a series of explosions rocked the Valley. Explosions continued over the next few months, augmented by organized strikes and antigovernment riots in which protesters clashed with security personnel. These activities increased almost sixfold during 1989. According to Robert Wirsing, who quotes a source in the Indian Ministry of Home Affairs, violent incidents totaled 2,154 in 1989 compared with 390 in 1988.[3]

In May 1989, separatists launched a "Quit Kashmir" movement patterned after Mahatma Gandhi's "Quit India" call against the British in 1942. Assassinations became more frequent, many of the targets being policemen, judges, and other government officials. Abdullah seemed unable to halt the violence, which New Delhi blamed on Pakistan-sponsored militancy. Pakistanis countered that they were only providing diplomatic and moral support. For two years running, protested New Delhi, Pakistan's Independence

Day had been celebrated with enthusiasm, while India's was marred by a complete *bandh* (strike) in the Valley. Pakistan, it also pointed out, had many sympathizers in Kashmir in areas such as Borikadal, Kahnyar, Zainakadal, and Naikadal, which were referred to as *chhota* (little) Pakistan.

In December 1989, the separatist militants achieved what Asia Watch later termed a "major political victory" in connection with their December 8 kidnapping of Rubaiya Saeed, daughter of India's home minister.[4] When they demanded that five members of the prominent militant group Jammu and Kashmir Liberation Front (JKLF) who had been in jail be released, the state government decided to acquiesce, a move that opened it and India's central government to much criticism, focused heavily on the center's "soft" policy regarding the involvement of a "foreign hand" (namely, that of Pakistan).

Military Maneuvers

Early in August 1989, the Indian government, concerned about the insurgencies in Kashmir and Punjab, decided to augment its security forces there, primarily with paramilitary forces, and later with infantry from the Indian army. The army, according to its chief, General V. N. Sharma, did this to stem the flow of Pakistan-backed Sikh and Kashmiri terrorists into India, which threatened to overwhelm the local police forces, endangering India's integrity and its mobilization and war plans. A very senior Pakistani general rejects this, noting that while some volunteers may have participated in the jihad, Sharma had misrepresented the facts by branding them government-sponsored infiltrators.[5]

To add to the friction, in December 1989 Pakistan conducted the largest military exercise in its history in Punjab. Named Zarb-e-Momin, the maneuvers involved about 200,000 soldiers, four army corps, seven infantry division, one armored division, three independent infantry and armor brigades, a squadron of the army's Cobra helicopters, air defense units, and several air squadrons. Their declared aim was to test Pakistan's strategy of "offensive defense," but they were clearly designed to demonstrate Pakistan's conventional military prowess and dissuade Indian military planners.[6] In addition, a Pakistan air force exercise (Highmark) was merged with Zarb to create a realistic air-threat environment. Highmark consisted of a large number (some say thousands) of sorties by combat and transport aircraft firing live missiles, rockets, and bombs. The purpose was to allow pilots to test their wartime ordnance, ground crews to ensure peak serviceability of equipment, radar units to provide timely warning of enemy aircraft, and ground controllers to guide pilots onto their targets.

The exercise resembled the 1986–87 Indian Brasstacks exercise, which had made a deep impression on Pakistan. Both exercises placed battle-ready troops within striking distance of the border. Also, both were linked to critical ethnic conflicts on either side of the India-Pakistan border: in India's Punjab and Kashmir, and in Pakistan's Sindh. Thus the need for countermeasures suggested itself to the Indian military, as it had to Pakistan during the Brasstacks exercise, lest Zarb become the "real thing."

1990: The Onset of the Crisis

With fragile governments in both India and Pakistan, military maneuvers near the border, and violent clashes in Kashmir, the 1990 crisis seemed an event waiting to happen.

Kashmir: Rapid Deterioration

The events of that year were calamitous compared with the 1989 upheaval in Kashmir. As Robert Oakley, the U.S. ambassador to Islamabad during the crisis, recalls, before 1990 "Kashmir was so calm it was not discussed . . . there was a series of meetings during 1989 between the two prime ministers and the defense ministers and the foreign ministers and the foreign secretaries—no one raised Kashmir. Punjab always; but Kashmir, no."[7] In early 1990 all this changed.

Jagmohan, who had been appointed governor again, launched a major crackdown on the violence and its perpetrators, now so prevalent that "every component of the power structure had been taken over by the terrorists. Subversive elements had infiltrated the police ranks and a portion of the police was on the verge of mutiny. Civil services had broken down completely. Lawyers, doctors and even the press were dominated by militants."[8] In February 1990 he dissolved the state assembly and over the next few months brought in the army. But the clashes only worsened. Between January 20 and the end of March, 217 lives were lost in the violence. Although curfews were imposed, they merely added to the general hardship, making it difficult for people to obtain food or run their businesses, many of which had to shut down.

If anything, Jagmohan's brutal approach helped build greater support for separatism. An all-party delegation that traveled to Srinagar in March witnessed this firsthand as Kashmiris who had been confined to their homes by the curfew shouted slogans in support of self-determination from rooftops and windows. Critics also complained that Jagmohan seldom reprimanded errant soldiers or policemen.

As April rolled around, conditions deteriorated. Militants abducted and killed Mushirul Haq, vice chancellor of Kashmir University, his secretary, and H. L. Khera, general manager of Hindustan Machine Tools. In response, Jagmohan clamped an indefinite curfew on Srinagar and launched another crackdown, which led Farooq Abdullah to refer to him as Genghis Khan.

Perspectives on Kashmir

The factors that in late 1989 and 1990 brought Jammu and Kashmir, and eventually India and Pakistan, to the brink of war remain surrounded by controversy. What does seem clear, however, is that the question of Pakistani support to the Kashmiris and the degree to which they facilitated the transfer of militants from Afghanistan to Kashmir lay at the heart of the subsequent crisis between India and Pakistan. The suspicion that India would move militarily against the training camps organized for the militants raised the possibility of Pakistani military escalation, which in turn could have led to a nuclear response.

To India, Pakistan appeared to have developed a low-cost strategy to destabilize its stronger neighbor by fueling "the main spring of insurgency . . . within Kashmir . . . from across the border." Pakistan, India alleged, was arming and training the Kashmiri Muslim separatists through its deep involvement in the growth of madrassas (Islamic religious schools) in the Valley and its military and financial cross-border support, turning them into "terrorists." According to India's hard-liners, Pakistan's Inter-Services Intelligence (ISI) agency and right-wing religious parties had a large hand in these developments, but their own government was also partly to blame for being too tolerant of separatist inclinations.[9]

From the Pakistani perspective, Kashmir represented the unfinished business of the 1947 partition, in that India had not fulfilled its promise to allow a plebiscite under UN auspices to determine the future of the state. By the late 1980s, Pakistanis had become tired of waiting and demanded resolution of the dispute, especially in view of India's apparent resolve to dig in further instead of pursuing credible self-determination, which they saw as the primary cause of Kashmiri discontent. The insurgency, they charged, was the result of "decades of Indian abuses in the state," and they were merely providing diplomatic and moral support to the Kashmiri "freedom fighters." Some leaders argued that Kashmir was an "emotional" issue for Pakistan, and it was their "duty" to help Kashmiris who were not content with India.[10] A few also considered this support a kind of revenge against India for its role in the activities leading to the bifurcation of Pakistan in 1971.

A number of observers—Indians and others—are of similar mind, arguing that the Kashmir insurgency was largely due to India's inability or unwillingness to accommodate reasonable Kashmir demands.[11] In their view, New Delhi's failure to offer Kashmiris the same freedoms granted to other Indians led to their ultimate alienation, pushing them into Pakistan's arms.[12] Others attribute the ferment to the disenchantment of young Kashmiris and increasing receptiveness to radical views when they found their rising educational and social aspirations thwarted and their path to economic and political empowerment blocked or manipulated. Subscribing to this view, U.S. ambassador Robert Oakley considered the Kashmir insurgency a "primarily spontaneous" development, though "Pakistan, willy-nilly, began to play a much more active role."[13]

Early Attempts at Diplomacy

Despite the inflammatory rhetoric on both sides, some attempts were made to resolve the bilateral tensions diplomatically. In December 1989, in an effort to "maintain amicable relations with India," Benazir Bhutto sent a Pakistani diplomat, Abdul Sattar, to New Delhi, but with little evidence of progress in this direction. While Sattar claimed that his mission of cultivating friendly relations with India had been successful, V. P. Singh had reportedly "conveyed a warning to Pakistan to stop supporting the freedom movement in Kashmir or face the consequences."[14]

The next Pakistani mission to India was a three-day visit by Foreign Minister Sahibzada Yaqub Khan from January 21 for talks with the Indian leadership. While the Pakistani leadership directed Yaqub to convey a "tough message" to India, he requested (and received) some flexibility, knowing that such a message could trigger a needless crisis.

Yaqub Khan had three meetings with Indian leaders. In the first one, with his counterpart Inder Kumar Gujral, he adopted a hard tone, suggesting that India needed to resolve the Kashmir problem by giving Kashmiris a free choice in whether to continue their association with India. He conveyed Pakistan's concerns, emphasizing its strong support of Kashmiri self-determination. Gujral appeared to be somewhat unsure of his own government's line, possibly because it was still a relatively new administration. He seemed to show some understanding of Pakistan's domestic political need to express sympathy for the Kashmiri militants, but those back home thought his reply to Yaqub Khan was not resolute enough.

Prime Minister Singh, who also held the defense portfolio, as he had at the time of the Brasstacks crisis, corrected this in his own meeting with Yaqub. The domestic politics of Pakistan, Singh stressed, were its internal matter and of no interest to India. Yaqub, in turn, warned of the pitfalls of India's Kashmir policy.

The Indians found Yaqub Khan cold and unfriendly and were further displeased when he repeated his warnings publicly. Equally disturbing were reports coming out of Kashmir that the JKLF leader, Amanullah Khan—who was living in Pakistan at the time—threatened to march thousands of his supporters into the Valley. At a subsequent meeting, the Indian cabinet decided to reciprocate by warning Pakistan to "keep off Kashmir." Gujral conveyed this tougher message to Yaqub Khan in their next meeting later in the day. At a subsequent meeting attended by the press, Gujral and Yaqub quoted verses by the poet Faiz Ahmed Faiz that seemed to convey an oblique warning: Gujral referred to "lovers who had lost each other," while Yaqub spoke of "lovers being separated by objective circumstances." In the perception of some Pakistanis, on the other hand, Gujral was hoping, somewhat optimistically, to reverse the long and hostile India-Pakistan relationship during his tenure and was disappointed when this did not happen. This disappointment might have colored his later judgment about these exchanges.

Close observers of these events are divided on whether Yaqub would have indulged in such threat-mongering, given his cultivated style and long experience in foreign affairs, or whether he was especially suited to perform this task in an aptly circumlocutory and ambiguous manner. One cannot rule out the possibility that too much was read into these statements at the time, but some anxieties undoubtedly arose in the Indian leadership.

One informed Pakistani account has it that Yaqub exceeded the limits of his mandate to "placate" New Delhi and instead delivered an ultimatum, something that Yaqub denied in our interviews with him. Others claim he told Gujral that if New Delhi did not meet a certain "deadline," the "subcontinent would be set on fire." Among the many contradictory versions of these meetings, some suggest that he was misunderstood, that he exceeded his brief, or that he delivered the intended message and that it was correctly perceived by the Indians. If his mission was to calm the Indians down, it certainly produced a contrary result. After an emergency meeting of his cabinet, V. P. Singh declared that India would "retaliate even if it meant war."[15]

In Pakistan, press reports of Yaqub Khan's visit gave some hint of his dialogue, usually buried in the more extensive coverage of his unprecedented national television address to the nation after returning from India. This address was clear, forceful, and unambiguous; it had the effect of appealing to, and further exacerbating, Pakistan's hawkishness toward Kashmir. The *Frontier Post,* one of the first to mention the possibility of war between India and Pakistan, quoted Yaqub as having told Gujral that even when wars are not intended they break out and warned the Indians of "strong retaliation" if there was any "mischief" along the LOC.[16] Did he deliver one message to the Indians, and did he report another one back to Islamabad? As in so many other instances presaging this and other crises, one may never know the truth.

The Crisis Escalates: More Military Moves

As the level of violence in Indian-administered Kashmir increased and diplomatic efforts to defuse the tensions faltered, the rhetoric became more heated. To ward off political pressure from opposition parties and assuage the concerns of the Kashmiris in Pakistan-administered Kashmir, Benazir Bhutto repeatedly proclaimed that the Kashmiris across the LOC had the right of self-determination.[17] On March 13, she went further: addressing a rally in Muzaffarabad, Ms. Bhutto promised a "thousand-year war" in support of the separatists and pledged $4 million to their cause.[18]

In India, the Bharatiya Janata Party (BJP) pressed for "hot pursuit" across the LOC to shut down training camps. On April 10, addressing the Indian parliament, V. P. Singh asked his compatriots to be "psychologically prepared" for war: "I warn them [that] those who talk about a thousand years of war should examine whether they will last a thousand hours of war."[19] Home Minister Mufti Mohammed Sayeed contended that war with Pakistan would be "fully justified if the objective of freeing Kashmir from the stranglehold of the secessionists was achieved."[20] BJP leader L. K. Advani further warned that Pakistan would "cease to exist" if it attacked India.[21]

One of Pakistan's concerns throughout the crisis was that New Delhi, unable to fight the militancy, might take the battle to the alleged training camps in Pakistan-administered Kashmir, thus posing a security threat to Pakistan. Singh's speech brought back memories in Pakistan of the earlier Brasstacks episode.

Following Prime Minister Singh's speech, Pakistan's chief of army staff (COAS), General Beg, convened a meeting of his corps commanders to carry out a "detailed threat assessment."[22] He told his subordinates that India, in an act of intimidation, had deployed a strike force of up to 100,000 men within 50 miles of the border in Rajasthan. He was referring to the Indian army units that had been on winter exercises in the Mahajan area, which Pakistani officials claimed had been extended. Pakistan army sources believed that the Indian force comprised several infantry divisions, one armored division, and three or four armored brigades, all deployed in such a way as to "halve India's normal mobilization time to one week." In addition, Islamabad noted, India was continuing to move large numbers of paramilitary forces into Kashmir.

In response, Beg put his troops on alert. In his estimation, the presence of 100,000 soldiers was not yet threatening enough to warrant strong reactive moves, whereas the presence of 1,000 tanks, say, would indeed have constituted a major threat. Nonetheless, on April 14, a senior Pakistani official informed a parliamentary committee that the country's military forces were in a "high state of preparedness and vigilance to meet any external threat," thus reflecting a fair amount of concern about India's troop deployment and seemingly provocative statements from across the border.[23]

The feeling in India was that Pakistan was overreacting. India clarified that it "just had two newly equipped tank units there [on the Mahajan range] as they had to be trained in tank firing. They had been sent for this [training] in Feb.-Mar. 1990."[24] According to India's army chief, General Sharma, the troops were actually in their peacetime stations or cantonment locations. The two Indian strike corps were also still at their normal locations in Ambala and Jhansi; any move to shift them to the border would have entailed extensive disruption of the Indian railway system.[25] With the situation in Punjab and Kashmir deteriorating, however, the army felt reinforcements were needed to quell the insurgencies there. Even then, only the Eighth (Mountain) Division was moved into Kashmir, without its divisional artillery and heavy vehicles.

India may also have been responding to Pakistan's troop movements following its Zarb-e-Momin military exercise. Instead of returning to their peacetime locations, Pakistan's reserve forces moved to positions that permitted easy strikes across the international border. India's fear of an attack is reflected in a civilian bureaucrat's remarks: "We got definite information that Pakistan was planning to make a pre-emptive attack in Northern Punjab as soon as the monsoon season broke there which would make movements on the Indian side difficult."[26] Thus although Western military analysts reported no major Indian troop mobilization near the international frontier, they speculated that by extending its exercises, India's military may have pre-positioned its tanks and heavy artillery near the border. In the words of one analyst, "everything the Indians have been doing fits under the category of defensive preparedness, but some of it is ambiguous."[27]

As for the two air forces, India put its squadrons on high alert in the border areas and especially in Rajasthan, as the opposite air bases in Pakistan had gone on high alert. Accordingly, radar activities were upgraded. However, reconnaissance trips by the U.S. military attaché in Pakistan confirmed that India had not opened the forward operating bases for its air force or moved the strike corps out of their usual stations. The Pakistanis, still obviously alarmed, decided to talk to their Indian counterparts on the hotline. When India explained that its actions were part of its annual armor training exercise, the alarm bells apparently stopped ringing.[28]

On April 14, V. P. Singh, in discussions with the press, elaborated on the logic of India's preparations. Pakistan, he noted, had deployed new armored regiments and sophisticated radar along India's western border and seemed to be getting ready to launch an attack there. Furthermore, Pakistan's army and air force were on "red alert" along the cease-fire line dividing Kashmir, and Pakistani artillery had been moved to forward positions across from Kashmir and Punjab.[29]

According to a Pakistani general involved in these events, the armed forces would understandably be asked to be vigilant in a crisis situation, but ordering a "red alert" implied preparations for war. He asserted, however, that the Pakistanis had ordered no red alert and that both directors-general of military operations (DGMOs) were regularly in touch with each other on the hotlines. Several senior Pakistani officers interviewed for this study claim that they had not considered war inevitable at the time, despite the growing concern that India might launch an attack on Pakistan-administered Kashmir and Sindh. Because India had committed so many troops to coping with the separatists in Kashmir, said one, it would have been extremely unwise for Delhi to contemplate a war with Pakistan. Indeed, a number of officials felt that a war with India would have been disastrous for both sides and still have left the Kashmir dispute unresolved. Even the corps commander of Lahore did not view the increase in Indian deployment as an offensive move, although it meant India could put its forces on a war footing one or two weeks faster.[30] According to a senior Pakistani officer intimately involved with these events, Pakistan's goal was less to prevent an Indian military attack across the LOC or even across the international border itself than to keep the Indians from clamping down too firmly on the Kashmiri separatist movement. This relaxed position was evident to one of the authors during a series of visits to various Pakistani military facilities at that time.

In the first public discussion of the role of nuclear weapons in the crisis, India's former COAS, General K. Sundarji, suggested that war was not too likely because nuclear fears would deter Indian and Pakistani leaders from such action.[31] Several senior Indian generals apparently admitted that many of their commanders had been reacting to newspaper reports and only taking precautionary measures in congruence with their own assessment of the then prevalent situation and what was likely to happen.[32] Both sides were well aware of the many factors that cautioned against a drift toward war. In the absence of clear directions from political bosses, however, political statements were ambiguous enough to allow for unnecessary saber rattling, which continued for quite some time.

Although the media made much of the military movements, the essential steps toward war—such as canceling leaves, disrupting train schedules, calling up reserves, moving the strike forces, making the forward air bases fully operational, and holding daily meetings of defense committees—were all missing from the scenario. On the contrary, the prevailing sentiment seemed to have been a desire to avoid war. Throughout the crisis, Indian and Pakistani diplomats and officials remained in touch, despite the inflammatory speeches and changes in force deployment. India sent its defense secretary, Naresh Chandra, on a quiet mission to Islamabad to reassure the Pakistanis that its forces were not moving. Both countries also allowed the United States to verify the positions of their troops, each assuming, correctly, that the United States could reassure the other country on this count.

Evidently neither side wanted a full-fledged conflict at this time, but both were apprehensive about the situation inside Kashmir or along the LOC and seemed to think it necessary to move toward a defensive posture. On April 25, 1990, with international pressure mounting, Foreign Minister Inder Gujral and Yaqub Khan met in New York and agreed to work toward reducing the military tensions by employing existing CBMs and keeping open all channels of communication, especially those between senior military officers. There was no subsequent troop redeployment.

On May 16, the White House announced that it would send Deputy National Security Adviser Robert Gates as its special envoy to South Asia. Before then, Pakistan had tended to seek a U.S. role in the Kashmir crisis, whereas India had firmly resisted U.S. involvement in what it regarded as a domestic political dispute. During this crisis, however, both India and Pakistan seemed open to U.S. assistance in managing the military dimension of the crisis. Pakistan was reportedly the first to approach the U.S. government about Indian troop movements, and the National Front government in India, disregarding the "Indira Doctrine," did not seem to object to the United States acting as a facilitator (not as a mediator) during a crisis.[33]

The "Gates mission" traveled to India and Pakistan to meet with their leaderships from May 19 to 20 and included Assistant Secretary of State for Near Eastern and South Asian Affairs John Kelly and Richard Haass, the senior National Security Council (NSC) staffer responsible for the region. The mission's primary objective was to deliver presidential messages to the leaders of both countries and gain a firsthand understanding of the situation.

Within two weeks of the Gates mission, the crisis had subsided. In early June, India announced that armor sent to the Mahajan range would return to its normal stations and proposed a package of military/nonmilitary confidence-building measures to Pakistan. These included (1) information sharing, (2) increased communication between local commanders, (3) joint border patrolling, (4) prevention of airspace violations, and (5) exchange of delegations to reaffirm these arrangements. Pakistan responded cautiously at first but grew more enthusiastic when it became clear that the Indians were, in fact, pulling back their forces. Pakistan suggested foreign secretary–level talks to resolve all the issues in contention between the two countries. New Delhi also submitted a package of CBMs for diplomatic discussion, which helped dissipate the aura of crisis.

Unwinding the Conflict: American Engagement

The atmosphere changed so quickly in early June that both sides indeed seemed anxious to back away from the brink of war without appearing weak, and Gates provided them with a mechanism for doing so. However, they delayed these decisions for a week or two after the mission's visit, probably for domestic political reasons. Neither side wished to appear too influenced by the United States.

Other governments had closely watched the crisis unfold and the movements of forces on both sides of the border. The U.S. administration first voiced its concern in January 1990, when Undersecretary of State for Political Affairs Robert Kimmett visited the region and discussed events in the Valley with interlocutors in New Delhi and Islamabad. Over the next few months, Central Intelligence Agency (CIA) analysts puzzled over the covert nuclear developments in Pakistan, the kaleidoscopic changes in both Indian and Pakistani politics, the termination of two major cross-border operations (the Pakistan-supported mujahiddin in Afghanistan and the Indian Peace Keeping Force in Sri Lanka), the troop movements, and the press references to nuclear threats. After having failed to predict the Brasstacks crisis, elements of the U.S. intelligence community took greater note of the growing political instability in the region, the further development of Pakistan's nuclear program, and the fragile nature or inoperability of the CBMs earlier agreed upon by the two countries. Some predicted war, if not in May when rising temperatures would have made operations impractical, or in June or July when the monsoon would have made major roads and the desert impassable, then most likely "in the fall."

However, the State Department's Bureau of Intelligence and Research did not fully share this assessment. On the basis of their own observations and contact with leaders in the countries, the embassies were fairly certain that war was highly unlikely and, in the absence of hard evidence to the contrary, they were not predicting a nuclear crisis; instead they expected a rerun of the 1987 Brasstacks crisis.

In March 1990, Assistant Secretary of State John Kelly expressed concern about the tensions between India and Pakistan and a possible conflict but indicated that the United States did not think they would actually go to war over Kashmir. The Defense Department concurred: "Heightened charges and increased incidents along the border might lead to a lower flashpoint for a conflict on the subcontinent" but not all-out war.[34] Many in Congress had grown apprehensive as well, especially since both antagonists in this case possessed nuclear capabilities, as pointed out by Stephen Solarz, chairman of the House Subcommittee on Asian and Pacific Affairs.

In early April, Pakistan once again asked the United States to verify whether India had moved its forces into threatening positions. These requests, said one American official, sounded "panic-stricken" and the Pakistanis "very alarmed." There was a "what if" meeting to discuss U.S. responses should a regional war break out. Over the next few months U.S. diplomacy focused on "crisis prevention" in place of the State Department's earlier low-level discussion about how Washington might play a more active role in settling the Kashmir dispute. The United States received tacit permission from the highest authority of both countries to confirm that neither side had deployed troops provocatively. The respective U.S. ambassadors, Robert Oakley and William Clark, conveyed the results of the verifications, assuring each that no major military movements were taking place.

Nonetheless, friction between the two countries continued to increase, and on April 18 Kimmett warned both that "there is a growing risk of miscalculation which could lead events to spin dangerously out of control," urging them to focus on "dialog and negotiations," "lower the rhetoric," and ensure that their troop deployments were "not seen by the other side as intentionally or unintentionally provocative."[35] This was the first public caution from the U.S. government during the crisis.

By May, President Bush was apparently receiving differing assessments of the crisis. The U.S. ambassadors in New Delhi and Islamabad, by then deeply involved in prevention through their independent review of military positions and their reassurances to the respective governments, believed that hostilities were not imminent, although there was a risk of war later in the year. The Department of State was slightly more concerned, while the CIA saw the possibility of a conflict that might eventually have nuclear overtones. Still, even in the most pessimistic view the prospects of a conflict were at the 20 percent level. In sum, the situation in South Asia in general and the *prospect* of escalation to a nuclear confrontation in particular were creating some concern, but not panic. As one former senior Bush administration official recalls, the Indians and Pakistanis "were not acting with sufficient sobriety. There was a little bit of recklessness in the air. There was a little bit of blindness or forgetfulness about how destructive wars can be." Accordingly, in May the White House sent the Gates mission to the region

> to help both sides avoid a conflict over Kashmir, which would entail great loss of life, and damage to both countries, and to begin the sort of political dialogue which would not only reduce tension but could lead to a peaceful and permanent resolution of the Kashmir problem, as called for under the Simla Agreement.... We are urging both sides to restrain their rhetoric and to take confidence-building measures on the ground to lower tension.[36]

Three years later, Gates said his mission was "a rare but classic example of 'preventive diplomacy,'" a term popularized by the former UN secretary general, Boutros Boutros-Ghali. The NSC's Richard Haass also felt the trip was a "good example of pre-emptive diplomacy designed to reduce the likelihood of a more serious crisis later in the fall of 1990."[37] The Gates mission made six points to its Pakistani interlocutors:

—Washington had war-gamed a potential India-Pakistan conflict, and Pakistan was a loser in every scenario.

—In the event of war, Pakistan would not receive American assistance.

—Pakistan must refrain from supporting "terrorism" in Indian-administered Kashmir, avoid military deployments that India could interpret as threatening, and tone down the war rhetoric.

—Both sides needed to adopt confidence-building measures.

—If both India and Pakistan agreed to withdraw their forces from the border area, the United States would offer intelligence support to verify this.

—Finally, Gates would carry a message from Pakistan to India, if the Pakistanis desired this.

President Ghulam Ishaq Khan and General Beg responded that India was using terrorist tactics in Kashmir, that Pakistani public statements had been moderate, and that Pakistan's military movements had been less menacing than India's.

In Delhi, Gates and his team met Prime Minister Singh, Foreign Minister Gujral, COAS General Sharma, and Minister of State for Defense Raja Ramanna, one of the key figures in the development of India's nuclear weapons program. Gates's message was essentially the same as the one delivered to Pakistan, namely, avoid provocation that could spiral out of control. Gates reiterated that it would be to neither side's advantage to go to war. Even if India won a war, the long-term costs would greatly exceed any short-term benefits.[38]

India, in turn, alleged that the crisis had been generated by Pakistan's proxy war in Kashmir and Punjab, and hence tensions would not ease until it ceased these activities. India wanted joint patrolling along the border with a right to hot pursuit, the elimination of training camps in Pakistan with verification, and the arrest and extradition to the United States of a Sikh terrorist who had operated in the United States and had taken refuge in Pakistan.

Opinions as to the success of this mission vary. According to a senior Bush official, "The facts speak for themselves. If one looks at what South Asia was like, say June 15, it looked a lot better than it looked May 14." Gates's own summary highlighted the successful prevention of a conflict that might have had dangerous consequences, the face-saving measures provided to both parties, and suggestions for a number of CBMs to keep border tension under control.[39] Others, such as journalist Seymour Hersh, agreed that "by the end of June, the crisis was over," and that the Gates mission had "defused what looked to be inevitable warfare."[40] However, interviews with key Indian and Pakistani leaders involved in the crisis show that the Gates mission was regarded as helpful but not critical to the termination of the crisis; instead, they stress the early and active intervention of the two American embassies, plus the evolution of talks between Indian and Pakistani officials from cold hostility to accommodation.

Overall, in this instance, the U.S. government had a fairly accurate understanding of the magnitude of the crisis brewing in South Asia. The Gates mission was built on a strong foundation of regional American diplomacy (dominated by regional specialists), utilizing both diplomatic and military assets. Gates did succeed in extracting pledges from both sides that they would exercise restraint in their military deployment, although these pledges were already being considered before his visit. Thus even though it might not have been decisive, Washington's role in defusing the tension was undoubtedly constructive, bolstering the impulse for peace in South Asia.

During the crisis, other countries, including Britain, China, France, and the Soviet Union, counseled restraint as well. Prime Minister Toshiki Kaifu of Japan, visiting both countries in April, also urged both India and Pakistan to exercise self-restraint and resolve their dispute through negotiations.

A Nuclear Crisis?

The belief that India and Pakistan could enter into crisis led many foreign observers, especially Americans, to view Kashmir as the most likely issue to trigger a larger India-Pakistan nuclear war. This was not a new argument. In the 1950s, Josef Korbel, a former Czech diplomat turned professor who had worked on Kashmir under UN auspices, warned that Kashmir could lead to a larger war and ultimately to a nuclear confrontation.[41] The scenario offered at that time was that the United States and the Soviet Union, each backing a regional client, might be dragged into a regional dispute having the potential to escalate to a nuclear war. The scenario in 1990, however, was that India and Pakistan, acting on their own, might have escalated the Kashmir dispute to the nuclear level. The regional perspective was very different by then. For Kashmiris and most Indians and Pakistanis, *Kashmir*, not nuclear war, was the region's biggest security problem. For almost all South Asians, the nuclear dimension of the 1990 crisis was an afterthought and, some would argue, a stabilizing development.

Capabilities and Intentions

By 1990 many outside observers adjudged India and Pakistan to be nuclear-weapon *capable*, implying that they either possessed a small number of nuclear weapons or could assemble them quickly. How long they had been in production and what kinds and how many were available in 1990 are questions still in the realm of speculation. More is known about their delivery systems: Pakistan had the Chinese M-11 missile, in addition to its own fleet of high performance F-16 aircraft and newer missiles developed with outside technical assistance, such as the Shaheen, the Hatf, and the Ghauri; and India had a wide range of capable aircraft. According to K. Subrahmanyam, a former Indian official, "the first Indian nuclear deterrent came into existence in early 1990." Citing key figures in India's nuclear program and others, including Subrahmanyam, American scholar George Perkovich indicates that between 1988 and 1990 India had readied at least two dozen nuclear weapons for quick assembly and potential dispersal to airbases for delivery by aircraft for retaliatory attacks against Pakistan.[42]

In a 1994 comment on India's nuclear preparedness and planning, senior Indian official B. G. Deshmukh noted that before the crisis Rajiv Gandhi had directed the defense establishment "to prepare plans for meeting any foreign threat or aggression on the basis of [our] not having any nuclear weapons."[43] The Pakistanis, Deshmukh adds, were told that if they did use their nuclear weapons to attack any part of India, "our clear mandate to our Service Chiefs would be go full steam ahead and dismember Pakistan once and for all." Thus the implication is that at the time of the crisis India did *not* have any nuclear weapons, but, as revealed in subsequent briefings, especially by India's army, its forces felt that they would be able to destroy Pakistan as a state by conventional means.

Raj Chengappa, a journalist who has talked to many of the key figures in the Rajiv Gandhi and V. P. Singh governments, also concludes that India's nuclear option was not ready at the time and quotes an unnamed senior official as saying: "We could have tightened the bolts [of the bomb] but admittedly we were far from ready [to deliver it]."[44] Chengappa's extensive interviews led him to believe that if push came to shove, India could have heaved a bomb off a fighter aircraft as the United States had done in the 1940s.[45]

On the other hand, Pakistan's nuclear capability, in the view of the nonproliferation community, seemed to date to the mid-1980s. Strong hints came from senior Pakistani officials themselves, including President Zia ul-Haq and A. Q. Khan, after the 1987 Brasstacks crisis in a declaration to India and the rest of the world of Islamabad's nuclear muscle. Between 1987 and 1990, officials would often deny that Pakistan was a nuclear weapons state in one breath but then speak of mutual nuclear deterrence on the subcontinent in another. In a meeting with Gates and his team, with Ambassador

Robert Oakley present, General Beg admitted that Pakistan had crossed the line in regard to manufacturing weapons-grade uranium in 1987, and stated that in February 1989 Pakistan had decided to reduce the level of enrichment because the objective of obtaining nuclear capability had already been achieved. Nevertheless, some doubts exist about exactly how prepared Pakistan was in 1990, and whether it had actually deployed nuclear weapons at that time.

India's statements about its nuclear capabilities were less pointed, but their net effect was the same. Public statements emanating from New Delhi and Islamabad during the late 1980s left no doubt that the two sides were prepared to at least contemplate the nuclear dimension in the event of a major conflict and definitely believed that the other side was already indulging in such contemplation.

The Yaqub Visit

As already mentioned, the importance of Yaqub Khan's visit to the nuclear dimension of the 1990 crisis remains unclear. Some participants believe that he issued a veiled nuclear threat to India during his meetings in Delhi. But that assessment requires large inferences to be drawn from the ambiguous language used in these conversations, such as "the clouds are roaring with thunder," and "there is lightning in the skies." These remarks might have suggested a nuclear threat, but much lies in the ears of the listener.

Gujral and V. P. Singh may well have detected a threat in Yaqub Khan's words, which might explain the prime minister's subsequent inquiry as to whether the air force was certain that it could repulse a "sneak nuclear attack" launched by Pakistan against India. Air force authorities informed Singh that no such guarantee could ever be given since a nuclear-capable aircraft could launch a successful attack if executed at low (treetop) level to evade radar. To prevent such an attack, the officials informed Prime Minister Singh, India would need to develop a nuclear deterrent.[46] Surprisingly, Singh did not direct any such questions to the army or navy.

These circumstances give added significance to Singh's subsequent statement that "India would have to review its peaceful nuclear policy if Pakistan employed its nuclear power for military purposes."[47] Presumably this public warning was prompted by the perception of a nuclear threat in Yaqub Khan's remarks that needed an explicit, public response. When Singh was later asked whether he was apprehensive about the possible use of nuclear weapons if India-Pakistan tensions escalated, he replied: "We want to avoid conflict, but if it comes we have nothing to fear."[48] Furthermore, if Pakistan were to go nuclear, "we will have to take stock of the situation and act accordingly."[49] These replies can, of course, be interpreted in many ways. Later in April, to dispel any notion that Pakistan's nuclear weapon capabilities would give Islamabad a deterrent umbrella under which to carry out offensive operations against India, Singh said that if Pakistan deployed nuclear weapons, "India will have to take a second look at our policy. I think we will have no option but to match. Our scientists have the capability to match it."[50]

Just before the Gates mission arrived in New Delhi, BJP leader L. K. Advani strongly advocated that India weaponize its nuclear capability.[51] However, India's minister of state for defense, Raja Ramanna, ruled out the use of nuclear weapons in the subcontinent—emphasizing that the long-term effects of a nuclear exchange would make continued human habitation in the region very difficult.[52] All the same, mutual worst-case analyses ensured that for both sides the opponent's capabilities loomed even larger than objective circumstances strictly warranted and might have induced caution. India had no or very few nuclear devices—as distinct from weapons that are tested and deliverable—yet most Pakistani officials believed that its nuclear program was very mature and advanced.

Washington's warnings about Islamabad's nuclear progress and its exhortations to Pakistan to refrain from developing nuclear weapons had inadvertently lent credibility to the idea of a Pakistani nuclear deterrent where it mattered most—in New Delhi. At this time, the Indian army's leading expert on nuclear weapons, Retired General K. Sundarji, asserted that "any sensible planner sitting on this side of the border is going to assume Pakistan does indeed have nuclear weapons capability. And, by the same token, I rather suspect the view from the other side is going to look very similar." Sundarji acknowledged that "on the other side, there may be the odd person who has kidded himself into believing that they have the nuclear weapon capability and we do not" but called this view "stupid," adding: "The sooner they wake up to this reality, the better."[53] Although both sides believed that the risks of nuclear confrontation were distinctly low, they were aware that the potential damage of a nuclear conflict in the subcontinent was unconscionably high. By 1990 both sides had probably acquired limited or primitive nuclear capabilities, but neither had a credible delivery system or a nuclear strategy or doctrine, and both sides doubted whether the other was nuclear capable in the sense of having an operational nuclear weapon; however, neither of them had conclusive evidence that this was the correct assessment.

To reiterate, though concerned that the crisis might develop a nuclear dimension, neither side appears to have seriously believed that this was likely to occur. General Sharma scoffed: "There is a lot of bluff and bluster from Pakistan. It is different to talk about something and totally different to do something. In return it is bluff and bluster from India that we would do this and that. In hard military terms your capability is not judged by the bluff and bluster, but by what you have in your pocket and what you can do with it."[54] This was the general perception of the military and intelligence community, though we have reason to believe that India's political leaders were somewhat more alarmed. However, Pakistan's senior military and political leaders were not unduly alarmed aside from perhaps Benazir Bhutto, whose views are hard to determine and were in any case not central to Pakistani policymaking on the crisis itself.

The Hersh and Other Accounts

The most significant and influential American account of the 1990 crisis, by Seymour Hersh, viewed it entirely in nuclear terms, with "the Bush administration . . . convinced that the world was on the edge of a nuclear exchange between Pakistan and India." According to Hersh, Deputy Director Richard J. Kerr of the CIA called the crisis "the most dangerous nuclear situation we have ever faced since I've been in the U.S. government. It may be as close as we've come to a nuclear exchange. It was far more frightening than the Cuban crisis."[55]

Hersh's account reflects the most alarmist point along the spectrum of American views but fails to comport with a number of facts. For example, his statement that Pakistan, in response to India's buildup of conventional forces in Kashmir and Rajasthan, "openly deployed its main armored tank units along the Indian border and, in secret, placed its nuclear-weapons arsenal on alert" is incorrect. Such assertions reflect the worst-case assessment of some individuals at that time, but that does not make them true.

American officials familiar with the flow of intelligence at that time recall seeing some reports of activity at Kahuta, Pakistan's main nuclear facility—which Hersh takes to be proof of a nuclear dimension—but like most intelligence, it was not indisputable evidence of an impending nuclear war. American thinking at the time was that a nuclear war was possible, but only if either side miscalculated and thought that the other might launch an attack "out of the blue," or if there were to be ground warfare and one side or the other were to fare badly. In Washington's judgment, neither Pakistan nor India had fully deployed nuclear forces, nor did they have a doctrine or strategy for the use of nuclear weapons. There was also no evidence that India was aware of any Pakistani preparations to launch a nuclear strike, although the Yaqub Khan conversations did alarm V. P. Singh and Gujral (conversations that the United States was not aware of).

Officials on both sides indicate that each side recognized the feebleness of its own nuclear capabilities but was somewhat more uncertain about those of the other side. Furthermore, neither believed that the other would launch a preemptive, nuclear strike out of the blue, and neither attempted to attack the other's nuclear forces with its own conventional airpower. A surprise attack would not have been possible without scientists' assurances that the crude nuclear devices then in each country's possession would have worked as a weapon—that is, they would have to have been safe for air crews to handle, capable of being armed after takeoff, and certain to produce the desired yield and effect on the appropriate target. That certainty, moreover, would depend on having completely accurate information on the location of the other's nuclear weapons, which would have been almost impossible for either side to uncover, especially if nuclear devices were no longer in the facility where they were assembled.

Some of Hersh's allegations found their way into print before his article was published. In May 1990 the London *Times* reported that "new information in the hands of both superpowers suggests that both India and Pakistan 'have been readying their nuclear arsenals.'[56] The *Far Eastern Economic Review* reported in 1992 that "according to leaks from the then V. P. Singh government in New Delhi, Gates was told by Pakistan's president Ghulam Ishaq Khan that in the event of a war with India, Pakistan would use its nuclear weapons at an early stage. Gates subsequently relayed this to New Delhi."[57] None of the members of the Gates mission that we have interviewed, let alone Pakistani officials, support this assertion.

Hersh's account has also been widely criticized by U.S. diplomats and military attachés posted in Islamabad and New Delhi during the spring of 1990, and also by regional strategists, some of whom claim that the whole nuclear dimension of the crisis was exaggerated, if not fabricated, by the Americans. Referring to Hersh's account of F-16s on strip alert, the U.S. Air Force attaché in Islamabad, Colonel Don Jones, called it "the silliest allegation I read in the article, and there were a lot of silly things in the article . . . some of the things he said were just on the face of it, ridiculous. It's not true."[58]

On the face of it, conversations with senior American, Indian, and Pakistani officials seem to indicate that the facts reside somewhere between the

Hersh account and the concerned, but less alarmist portrayal of the 1990 crisis by the Stimson Center of Washington, D.C. Their differences are rooted in uncertainty within the U.S. government about exactly what the Pakistani leadership was doing with its nuclear capabilities, as well as within India and Pakistan about the capabilities of their respective states, not to mention their intentions. Furthermore, the views of some Americans may have changed between 1990 and 1993, when Hersh's account appeared. In 1990 there was incomplete and fragmentary evidence—some of it alarming (though inconclusive)—to the effect that India or Pakistan were thinking of, or were even capable of, using a nuclear weapon against the other. After 1993 the understanding of the crisis became more balanced.

Clearly, however, Pakistan was doing something. Clues to this can be found in Ambassador Oakley's discussion with Hersh, in which his denials of Pakistani nuclear preparations are substantially more tepid than his comments during the Stimson proceedings. Hersh quotes him as saying that "the evacuation of Kahuta is not necessarily evidence of war," because Pakistan had long feared an Indian first strike against the enrichment facility.[59] This would imply either that an evacuation had taken place, or at least that intelligence data suggested Kahuta was being cleared out. An oblique exchange between Oakley and Colonel Jones is also suggestive. According to the Stimson account, Oakley facetiously said: "Don, I do not want to put words in your mouth, but with respect to Seymour Hersh's allegation or claim that Pakistani nuclear devices were starting to be deployed from Kahuta to the various airfields—that's because they were in big crates on big trucks. And on top of each crate it said, 'Pakistan Nuclear Devices,'—headed for airport." A moment later Jones replied: "Mr. Ambassador, you probably remember when we found out the trucks were being moved—and how that got blown out of proportion."[60] Oakley did not respond. These comments imply that U.S. intelligence had picked up signs of some unusual movements suggesting at least the possibility that nuclear material was being moved. Oakley himself says, "ISI [Inter-Services Intelligence] was putting out all sorts of messages," and intelligence analysts in Washington found these messages more credible than those of U.S. diplomats in the field.

Is it possible that these Pakistani actions suggesting preparations to deliver nuclear weapons were a colossal bluff? Without corroboration from Pakistani leaders, only a circumstantial case can be made that it was a clever hoax devised to achieve Islamabad's objectives in 1990. Pakistan certainly had the motive: it interpreted Indian deployments in Rajasthan as possible preparation for a conventional assault that could sever the strife-ridden

Sindh Province from northern Pakistan. As tensions rose, Pakistani officials may have believed that only a dramatic move could deter India, which after all had already tested a nuclear explosive device whereas Pakistan had not. Faking nuclear delivery preparations would spur the United States into action; a precedent for this could be found in South Africa, which had done something similar a few years earlier, with considerable impact on U.S. policy. Pakistan may have calculated that Washington would intervene to ease the tension, or at least pass along its observations to Indian leaders, who would then be deterred from any aggression they might have been contemplating. According to Hersh's anonymous source, the "big mistake" of the Pakistani truck convoy that Oakley mentioned leaving from Kahuta "was putting on more security than they needed." Another interpretation could be that the Pakistanis put on just the right amount of security: enough to set off alarm bells in Washington. William Burrows and Robert Windrem note that the idea of a Pakistani bluff "was later given credence in some intelligence circles," especially since "the data collected by U.S. intelligence systems, far from being ambiguous, were almost unbelievably explicit."[61]

Was there any link, at that time, between Washington's response to the crisis and its concern over the expanding covert Pakistani nuclear weapons program? Pakistan was, after all, "sanctioned" later in the year when President Bush was unable to certify to Congress, as required by the Pressler Amendment, that Pakistan did not possess a nuclear weapon, and that continued American assistance to Islamabad would be helpful in ensuring that it did not acquire one. The general belief within the administration was that hostilities between India and Pakistan could easily flare up—arising from the long-standing Kashmir dispute—and could escalate into a nuclear exchange between the two countries. Amplifying this view in dramatic testimony to the U.S. Senate, Director of Central Intelligence James Woolsey stated that a nuclear arms race between India and Pakistan posed "the most probable prospect for future use of weapons of mass destruction, including nuclear weapons. Both nations have nuclear weapons development programs and could, on short notice, assemble nuclear weapons."[62]

Hersh claims the Gates mission was a direct outcome of signs picked up by U.S. intelligence that Pakistan was making nuclear delivery preparations. These claims are neither provable nor disprovable on the basis of available evidence. A senior administration official commented:

> I think for most of us who were involved, nuclear weapons formed the backdrop for the crisis . . . the concern was not that a nuclear exchange

> was imminent; the concern was that this thing was beginning to spin out of control and that would lead to clashes, potentially conventional warfare. Most of our analysis suggested that India would fare better than Pakistan, and that very early on, as a result, Pakistan might want to consider threatening . . . a nuclear action. Or, that India, thinking about that, would escalate conventionally very early on, to eradicate it.[63]

However, the U.S. embassies (and the NSC) had a different concern: without timely intervention, they believed, the India-Pakistan tension would develop an inexorable momentum toward war in the fall of 1990. Several U.S. officials interviewed for this project deny that the nuclear link existed, arguing that the crisis had been treated on its merits. Decisive evidence about Pakistan's nuclear program came only in July, according to senior officials.

Yet one can speculate that Pakistan's nuclear program influenced attitudes deeper in the bureaucracy. Those familiar with Pakistan's nuclear program were aware that American officials had "seen no evil, heard no evil, and spoken no evil" for nearly ten years, despite conclusive evidence of Pakistan's burgeoning nuclear program. The CIA, in particular, had been angry at the failure to sanction Pakistan in 1988; it had even prepared a video for senior officials showing how Pakistan had not only violated U.S. law but had also broken its promises to two U.S. administrations. CIA officials had been stressing how serious the South Asian nuclear crisis was and were among Hersh's most important sources.

A number of conclusions can be drawn about the nuclear component of the 1990 crisis.

—American and South Asian perceptions differed in this regard. Washington thought the crisis was made worse by the existence of nuclear weapons. New Delhi and Islamabad seemed less anxious about a possible nuclear confrontation. Rather, the dominant view—with one or two important exceptions—was that the two states were never, in truth, close to war, let alone a nuclear exchange. If anything, Indians and Pakistanis seem to concur, nuclear weapons may have limited the risk of war, making the crisis of 1990 not unlike the situation during the cold war.

—Whether nuclear weapons were actually brandished during the crisis (notably via Yaqub's remarks), the suspicion remains, in the absence of hard evidence, that a nuclear threshold of one sort or another had been crossed. Was that threshold an actual mating of warheads and delivery vehicles? Was it the movement of nuclear weapons from one place to another? Or were policymakers (on both sides) suddenly persuaded of the need to speed up their nuclear weapons programs to ensure that they would be fully prepared to deter the other side when the next crisis came?

—Notwithstanding the ambiguities concerning thresholds, intelligence was decidedly bad on all sides and contributed significantly to the shaping of this crisis.

Internal Politics

The 1990 crisis was both a product and a cause of domestic political crises in India and Pakistan. India was struggling with its first minority government, an unstable non-Congress administration, while Pakistan was in the hands of a very weak civilian government after thirteen years of military rule. Both had opposition parties waiting to displace them. Various elements in each regime were also playing political games, with intelligence services "on the loose," especially in Pakistan, and foreign affairs and defense bureaucracies losing confidence in the quality of leadership provided by their respective prime ministers. Perhaps out of insecurity, newly elected officials in India and Pakistan made public statements suggesting brinkmanship and worst-case thinking. It is hard to recall another period in which leaderships were so tenuous in both countries simultaneously, which suggests a possible relationship between political coherence and regional stability.

During the crisis, the atmosphere crackled with rhetorical excess and populist proclamations at the highest levels. No doubt these verbal pyrotechnics were intended to meet the opposition's charges of "softness" toward the adversary. The loudest criticism came from right-wing parties, and in Pakistan's case, elements of the intelligence community. Benazir Bhutto's outbursts during her March 1990 tour of Kashmir and Singh's rhetoric in the Indian parliament greatly heightened the tension between the two countries. Paradoxically, it only made their position worse over the longer run. As perceptively noted by Indian journalist Shekhar Gupta: "For Benazir the dilemma is: if she relents on Kashmir she is damned at home: if she does not she could be headed for a war she may not want."[64] Singh was in a similar position. He needed to play up the Pakistani threat and its involvement in Kashmir to counter the criticism of the BJP and Congress Parties that he was not resolute enough. But he, too, did not want a purposeless conflict with Pakistan.

As already mentioned, both leaders had failed to win a clear "mandate" and were facing powerful groups on the sidelines waiting to topple their governments—the military and the defeated Nawaz Sharif in Pakistan, and the just-ousted but long-in-office Congress Party in India. Singh also had to grapple with the demands of the conservative Bharatiya Janata Party (BJP), which was providing crucial parliamentary support to his government.

Although upon assuming office Bhutto had made the usual pro forma statements about the need to settle the Kashmir issue, it did not become a major concern until rebellion broke out in the state. After surviving a no-confidence vote on October 21, 1989, she turned notably more hawkish, especially when the opposition flailed her for her "so-called compromising attitude toward India and [for] having failed to extract any compromise from Rajiv Gandhi, despite the alleged softness which he had shown toward Pakistan."[65]

One of her leading opponents was Sharif, who had assembled a center-right coalition heavy with Islamic conservatives and former Zia officials, and supported by many in the military. The Kashmir crisis seemed tailor-made for Sharif, who used it to weaken Bhutto's government and further strengthen his ties with the other power centers in Pakistan. Others were also critical. A former air chief, Air Marshal Asghar Khan, president of the centrist/secular Tehrik-e-Istiqlal Party, for example, criticized Bhutto's "vacillating" foreign policy, pressing her government to stop being a silent spectator and instead mobilize world public opinion in support of the Kashmir liberation movement.[66] From the Islamist side, Qazi Hussain Ahmad, the *amir* (leader) of the militant Jamaat-i-Islami, "urged the government to request the Organization of Islamic Conference (OIC) to call a summit of the member states to discuss the Kashmir issue and draw the attention of the world community towards this burning question."[67]

In India, V. P. Singh was also being pressured to take a more hawkish stance. The BJP's national executive committee passed a resolution urging the Indian government to "knock out the training camps and transit routes of the terrorists" and dispense with the doctrine of "hot pursuit . . . [as] a recognized defensive measure."[68] Joining in the clamor, former prime minister Rajiv Gandhi said the government needed to take "some very strong steps on Kashmir," adding, perhaps with reference to India's secret nuclear weapons program, "I know what steps are possible. I also know what is in the pipeline and what the capabilities are. The question is, does the government have the guts to take strong steps?"[69]

In retrospect, the Indian government's preoccupation with its survival may well have eroded its capacity for the patient diplomacy needed to address long-existing problems such as Kashmir or India-Pakistan relations. Instead of supporting Foreign Minister Gujral's committed efforts to improve India's relations with its estranged neighbors, for instance, the Janata government tended to let matters drift until they came to a head—and even then would just take the least action necessary to prevent the situation from going out of control. The confusion within the political system during the last half of 1989 and first half of 1990 might explain the government's lack of attention to the building crisis.

Decisionmaking

The change in government in both countries in 1988–89 brought to power many new personalities: new ministers, army commanders, senior civilian bureaucrats, and an entirely new cast of politicians. They voiced new perspectives on every issue confronting their respective decisionmakers: the lessons of recent conflicts, the nature of their security situation, the interests of their own country, and the steps, unilateral and bilateral, required to advance these interests.

At the time of the crisis, India's decisionmaking was under the influence of three major groups: the National Front government, the Congress opposition, and the permanent bureaucracy, especially in the foreign ministry. The lead voice, of course, was that of Prime Minister V. P. Singh, an experienced politician who had earlier served as Rajiv Gandhi's finance minister, then as defense minister. As foreign minister, Gujral undoubtedly had a major influence on shaping foreign policy, although he shared Singh's primarily inward, domestic-looking orientation. Another important figure was the deputy prime minister, Devi Lal, who had prime ministerial ambitions himself.

Almost all the policies of the National Front government were vehemently criticized by the opposition Congress Party, led by Rajiv Gandhi, as well as by the BJP, even though the latter had pledged to support the government. The BJP's principal parliamentary spokesman, Atal Bihari Vajpayee, had served as foreign minister in the late 1970s in an earlier coalition government (he was to be prime minister in the next two crises). Congress was still the largest party in parliament but had been unable to form a government. Both Congress and BJP spokesmen argued in parliament and the press that India had become a power in decline, that elements of the Janata Dal (the party Singh belonged to and the main constituent of the coalition) in the government had allowed foreign agents and powers to meddle in the country's internal affairs, especially in Kashmir and Punjab. They demanded that India reassert its regional dominance. Although still reeling from a defense procurement scandal, Gandhi remained assertive in foreign policy matters, arguing (as did the BJP) that a strong India (that is, an India led by him) would deter others from undercutting India in its own region. The permanent bureaucracy was closer to this perspective than to that of the new government. Note, too, that the bureaucracies of both countries—always significant in India and Pakistan in hitherto stable times—had begun to assume greater powers in the increasingly uncertain political environment.

Pakistan's decisionmaking, as mentioned earlier, was largely in the hands of a troika consisting of Prime Minister Bhutto, President Ghulam Ishaq Khan, and General Aslam Beg, each of whom believed that they were acting on behalf of the national interest and represented "the people" (or at least the state) of Pakistan. The military in particular viewed itself as the last bastion of stability and security. Bhutto had a few liabilities. For one thing, her only experience in politics was gained during the traumatic period before and after her father's imprisonment and execution. Her earlier career plans were to enter the Pakistani Foreign Service. Very few of her advisers were experienced in government. Her father's style was, at best, autocratic, and many of his wisest advisers had long since left the Pakistan People's Party. Bhutto was therefore heavily dependent on the civilian and military bureaucracy for advice and direction and never developed a coherent domestic and foreign policy of her own. On crucial matters of national security and the nuclear program, she was clearly a junior partner and not fully informed, especially about the latter.

Hence the other two members of the troika, President Khan and General Beg, dominated Pakistan's crisis management apparatus. Khan had been one of General Zia's closest civilian advisers and had been elevated from the chairmanship of Pakistan's Senate to acting president. He was the first Pakistani politician to call for a plebiscite in Kashmir (in 1989) and had reintroduced the "unfinished agenda of partition" argument. He had power over Bhutto—the constitution allowed Pakistan's president to dismiss an elected government at his (or her) pleasure—and he was associated with Pakistan's nuclear program since its inception. It is notable that the Gates team met with him (and General Beg) in Bhutto's absence.

The army, led by Beg, had well-formed foreign policy views and, unlike its Indian counterpart, had the means to implement them. Most of Pakistan's army officers believed that a dominant India needed to be balanced against a dominant Pakistan if there was to be peace in South Asia and if the chief India-Pakistan grievance, Kashmir, was ever to be resolved. But they had little faith in the good offices of outsiders, such as the United States, in helping Pakistan achieve justice for the Kashmiris and doubted Washington's reliability as an ally. While some privately worried about the increasing political disorder in Pakistan (stemming from the spillover of arms, narcotics, and combatants from Afghanistan, as well as from India's involvement in purely Pakistani ethnic and linguistic quarrels), most senior officers were proud of Pakistan's recent military performance and confident that a smaller Pakistan could hold off a more powerful India if it remained firm and true to its core principles. This implied a continuation of the nuclear program, which was widely understood to be Pakistan's "equalizer" against not only India's suspected nuclear program but also its much larger conventional force.

Some army officers and members of the intelligence community felt that Pakistan should take the offensive against New Delhi and carry the war into India by expanding support to Sikh dissidents and separatists. The view taught in army schools was that India was an artificial creation and might yet unravel.[70] Indeed, the creation of Pakistan at the time of partition was considered but the first step toward creating a South Asia of many states and eliminating a regionally dominant India. After 1984 Zia had allowed his intelligence services to give Sikh separatists some support, and a number of officers, including many who had supported the gigantic operation in Afghanistan, were eager to apply their techniques to vulnerable "India-held" Kashmir.

Pakistan's civilian foreign policy establishment had a somewhat different perspective on the question of relations with India and the United States. Since 1977 this establishment had served as the interface between a military regime and the rest of the world. As mentioned earlier, it comprehended Pakistan's larger political and strategic vulnerabilities better than the military and remembered well the years before the Afghan war when Pakistan had the reputation of a third-rate country. Somewhat embittered by the way in which the armed forces had brushed them aside, most in the civilian establishment were eager to see Bhutto succeed, as it would represent the further "civilianization" of Pakistan. They were also willing to negotiate with India on critical issues, including Kashmir, but had no clear idea themselves of what a normal relationship with India would be like. Like most foreign services, Bhutto's civilian bureaucratic advisers were superb on tactics but short on strategy.

Media and Public Opinion

Although the elections brought two relatively weak governments to power in Islamabad and New Delhi, they gave the media new attention that changed the context in which decisions were made. Most notably, the new prime minister, Benazir Bhutto, liberated the Pakistani press, while India permitted enhanced television and electronic coverage of public events.

The Press

As the Kashmir crisis unfolded, both countries experienced increasing media coverage, which was by and large nationalistic in both countries and fairly incendiary. Whereas the radio had played a strong propaganda role in the campaigns of 1971, the parties to the 1990 crisis, especially Pakistan, relied more on the emerging visual media (film, television, and videotapes) to whip up support for the militants in Kashmir and to highlight the atrocities purportedly committed by the Indian forces. These programs were available to the population in the border states of India. India's countermeasures were of the same genre: mainly radio and TV campaigns, which were easy to organize because certain aspects of the media were state-controlled at that time. In 1990 cable TV was not as extensively available as at present to offer wider and more balanced fare to the viewer.

The print media also served as a conduit for the public relations machinery of both governments, presenting a distorted image of the "Other." This was easily achieved in India by setting up several dozen "defense correspondents" accredited to the Ministry of Defense and feeding them tidbits of information. Consequently, they felt obliged to carry the handouts and leaks put out by the ministry, lest they be excluded from this government-controlled information. Although India has a free press and its democratic form of governance is well established, information on national security is selectively disseminated. The role of the so-called defense correspondents in exacerbating the crisis of 1990 and other crises is noteworthy.

Press coverage of the 1990 crisis (figure 4-1) was significantly more intense than that during the Brasstacks crisis, especially in India. The elite Indian papers more than quadrupled their coverage compared with that during Brasstacks, perhaps because this was considered a crisis of larger proportions, extending beyond the military to the domestic political sphere and involving the integrity of the Indian state and its position in Kashmir. Pakistani coverage doubled and continued at a high level for a long time,

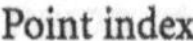

Figure 4-1. *Press Coverage of 1990 Crisis*[a]

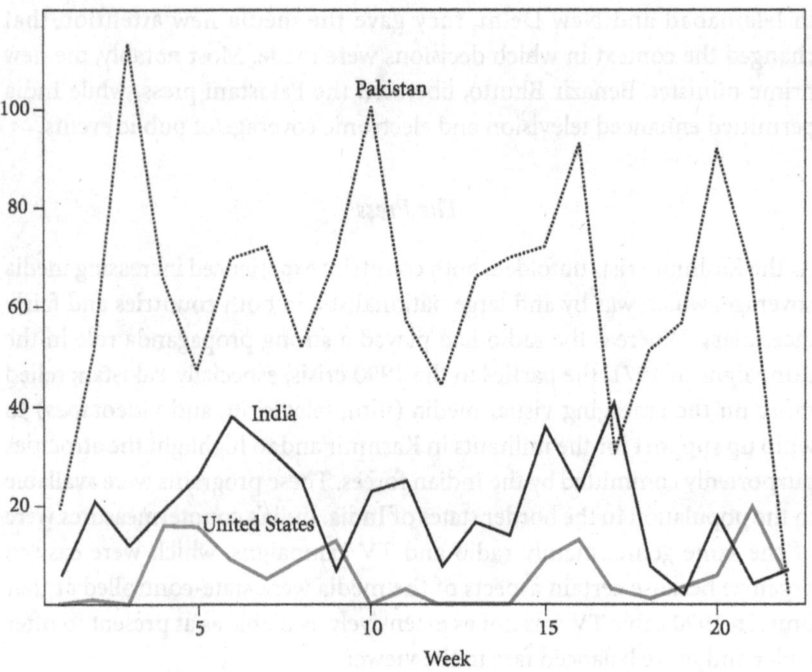

a. Two weeks of data for Pakistan were unavailable for this period.

exceeding that in India. American coverage was more intense than in 1987 but was very episodic, with a few peaks and many valleys. Although the Gates mission did draw attention in the U.S. media, it was modest compared with that in South Asia's press, or that given to events in the Balkans, the former Soviet empire, or the Middle East. This is not surprising since, as mentioned earlier, fevered speculation about Pakistan's movement of nuclear assets did not begin until the crisis had ended.

Public Opinion

By 1990 India and Pakistan had hardened their attitudes toward each other. Anti-Pakistan sentiment in Delhi grew especially strong when it became inundated with a new flood of Kashmiri Hindu refugees, while Pakistani feelings ran high in Punjab and other cities with large numbers of Kashmiris from

Jammu and Kashmir. Reflecting this hostility, massive protest rallies were held in Pakistani cities, demanding that the government liberate Kashmir.

Much of the rhetoric that issued from the political leadership was targeted at assuaging this domestic public sentiment. However, both countries also tried to shape world opinion. Pakistan made a considerable effort to do so regarding the developments in Kashmir. Bhutto went on a tour of Islamic countries to garner support, but some also came from the sizable Kashmiri population living outside South Asia, especially in Great Britain. To counter these efforts, the Indian government intensified its diplomatic activity and regularly briefed New Delhi–based envoys from China, the United States, the Arab countries, the European Community, and the Soviet Union; it also sent special envoys to a number of key countries to control the anticipated damage of the Pakistani diplomatic onslaught. In response, the president of Pakistan-administered Kashmir, Sardar Abdul Qayyum, accused India of deliberately distorting Pakistan's actions by giving the international community the impression that Pakistan was patronizing the separatist movement. He called on the Pakistani government to intensify its diplomatic efforts so as to dispel this "mischievous impression being given by India."[71]

Observations and Lessons Learned

The 1990 crisis was a *composite* or *compound* one. It came at a time when the world was rapidly changing. The two superpowers were shifting their attention away from the region and focusing more on nuclear proliferation. Unlike the conflict of 1987, the one in 1990 involved the contested state of Kashmir, which was in the throes of a separatist uprising. This uprising interacted with and contributed to the domestic political crises in India and Pakistan, both of which were plagued with weak governments. In sum, the crisis was not merely the outgrowth of historically persistent hostility between the two countries; it resulted from a specific confluence of events, trends, and personalities. The complexity of the 1990 crisis raises questions about the difficulty of predicting compound crises, as well as about strategies for resolving them.

Neither India nor Pakistan seemed to want to go to war in early 1990, yet participants and observers alike believed events were progressing in a way that portended a conflict. Among the factors often cited as evidence that the crisis could have escalated to the nuclear level are (a) the weak state of the minority governments on both sides, which engaged in fiery rhetoric to appease their domestic constituents and keep at bay their domestic opposition groups; (b) the provocative role of the media in both countries; and (c) the gap between the conventional capabilities of India and Pakistan, which might have led Pakistan to quickly—even preemptively—use its nuclear arms. However, a number of developments reduced the prospect of war between India and Pakistan and helped defuse the crisis.

First, both sides recognized that the military balance had changed and that the Indian army could not count on a quick victory. Having redressed some of their serious military deficiencies with the help of American aid in the 1980s, Pakistani officers calculated the army could sustain and fight a war for eleven to forty days. The 1989 Zarb-e-Momin exercise confirmed the enhanced fighting capacity of the Pakistan army. In addition, the defense production sector had also been improved with assistance from a number of European states, as well as China and North Korea. Furthermore, many Indian troops were just coming back from Sri Lanka and a failed counterinsurgency operation, which had demoralized the Indian army and embittered the officer corps.

Second, both states were uncertain of the diplomatic support they might receive from abroad if the crisis escalated. During the cold war, bloc leaders could be expected to come to the assistance of their followers, but subsequently that kind of support to friends was no longer a foregone conclusion. A war was, in fact, likely to attract condemnation more than anything else. The leaders of the United States, the Soviet Union, and China were extremely reluctant to see another conflict in South Asia.

Third, internal political confusion in both countries checked what some outsiders considered a drift toward war. Paradoxically, the same factor that precipitated the crisis may have stopped it from evolving into a military confrontation. For India, the disturbances in Punjab and Kashmir discouraged it from contemplating a war with Pakistan. Wars are rarely won if the local population is opposed, let alone completely hostile, to them. This was definitely a factor three years earlier in the Brasstacks crisis, when Pakistan made a feint toward India's then-rebellious Punjab state in response to a threatened Indian move toward the similarly restive Sindh Province. By 1990 India had a full-scale insurrection on its hands in Kashmir, and a still-unhappy Punjab besides; both these states are situated on the borders of Pakistan. An equally important consideration for Pakistan was the situation in Sindh, where it would have had to fight a war on three fronts: Kashmir, Punjab, and the Rajasthan-Sindh area. Aware of India's strategic advantage in the latter sector, Pakistani planners could not afford to leave it undefended. Behind these calculations, in both states, lay the memory of the

Indian intervention in East Pakistan, which had led to the formation of Bangladesh. That and other empirical evidence indicates that war in South Asia has been linked to ethnic or regional separatism; in 1990 (as in 1987) the vulnerabilities as well as the opportunities were mutual for both India and Pakistan.

Fourth, both countries recognized that war would wreak havoc on their economies. At that time both states were just beginning to liberalize, privatize, and deregulate their economies to attract foreign investment. A war would not only have scared away investors but also have had an adverse effect on investments by any new trading partners.

Fifth, the existence (and deterrent effect) of nuclear capabilities could not be ignored, although it does not appear to have been a determining factor. The 1990 crisis was, in the view of some at the time, the world's second nuclear confrontation. This aspect of the crisis has attracted the most publicity in the West, although the "nuclear" dimension was smaller than is made out in some accounts.

All these factors made decisionmakers on both sides wary of moving down the path of confrontation. Nevertheless, they engaged in brinkmanship, although with meticulous care and with primarily a domestic audience in mind. Their behavior (and the crisis as a whole) convinced many outside observers that South Asia was *the* area in the world where nuclear war was most likely to occur. Despite the less alarmist assessment of many important regional analysts, this understanding of the crisis strongly shaped later beliefs and policies, especially in the United States.

CHAPTER FIVE

The Kargil Conflict

Three months after the Lahore Summit of February 1999, the armed forces of India and Pakistan clashed along the Line of Control (LOC) in the Kargil-Dras region of the state of Jammu and Kashmir (map 5-1). This was a small war, but with numerous casualties and global interest in its outcome. The crisis atmosphere was heightened by concern that it might expand geographically from the remote vastness of Kargil to the rest of Kashmir or across the international boundary, or that it might escalate to higher levels of violence, even a nuclear exchange.

Initially, a force of Pakistan army paramilitaries and "mujahiddin," supported by locally recruited porters, occupied the heights dominating the Srinagar-Leh road. Once they were detected, New Delhi mounted a counteroffensive that escalated into an intense battle involving artillery, infantry, and some air-ground action. This action continued until July, when Pakistan made a U.S.-brokered announcement that it was withdrawing its troops from their forward positions. The crisis had major domestic consequences in the region, especially in Pakistan.

The Crisis

Rather than add to the numerous studies of the military dimensions of this crisis, this chapter focuses on its political context and strategic consequences. Even more than in the case of other crises examined in this book, there were strikingly different versions as to what happened and why, and what lessons are to be drawn from the event. Briefly, Pakistan's military leadership viewed Kargil within the context of the wider India-Pakistan conflict and the dispute

This map is indicative and not to scale. The disputed areas shown in the map reflect the authors' judgement. The boundaries shown in the map may not confirm to the official boundaries of India. The printer and publisher bear no responsibility on the accuracy or otherwise of this map.

Map 5-1. *Kargil and Northern Kashmir*

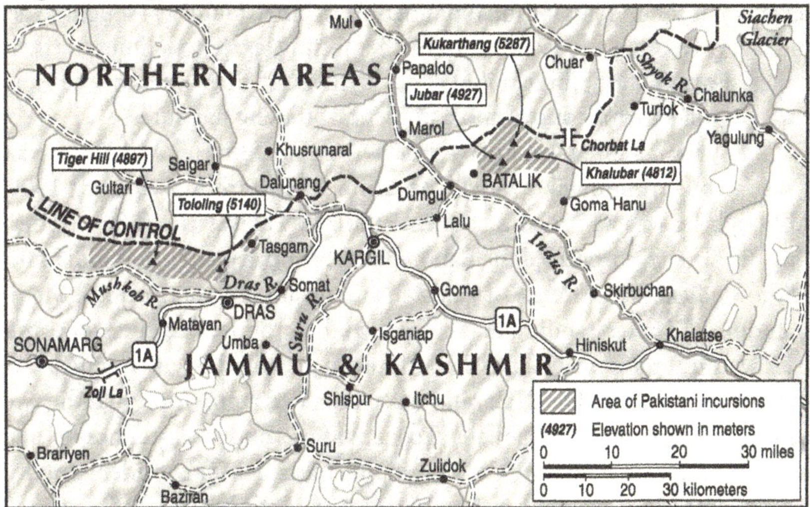

over Kashmir, and it tended to draw comparisons with past crises such as those over the Rann of Kutch and Siachen. General Pervez Musharraf has also argued that the occupation of the Kargil heights was a defensive military move in response to India's adjustment of its forces along the LOC.[1] Conversely, Indian officials not only characterized Kargil as an isolated incident but placed the entire blame on Pakistan, noting that planning for Kargil had been under way even as the two countries were engaged in peace talks in Lahore just a few months earlier.[2] Indian strategists also note that this was no minor incursion—because of its location, the operation threatened India's entire position in Leh to the east and Kargil to the north and could have precipitated a wider war. This latter point resonated strongly in Washington, and the crisis saw heavy American involvement and President Bill Clinton's personal engagement. The involvement of sympathetic outsiders was actively encouraged by India, a major departure from its stated policies and recent practices. Nuclear weapons played a significant role in this crisis, largely through threat and bluster, and the latent threat (sometimes made explicit) ensured intense and widespread coverage in the world's press.

Context

India's nuclear tests of May 1998 alarmed the international community, created a major diplomatic crisis, and brought U.S. involvement in the region as the Americans sought to prevent Pakistan from following suit. Subsequently, Washington engaged in extensive diplomacy with both India and Pakistan, described fully in the memoir-history written by Strobe Talbott, then deputy secretary of state.[3] Talbott (and diplomats from other countries) sought to get India and Pakistan to refrain from further testing, agree to a limit on fissile material production, limit military deployment of their nuclear weapons, and adopt new arms control and confidence-building measures.

One such measure taken up by India was Prime Minister Atal Bihari Vajpayee's "bus diplomacy," which took him to Lahore in February 1999. Although he was accorded a cool reception by Pakistan's military leadership, the journey produced the Lahore Declaration, a pledge that India fully acknowledged the existence of Pakistan and meant it no harm, and a Memorandum of Understanding that embodied the promise that the two countries would forge a new bilateral relationship premised on an atomic peace in the subcontinent. The declaration also included a provision that the two countries would "engage in bilateral consultations on security concepts, and nuclear doctrines, with a view to developing measures for confidence building in the nuclear and conventional fields, aimed at avoidance of conflict."[4] The objective in reaching these agreements was as much to address the concerns of the international community (both countries had been sanctioned by the United States, Japan, and other major states) as it was to bring about a genuine normalization of relations. However, after reports of intrusions into India across the LOC started filtering in, the hopes for normalcy embedded in the Lahore process were dashed for nearly four years.

Initiation

In October 1998 India claimed that it had beaten back two Pakistani attacks in the Siachen area.[5] According to President Musharraf, the Pakistan army's internal investigation of these claims found that they were "make-believe," and that there were no "official" incursions. However, as characterized by Musharraf, the army leadership was aware of repeated crossings of the LOC by mujahiddin from Kashmir, supported by freelance sympathizers from Pakistan and Afghanistan.[6] Presumably, these crossings extended to the Siachen region, which is not covered by the LOC.

For New Delhi, the earliest indication of intrusions into the Kargil-Dras sector from Pakistan seems to have been reports by local herders on May 6, 1999, of individuals lodged in bunkers usually vacated by Indian troops during the winter months.[7] There has been much controversy about the exact number and identity of these infiltrators. While *Keesing's Record* puts the number at about 600, the *SIPRI Yearbook 2000* gives 700–1,000.[8] Initially, Indian sources stated 600–800 infiltrators had occupied positions overlooking a key Indian supply route,[9] but later, in an interview with the *Financial Times,* India's foreign minister doubled that number to 1,200–1,500. President Musharraf writes of 100 new posts filling the "unoccupied gaps" along the LOC, each post consisting of 10 to 20 persons, suggesting that in the end there was rough agreement as to the total numbers involved on the Pakistani side.[10]

As for the identity of the infiltrators, initial reports cited a joint operation by Kashmiri mujahiddin and their sympathizers—mostly veterans of the Afghan war who had not yet left the area and some members of the militant wings of Pakistan-based religious parties. Subsequently, it became quite clear that these forces included Pakistan's Northern Light Infantry (NLI), which at the time of the Kargil clash was a paramilitary organization but was later integrated into the regular army for duties in the Northern Areas. Some Pakistani accounts aver that the mujahiddin slipped between established posts on their way to the LOC and did not necessarily need military support; Indian and several international accounts dispute this, stating that the entire region was under the control of the Pakistan army, and that no movement would have been possible without its knowledge and perhaps direct support.

The intruders were deeply entrenched: units of company and platoon strength ensconced in rudimentary fortifications held important heights, while smaller numbers or groups of section or half-section strength guarded the approaches to these areas from bunkers.[11] Indian troops stationed locally launched several unplanned and uncoordinated assaults to evict the intruders and to blunt the anticipated criticism of their lack of vigilance, but they were repulsed and suffered heavy losses. It took almost three weeks for the Indian army to assess the nature of the Pakistani action; Indian defense officials realized that the rugged terrain and virtual absence of cover would greatly hamper ground or air retaliation. As a result, they launched a series of minor but hard-fought operations against prepared positions and shifted troops from other sectors to achieve local superiority. Fighting also flared up near the Siachen Glacier.

The Confrontation Escalates

By the end of May, India had not only deployed a massive number of ground troops but had also started using its air force (IAF) to punish and evict the intruders.[12] The Cabinet Committee on Security did not authorize IAF entry until May 26, perhaps because of the risk of escalation. Following the early loss of two aircraft, the IAF changed tactics and began attacking Pakistani positions with air-to-ground missiles from heights of about 30,000 feet, thereby reducing their effectiveness. Indian sources note that one aircraft was lost in an accident and another in ground fire; the Pakistan version is that both were shot down as they crossed the LOC. Later, conventional 1,000-pound bombs using modified laser guidance kits were used with greater success. Indian pilots were handicapped by the political directive not to cross the LOC, which required skillful flying to remain within Indian-administered territory. The Indian navy also seems to have entered the picture at the end of May. Most notably, the Eastern Fleet was shifted to the Arabian Sea to be in a position to blockade the Makran coast and bottle up the Pakistan navy in Karachi if required. In the view of Pakistani naval officers, however, India did not have the capacity to blockade Karachi because of enhanced Pakistani air-sea capabilities, and because their submarines could have, if necessary, lurked outside of Indian ports on India's eastern and western coasts.[13]

Despite having to fight uphill against entrenched troops and being prohibited by political directive from crossing the LOC under any circumstances, the Indian forces managed to reduce the occupied positions sector by sector through innovative tactics and vast numerical superiority. By contrast, Pakistan was unable to resupply or reinforce its troops since the supply routes were vulnerable to Indian interdiction, and also because it needed to sustain the claim that the intruders were mujahiddin and not Pakistani army regulars.

Diplomacy

While these military maneuvers were taking place on both sides, diplomacy crept forward very slowly. After much haggling, India and Pakistan agreed to hold talks on June 12; Islamabad sent Sartaj Aziz, its foreign minister, to Delhi to discuss resolution of the issue. A taped conversation between Musharraf and his general chief of staff (see the next section) indicates that Aziz received his instructions from the army, which was fully in charge of diplomacy as well as fighting. These talks proved fruitless, whereupon Pakistan blamed India for closing the door to dialogue by rejecting Aziz's proposal that UN observers be allowed to identify the actual LOC. Pakistan knew that UN or other independent verification was traditionally anathema to India.[14] In the view of a senior Pakistani general directly involved in the crisis, his leaders also believed that the Indians were never interested in having the area demarcated—not just because they opposed third-party intervention in principle but also because a demarcation might require them to vacate areas in the Chorbatla, Qamar, and Siachen sectors.

A secret channel had also been established with special envoys—R. K. Mishra (a journalist in the confidence of Prime Minister Vajpayee) and Niaz Naik (a former Pakistani foreign secretary, meeting on behalf of Prime Minister Nawaz Sharif)—traveling to Pakistan and India, respectively, in an attempt to find a solution. Prime Ministers Sharif and Vajpayee also activated the hotline, holding at least three telephone conversations on it. India simultaneously embarked upon a vigorous diplomatic campaign aimed at influencing the international community, part of what one newspaper called "India's double act of war and diplomacy."[15] It also launched a media war, banning Pakistan television in India and strengthening its presentation of its side of events. Notably, it detached an articulate and telegenic Indian foreign service officer (Ramindar Singh Jassal) to the Ministry of Defense, where he conducted regular and informative briefings. India won South Asia's first television war.

By the beginning of July, Pakistan was being subjected to intense pressure to secure the withdrawal of its forces and the mujahiddin. After visiting China and later the United States, Prime Minister Sharif appealed publicly to the mujahiddin to withdraw from Kargil. On July 11, following an agreement between Sharif and President Clinton on July 4, Pakistan announced a troop withdrawal.[16] By mid-July, most of the occupied posts had been vacated and reoccupied by Indian forces. Fighting continued over three other positions that had been occupied by the intruders, but they were finally overrun by July 16, while fighting in the Haneef Uddin sector continued until August 3. Diplomatically, the international community by and large sided with India or blamed Pakistan for the crisis and the war; even China felt the crisis had to be resolved bilaterally and peacefully.

Origins and Lessons: Competing Views

No other South Asian crisis saw a greater gap between official Indian and Pakistani perspectives. As the following sections make clear, they were in agreement on only a few points, and the semiauthoritative government view has been seriously challenged, especially in the case of Pakistan.

Pakistan: A War of Defense and a Near-Strategic Victory

Head of the Pakistan army at the time of Kargil and subsequently Pakistan's president, Pervez Musharraf has provided an account of events in 1999 in both capacities. Musharraf's version has been supplemented by those of former colleagues, Pakistani scholars, and government officials. Together, they make four important points regarding Pakistan's motives and incentives. These pertain to the larger context of the crisis, Pakistan's concern about renewed Indian incursions, the success of the operation in weakening India's overall military position, and the importance of reviving the Kashmir issue. Further, the Pakistan establishment's version downplays the risk of a nuclear conflict and pins a great deal of responsibility on Prime Minister Nawaz Sharif.

The official Pakistani justification for its intrusions into the Kargil region was that the LOC is an artificial and temporary arrangement pending a final settlement of the Kashmir dispute and therefore that a certain amount of "nibbling"—crossing the LOC and encroaching on the other side's territory—is to be expected. Accordingly, despite the Simla Agreement's clear injunction that the LOC "shall be respected by both sides without prejudice to the recognized position of either side," India had breached this stipulation on at least three occasions. In Musharraf's opinion, "India had been 'creeping forward' across the LOC even after the Simla Agreement," and had "tested" Pakistan and violated Simla in the Chorbatla sector in 1972, and in the seizure in 1988 of twelve posts in the Qamar area, as well as the Bhimbet and Marpola posts in the Dras sector.[17] All these posts and areas were on the Pakistani side of the LOC (Pakistani officials also often include in this list the 1984 seizure of Siachen by Indian forces, although, as noted in chapter 2, the LOC did not reach up to the glacier).[18] Therefore, the Kargil intrusions fell within this genre of accepted "nibbling" operations that had acquired some legitimacy over the years and must be viewed in the context of the larger ongoing Kashmir dispute. Being a limited engagement and not the prelude to total war, Kargil resembles border clashes in the Rann of Kutch (1965) and Siachen (1984–89). These were also fought with limited means, for limited objectives, and in limited geographical areas.

The Kargil operation was also designed to meet specific Indian military threats: namely, to fill the gaps in Pakistani defensive positions and to redress the overall India-Pakistan military imbalance. As for the gaps, Musharraf has written:

> It was appropriate to allow the Rawalpindi Corps to prepare and present the FCNA [Force Command Northern Areas] plan of the defensive maneuver in the Northern Areas so as to deny any ingress across the LOC. A plan calling for plugging the gaps—ranging from nine to twenty-eight miles (fifteen to forty-five kilometers)—between our positions was formally presented and approved toward the middle of January 1999. Rawalpindi Corps and FCNA were to execute it.[19]

A variation on this Kargil-as-a-defensive operation offered by the then Pakistan minister of foreign affairs, Sartaj Aziz, was that it was a local operation in response to (and in retaliation for) India's regular firing in the Neelam Valley.[20] As Shireen Mazari, a leading Pakistani scholar, noted, army intelligence had reported that India was planning to occupy two more posts in the Shaqma sector to restrict Pakistan's ability to interdict the Kargil-Dras road. Thus Pakistani intrusions were really a defensive operation.[21] In this view, Pakistan's sole purpose was to prevent anticipated Indian attempts to occupy more area on the Pakistani side of the LOC.

The pattern of India's nibbling supposedly consisted of the concentration of troops followed by the quick supply of weapons and other necessary material deemed essential for sneak attacks and planned encroachments. By late 1998, Indian forces appeared to be contemplating another such operation in the areas being looked after by the Force Command Northern Areas. Soon Pakistani intelligence sources were pointing to the Shaqma sector, where they thought India had already started increasing forces and equipment.[22] An apprehensive Pakistani leadership then asked the FCNA to carry out a realistic assessment of likely Indian moves for defensive purposes. According to some of those involved in the planning, the FCNA did execute a defensive move, but only after confirming Indian plans, and put in a request for extra troops only after Pakistani posts were faced with massive Indian attacks. Some of the junior commanders, Mazari states, progressed to more dominating heights only after the Indians had attacked Turtok on April 30.[23]

India moved into the Batalik and Dras sectors on May 5 and 7, respectively. Thus some Pakistanis (especially those closely associated with its planning and implementation) consider Kargil a justifiable preemptive defensive move. This explanation resembles India's case for its preemptive occupation of the undemarcated Siachen Glacier in "no-man's land" on the grounds that Pakistan was planning a surreptitious occupation. In General Musharraf's assessment, the Pakistani maneuver was "conducted flawlessly, a tactical marvel of military professionalism."[24] Many observers agree that it was brilliantly executed.

There was apparently a *second* military objective behind the Kargil operation: to tie India down militarily, so that it could not mount an attack across the international border. As Musharraf wrote six years after the events,

> As a result of the foresight and alertness of our senior commanders, India's planned offensive was preempted. The initiative was wrested from India, and an imbalance was created in the Indian system of forces. The military assets committed by the Indians in the Kargil conflict in particular and in Kashmir in general brought about a near parity of forces both in the air and on the ground along the international border. This nearly ruled out the possibility of India's deciding on an all-out war.[25]

To reiterate, Pakistan's policies before, during, and after the Kargil crisis must be seen in the context of the overall situation in Kashmir, including its unresolved political status, the population's need for support in their struggle against what is perceived as unjust Indian rule and the need to pressure India to come to the negotiating table and resolve the Kashmir dispute. Pakistanis see New Delhi's refusal either to honor the original UN resolutions regarding a plebiscite or to move politically to accommodate Kashmiri sentiments, or to negotiate, as legitimate concerns.

From the beginning, the Kargil operation was considered a military-political operation that would revive the Kashmir issue. The idea for a Kargil-type operation had been circulating among Pakistani decisionmakers for some time and was defended by Musharraf's immediate predecessor, General Jehangir Karamat, shortly after the event. Although Karamat believed Pakistan had to seek an accommodation with India for its own political and economic progress, he felt it could not forsake the Kashmiris. He defended Pakistani policy as realistic: it had made the effort to keep the Kashmir issue alive, yet it wisely contained the conflict "by keeping it localized, and then, with U.S. involvement, stepped back from the brink—even though there were those who were advocating oblivion after the big bang."[26]

In one comprehensive account published shortly after the crisis, Shaukat Qadir, a retired Pakistan army brigadier, points out that the Kargil goal was to "provide a fillip to the Kashmiri freedom movement."[27] The operation was to use a military strategy (occupation of Indian posts along the LOC) to achieve a political objective (a just and permanent solution to the Kashmir issue). Brigadier Qadir faults Nawaz Sharif for both gloating over the initial

Pakistani military successes and failing to understand the political and diplomatic consequences of the Pakistani initiative, as well as for not seeking information beyond the briefings he received. In Qadir's view, Kargil's planners misjudged the international situation, but had it taken place a year earlier, before the Lahore summit, it might have had a different outcome. A former Inter-Services Intelligence (ISI) head, Lieutenant General Asad Durrani, took issue with the timing of the operation and the inept way in which it was justified internationally, and expressed guarded admiration for the way in which India responded both militarily and politically.[28]

Despite the apparent failure of the operation, Pakistan considered the outcome positive—the Kashmir dispute was once again internationalized, and many world leaders began talking about the urgency of resolving the problem. As succinctly stated on President Musharraf's website, the Kargil operation "with all its reality and distortions . . . proved a lesson to the Indians and a rude awakening to the world of the reality of Kashmir."[29]

The Pakistan army, with Musharraf at its head, has argued that the entire Kargil war was effectively lost by a political leadership (that is, Sharif) that displayed a lack of statesmanship and made no serious effort to rally the nation as had its Indian counterparts. Prime Minister Sharif is seen as having been demoralized by international pressure, and when the moment of truth came in Washington, "there was no negotiation at all": Sharif agreed to an unconditional withdrawal.[30] The military situation on the ground, asserts Musharraf, was not at all precarious (saying so was disinformation), as the Indians were in no position to launch a strong offensive, could not dislodge the "freedom fighters" and the NLI from their advanced positions, and overall, Pakistan was in an advantageous position in case of all-out war because so many Indian forces had been inducted into Kashmir. Thus on the eve of Sharif's trip to Washington, concludes Musharraf, the military situation was favorable, but Sharif buckled under American pressure and the phony accusation that the crisis might slip into a nuclear war. Musharraf himself has come under criticism from retired army officers, including Lieutenant General Javed Nasir, who was close to Nawaz Sharif. Nasir faults the operation for failing to hold on to some key posts long enough. Had the army done so, the Indians would have been forced to crawl, as in Nasir's view they could not have resupplied their posts in Leh and Siachen.[31]

President Musharraf's judgment that the Kargil conflict emerged out of a tactical maneuver of limited dimensions but had significant strategic effects is certainly correct. Still in dispute, however, is the question of who was responsible for the original "tactical" maneuver and what those strategic effects were, let alone whether the crisis had a nuclear dimension, which he denies.[32] We do agree that the Kargil conflict contributed, in a peculiar way, to the search for a solution to the Kashmir issue. Musharraf writes that he and Nawaz Sharif wanted to put Kashmir on the world's radar screen, politically and militarily, and that the Kargil initiative succeeded in doing so. He held Sharif responsible for buckling under American pressure, for failing to rally the country, for blaming the army, and even for denying any knowledge of the Kargil operations. This, says Musharraf, helped seal his political fate: "It was in dealing with Kargil that the prime minister exposed his mediocrity and set himself on a collision course with the army and me."[33]

Indian Assessments

To the Indian government and public alike, the facts of this crisis were as clear as daylight: Pakistan's paramilitary forces, along with Islamic militants, had crossed the LOC and blatantly occupied the Indian army's defensive positions in the mountainous Kargil-Dras sector in clear violation of the Simla Agreement and the sanctity of the LOC. In the view of Indian strategists and scholars, the Kargil intrusions were too extensive and widespread to constitute a "nibbling" operation—they were more like a huge bite. To suggest that this extensive and widespread operation was a local action, undertaken through local initiative, makes an impossible demand on credulity, they argue, disputing Islamabad's contention that the intruders were mujahiddin and that its soldiers were not involved. They find it difficult to imagine how mujahiddin could survive and fight at heights of 14,000 feet and provide themselves the necessary logistic facilities (Indian Army troops, incidentally, need to be acclimatized and especially trained for this kind of mountain warfare).

The consensus within India is that Pakistan's army planned the Kargil conflict much before 1999 and presented the idea to Prime Minister Benazir Bhutto, who rejected it outright.[34] General Jehangir Karamat, former chief of the army staff in Pakistan (1996–98), was also against this plan, but General Musharraf later revived it. When promoted to chief of army staff in October 1998, Musharraf decided to operationalize "Koh Pemah," which envisaged surreptitious intrusions across the LOC to occupy posts in the Kargil sector. This operation was apparently based on the prevailing belief, especially among the military, that the Indian army was exhausted and suffering from low morale because of its long-drawn-out involvement in counterinsurgency operations in Kashmir.[35] Though some believe that Sharif was only vaguely aware of the operation, Indians judge that he approved the plan in October 1998 and was briefed on its contours in January 1999 by GHQ Rawalpindi.[36] President Musharraf has stated that the army kept Prime Minister Sharif fully informed, and that Sharif was briefed in Skardu on January 29, 1999, and in Kel on February 5, 1999, where the army's "defensive maneuvers" and Indian actions were described. Subsequently, according to Musharraf, briefings took place on March 12 at ISI headquarters, on May 17 (by the director-general of military operations), and on June 2 and June 22. Musharraf himself briefed the Defense Committee of the cabinet on July 2, 1999, just before Sharif's trip to Washington.[37]

Koh Pemah was planned in great secrecy. Perhaps the secrecy was so great that India may have given it the wrong code name. It is consistently referred to as Operation Badr in Indian sources, but Pakistanis involved with the original operation insist that this is a misnomer. "Badr" was the Prophet's first battle at Mecca between Muslims and nonbelievers; it was also the name assigned by the Arab armies in their joint attack on Israel in the 1973 war. Besides the chief of army staff, only the chief of general staff, director-general of military operations, general officer commanding (GOC) of X Corps in Rawalpindi, and the GOC of Force Command Northern Area, whose 62 Infantry Brigade and some mujahiddin were involved in the operation, knew about it. "Throughout the winter, nominated regular troops of the Northern Light Infantry (NLI), Chitral and Bijaur Scouts and selected Special Service Group (SSG) commandos carried out extensive training in high-altitude warfare . . . [T]he northern areas were placed under Pakistan army rule to deny access to the media and facilitate optimal exploitation of resources."[38] The preparations for Koh Pemah were extensive: "Heavy weapons, ammunition, rations and other essential supplies were stockpiled, telephone cables were laid, and material for the construction of sangars (a defensive fortification constructed by piling up rocks in areas where it is difficult to dig down) was moved forward. In some areas, artillery field guns and mortars were dismantled and moved forward to gun positions close to the LOC to enable them to interdict NH 1A [Srinagar-Leh highway]."[39]

Indian analysts believe Pakistan crossed the LOC and occupied the heights above Kargil with several objectives in mind:[40]

—To interdict the Kargil-Ladakh highway and isolate Indian forces in Leh, the support base for Indian troops in Siachen, and thereby facilitate their later eviction.

—To emphasize that the LOC was essentially a temporary border and could be redrawn to reflect new ground realities created by the adverse possession of territory. Pakistan would then be able to keep the area it had "captured" by intrusion as the Indians had already done in the Chorbatla, Qamar, and Siachen sectors.

—To elicit a violent Indian reaction, which would alarm the international community and feed into its fears that the Kashmir conflict could escalate out of control and reach a nuclear flashpoint. These fears would ensure the involvement of external mediators who would act to defuse the crisis and internationalize the Kashmir issue to Pakistan's advantage.

—To excise, via "salami-slicing" tactics, territory in the Kargil sector that India would not consider important enough to escalate the conflict to the level of general war, much less to the nuclear level.

From India's perspective, Pakistan failed to secure these objectives except for managing to internationalize the Kashmir dispute—but in a way that lost it international support. The international community condemned Pakistan's evident violation of the LOC, an action that could have sparked an even greater conflict. The United States called its actions unprovoked and unjustified, as did the G-8 countries, which viewed "any military action to change the status [of the LOC] as irresponsible."[41]

America's Role

Just before the Kargil crisis, the U.S. government had already assembled a team to deal with the post-test nuclear negotiations between Washington and New Delhi. This team was centered in the Department of State and led by Deputy Secretary Strobe Talbott, along with Assistant Secretary Karl ("Rick") Inderfurth. In the White House, an NSC staffer, Bruce Riedel, was a major participant, joining in all of the high-level discussions; Riedel was to provide the first insider account of the July 4 meeting between Nawaz Sharif and President Clinton.[42] The president was very active himself, frequently telephoning Prime Ministers Sharif and Vajpayee and participating in lengthy planning sessions despite the growing domestic crisis stemming from revelations about his personal behavior. Some figures in the earlier nuclear dialogue with India and Pakistan, such as Robert Einhorn, had no significant role in the crisis, although they did try to ensure that the United States did not say anything that was incorrect as far as nonproliferation objectives were concerned. The Pentagon played little part in the process, except to provide an assessment of the tactical situation. With Congress focused more on President Clinton's personal affairs than events in South Asia, there was little, if any, congressional engagement.

For America, the Kargil crisis lasted just under two months, from the first démarches to India and Pakistan on May 24 to the final set of crisis-related telephone calls and conversations in mid-July. Over this period American engagement escalated steadily, reaching a peak on July 4, with the Sharif-Clinton White House meeting. Clinton's direct engagement began in early June, with presidential messages to Sharif and Vajpayee on June 3 (following earlier calls by Secretary of State Madeleine Albright to her counterparts, and to the British foreign secretary, Robin Cook). By June 15 the manner in which the course of events had unfolded was clear enough to persuade Clinton to call Sharif and urge Pakistan to pull out of Kargil—he followed this call up with one to Vajpayee, keeping him informed of developments. American diplomacy reached out to a wide circle: there were consultations with the Russians at the secretary level, démarches to several Gulf States and Turkey (states with close ties to Pakistan), and China. Senior U.S. officials also met frequently with their Indian and Pakistani counterparts in Washington, South Asia, and other venues. One meeting of note took place in mid-June in Europe between the American and Indian national security advisers, Sandy Berger and Brajesh Mishra, at which Mishra reportedly warned of the danger of escalation:

> The middle of June was the most anxious period of the war and possibly the closest when we came to enlarging the conflict area. Bitter fighting was going on in all sectors but we had yet to win any battle. On 16 June Brajesh Mishra informed the U.S. national security advisor, Sandy Berger, that India would not be able to continue with its policy of "restraint" for long and that our military forces could not be kept on leash any longer. He added that the Government of India might have to let them cross the border any day. According to Brajesh Mishra, the US administration took this message quite seriously.[43]

Apparently India's National Security Advisory Board had recommended to the Cabinet Committee on Security, through Mishra, that the military be allowed to "cross the border/LOC."[44] There is no evidence, however, that Indian ground forces crossed the LOC.

When the crisis began, the United States had no close strategic relationship with either India or Pakistan, and no outside issue loomed large to force it to tilt to one side or the other. Pakistan was not providing much help in countering terrorist groups, and its interlocutors were less than forthcoming with Talbott on the nuclear question. India was a new discovery—Talbott was deeply impressed during his talks with Jaswant Singh, and

Clinton had a strong desire to further improve relations with India, still not a strategic partner.

What did shape American policy was the belief in transparency when dealing with both states. Clinton's policy team saw America's role as that of an umpire, calling the plays as it saw them. This was the way the Talbott nuclear talks had been run, and there was no reason to give either India or Pakistan a pass on Kargil. In one exchange between Madeleine Albright and Jaswant Singh, Albright urged that India and the United States not "turn Pakistan into a pariah," to which Jaswant agreed, but needled her by saying that being an "umpire" was not enough—an umpire would not be able to bring Pakistan back into the ranks of decent and civilized states—to which Albright responded: "Don't blame the umpire, look to yourselves as players. Do something about the nature of the game."[45] From May onward, observed one Indian scholar, U.S. policy statements amounted to the following:[46]

—The United States regarded the infiltrators as "militants," not as "freedom fighters."

—The U.S. goal was, first, to bring the infiltrators back from across the LOC to the Pakistan side, and only then to look at the broader issue of Kashmir or India-Pakistan relations.

—The LOC was a critical line, inviolable and not to be crossed; it was Pakistan's crossing of the line that created the crisis.

—Because both sides were nuclear powers, there was always a possibility of misperception, and the costs of any miscalculation would be enormous.

The first articulation of the new American position on the LOC was a statement by Assistant Secretary of State Rick Inderfurth, on June 2, 1999, spoken to Indian ambassador Naresh Chandra. According to Indian sources, Inderfurth assured Chandra that the LOC had to be respected and the intruders must withdraw. From India's perspective, this was a major change in American policy, which, in Jaswant Singh's words, had not pronounced on Pakistani wrongdoing in 1948, 1965, or 1971. This was a major strategic gain and paved the way for subsequent closer U.S.-Indian ties.

From the beginning of the Kargil operation, the American intelligence and policy communities judged that Pakistan was both culpable and provocative. In the words of a close Western observer of these events based in the region,

> We thought that Pakistan could have put artillery observers in a place where they could have blocked Indian access to Siachen and Ladakh; this became a "red line" for India, and we saw it the same way. From the

> brigadier level down, the Pakistanis should have been awarded medals, from major-general and above they should have been court martialed because they did not understand the consequences of what they had attempted.[47]

At the same time, it seemed India was practicing coercive diplomacy in its relations with Washington. Via numerous public signals and private meetings India suggested it would have to escalate its military response, even attack Pakistan, unless the United States got Pakistan to pull its forces back from the LOC. While the American government did not have to be persuaded that Pakistan was initially responsible for the crisis, these threats gave U.S. policy a new urgency, accelerating the diplomatic process and bringing in the most senior policymakers, including the president.

In his memoirs, General Tony Zinni, the commander in chief of the Central Command, indicates the U.S. president directed him to persuade Sharif and Musharraf to withdraw their forces from Kargil. Of special importance were the contacts between Zinni and General Musharraf. These began on June 7 with a phone call from Zinni to Musharraf, followed by another call on June 20, and then a presidential mission in which Zinni and a midlevel American diplomat, Gib Lanpher, met with both Musharraf and Sharif. The mission was calibrated to impress the Pakistan army's high command, which is why Lanpher, not the assistant secretary of state for South Asia (Inderfurth), accompanied Zinni. Lanpher proceeded to Delhi alone, where he briefed officials there about the talks.

Of the mission, Zinni says, "I met with the Pakistani leaders in Islamabad on June 24 and 25 [1999] and put forth a simple rationale for withdrawing: 'If you don't pull back, you're going to bring war and nuclear annihilation down on your country. That's going to be very bad news for everybody.' Nobody actually quarreled with this rationale."[48] The problem for the Pakistani leadership, Zinni felt, was the apparent national loss of face. Backing down and pulling back to the LOC was considered equivalent to "suicide."

Zinni told his Pakistani interlocutors that before Sharif could visit Washington, something Sharif was desperate to do, he had to commit himself to a withdrawal from Kargil. Zinni left it at that but on the way to the airport was recalled for another meeting at which Sharif accepted the terms. According to Zinni, Washington

> needed to come up with a face-saving way out of this mess. What we were able to offer was a meeting with President Clinton, which would end the isolation that had long been the state of affairs between our

> two countries, but we would announce the meeting only after a withdrawal of forces. That got Musharraf's attention; and he encouraged Prime Minister Sharif to hear me out. Sharif was reluctant to withdraw before the meeting with Clinton was announced (again, his problem was maintaining face); but after I insisted, he finally came around and he ordered the withdrawal. We set up a meeting with Clinton in July.[49]

Pakistan's agreement to a withdrawal was an implicit admission that an official force had been involved, not a group of mujahiddin or irregulars, a further embarrassment for those who had conceived of the operation to begin with.

Musharraf sat in on the meeting but said nothing, although he knew of the conditionality of the invitation and its implications for Pakistan's army. According to many Americans involved in these events, the Pakistani general raised no objection then, or in one-on-one meetings with Zinni, to the American terms for Sharif's Washington visit.

Analyst Shireen Mazari suggests that Zinni may have given the Pakistani side some intimation that the United States was prepared to intervene between India and Pakistan because after the visit Musharraf referred to the possibility of a Clinton-Sharif meeting on Kashmir: the U.S. government, or Zinni, "must have given some assurance that the U.S. would be able to press India into starting a dialogue on Kashmir as a quid pro quo for Pakistani withdrawal" in Kargil. However, Mazari adds, Musharraf insisted there would be no unilateral withdrawal.[50] In the view of several Pakistani military commanders, this meant it was the United States that kept India from coming to the negotiating table at the time of the Sharif visit to China. Mazari also alleges that the United States sent Henry Kissinger to India with the message that New Delhi need not hurry in negotiating with Pakistan, a point strenuously denied by American officials interviewed for this project.

In fact, Zinni and Lanpher had no authority to promise an American involvement in Kashmir, nor do their accounts indicate any discussion of a solution for Kashmir. The term "prepared to intervene" in the White House statement seems to refer to an activist American role, but the United States had never been able to persuade India to negotiate with Pakistan on Kashmir, nor did it make much of an effort to do so, and it was New Delhi that set the terms for talks with Pakistan.

Our conversations with a number of American and other officials provide no evidence of a U.S.-India collusion against Pakistan, or suggestion that the United States (or Great Britain, China, Japan, and others) saw its role as anything but neutral. In public statements, American officials (and Chinese, for that matter) expressed their dismay that Pakistan had launched the Kargil adventure, had then denied any official connection with it, and persisted in doing so even after Pakistan's role in this episode had become abundantly clear, as had the fact that India's response would be vigorous. However, some American participants in these events offer a different version from that of Zinni. As far as they understood the situation, Sharif (let alone Musharraf) had not made a firm commitment to withdraw forces from Kargil. Thus in their view Sharif's mission to Washington was not a done deal designed to provide cover for him. It was only after his meeting with Clinton that he agreed to withdraw Pakistani forces.

The high point of American diplomacy came on July 4, 1999, when Sharif, along with some of his key advisers and family members, came to Washington for an intensive one-day meeting with President Clinton and his staff. One of Nawaz Sharif's key foreign policy advisers, Tariq Fatemi, recalls that the decision to travel to Washington was "made in consultation with the military leadership as well as prominent members of the cabinet who all felt that it was U.S. intervention alone that could save Pakistan from a major disaster that was looming on the horizon." Kargil, Fatemi also claimed, "played right into the hands of India" and retarded the effort to bring Kashmir to the negotiating table, all the more important because Pakistan's foreign office had recommended, after the 1998 nuclear tests, that Islamabad follow a "more mature and responsible foreign policy" and that "provocations and adventures of all kind be eschewed," as the international community would not tolerate irresponsible behavior from a state possessing nuclear weapons. Pakistan's actions, according to Fatemi, allowed India to portray it as an irresponsible and dangerous neighbor.[51]

The presence of Sharif's family led some Americans to fear that he might actually be planning to stay on in the United States rather than return to face his angry generals. The meeting with Clinton has been well documented by Bruce Riedel.[52] Conversations with others present confirm the essential accuracy of Riedel's account, despite Indian and Pakistani assertions that he distorted the truth or spread canards about the meeting. However, Riedel was the only one to take notes there, and he had access, as did other American participants, to intelligence reports regarded as authoritative. Indeed, some intelligence that came in on the morning of July 4 heightened American concern about regional nuclear developments.

Nuclear Developments

According to some American participants in these events, there was evidence that Pakistan had activated its nuclear weapons (in some unspecified way) during the crisis, but they could not be certain that Sharif knew of this move, which is why Clinton told him about it. Although several Indian and Pakistani sources dispute the suggestion of such a deployment, several former senior American officials state the Riedel account reflects what *the United States understood the situation to be at the time.* The uncertainty about what Sharif knew is not surprising since Kargil was an entirely military venture. Though briefed several times about Kargil and presumably about Pakistan's nuclear plans, Sharif obviously did not understand the significance of the operation, or perhaps it was kept from him by his army briefers and he was given only the barest details.[53] His position resembled that of Prime Minister Benazir Bhutto, who was also kept on the periphery regarding Pakistan's nuclear capabilities during the 1990 crisis.

One key participant, Jasawant Singh, recounts that India had received some information that Pakistan was operationalizing its nuclear-capable missiles, but this was regarded as a "desperate gambit." At the time, Singh writes, "a nuclear angle to this conflict simply did not exist." However, he goes on to cite Riedel's "authoritative" study, which, he says, concluded that "Pakistan had indeed resorted to nuclear blackmail."[54] Musharraf's version is that the American concern over a nuclear crisis was a "myth," that Pakistan's nuclear capability was not yet operational.[55] There remains the possibility that Pakistan was indeed bluffing, that it had no "operational" nuclear capability but moved its assets in such a way as to raise alarm.

Before the White House meeting, President Clinton had been reading John Keegan's *The First World War.* He pointed out to Sharif and others the analogy between the situation in South Asia and the way in which European generals and politicians stumbled into World War I, "when military plans went onto auto pilot and the diplomats couldn't do anything to stop it. We can't get into a position in which India feels that because of what you've done, it has to cross the Line of Control itself. That would be very dangerous. I genuinely believe you could get into a nuclear war by accident."[56]

In the meeting Sharif formally committed Pakistan to withdraw its forces from Kargil. According to the Americans present, he was visibly nervous, and his civilian advisers kept trying to renegotiate the deal, or to at least get the

United States to declare that it would take on a more active role in settling the Kashmir dispute. However, the most they could obtain from Clinton was a general statement that Washington could not impose itself on a dispute and play an active role in its resolution unless both parties involved invited it to do so.

Clinton did commit to a willingness, under the right circumstances, to help revive the peace process. He said that the United States was prepared to support "a resumption and intensification of the Lahore process and a commitment on the part of the U.S. to work hard on this," rejecting the idea of a definite date for the resolution of the Kashmir dispute.[57] This general American disinclination to get involved in the Kashmir dispute might have sealed Sharif's political fate. After all, the army's prestige was on the line, since bringing the Indians to the negotiating table was a major strategic objective of the Kargil operation from the beginning. Yet he received no face-saving concessions except a vague American offer to become more interested in Kashmir.

Nonetheless, the United States played a key role in this crisis. First, Washington had put together a solid policy team even before the crisis began. The Talbott nuclear talks had brought together an expert group centered in the Department of State. As the Kargil crisis heated up, the nonproliferation specialists stepped back to give the regional experts a greater role. When the president joined the crisis management team, his personal interest was not merely in avoiding a major war between the two parties but also in serving as a regional facilitator. He wanted to visit India some time during his term; speculatively, this may have shaped his view of the relative merits of the Indian and Pakistani cases, and the relative importance of the nonproliferation agenda versus his desire to improve relations with India.

Second, while the earlier nuclear dialogue had done much to help bridge the gap between American and Indian officials, it had further strained that between the Americans and their Pakistani counterparts. Hence American relations with the two South Asian powers experienced a major turnaround during the crisis: Indian officials had a much better working relationship with the American team than the Pakistanis did. This may have inspired the Indians to try to use the United States to apply pressure on Pakistan.

Third, American officials believed that they played the crisis "down the middle," serving as an umpire between two contending parties. In retrospect, however, this provided India with an opportunity to use the United

States as a vehicle to apply indirect pressure on Pakistan, even as Pakistan failed to use the Kargil crisis to galvanize American support against India, or to extract anything more than a limited commitment to investigate the pros and cons of the Kashmir problem.

Fourth, the position of umpire or neutral party did not address the region's real and continuing problems. While former Clinton officials indicate that they had planned to tackle the Kashmir issue anew, the administration was overwhelmed by domestic crises, the growing terrorist threat, and above all, a faltering Middle East peace process. It ultimately lacked the energy and the motivation to go beyond exhorting both sides to sit down and talk. Other countries, including China, adopted the American position, but one is left with the "what if" question as to what a more active American role in regional peacemaking could have achieved.

Other Observers

Senior Western officials with regional experience and many American participants in this crisis report hearing from various sources that Pakistan had a long-standing contingency plan for a Kargil-like operation, and that Musharraf simply dusted it off when he judged the time to be ripe. According to one well-informed observer, "this may have been triggered by his and the army's irritation about the Lahore Declaration and the Memorandum of Understanding of February 1999." Other foreign observers have suggested that Musharraf and his advisers might have felt international opinion was more sympathetic to Pakistan after the 1998 tests (since India had conducted tests first). They did not think that the international community would react too strongly if Pakistan were to acquire a bit of territory, just as the Indians had in Siachen in 1984. They could then use this territory as a bargaining chip in their negotiations with India, which they expected would follow from the episode. As a senior Western diplomat interviewed for this project noted, "Such lines of thinking betrayed deep political naïveté, on almost every count." According to still another Western official, Pakistan may have concluded that both the United States and India might offer only a tepid response to a move across the LOC; at the time President Clinton was embroiled in scandal, and India had a new and weak government. If this was in fact the Pakistani view before the crisis, then Islamabad gravely miscalculated both Washington's and New Delhi's crisis response.

Nuclear Calculations

The Kargil crisis did have a nuclear dimension, although its nature is contested. Strangely, India's Kargil Review Committee Report (commissioned by the government, but still not an official report) is silent regarding any nuclear threats being operative during the hostilities, despite devoting an entire chapter to the nuclear background to this crisis.[58] These may well have been discussed in the report's classified appendixes.

First, there was considerable public nuclear chest-thumping. At the height of the crisis, Pakistan's foreign secretary warned that his country "would not hesitate to use any weapon in our arsenal to defend our territorial integrity."[59] India is thought to have taken this threat seriously enough to place its nuclear weapons on "Readiness State 3," implying that assembled warheads were readied to be mated to delivery vehicles.[60] According to several senior Indian military officials involved in the crisis, however, "India had no concerns about going nuclear, there was no excitement and no looking at nuclear issues, there was no alert 3 status," and "India never believed that the other side would even contemplate the use of nuclear weapons."[61] Like their Pakistani counterparts, they regard the concerns detailed in the Riedel report as either a post hoc rationalization or a crude attempt to reinvent history so as to put pressure on responsible South Asian states.

In an address to the nation on the abatement of the crisis, Sharif himself drew attention to the hazards of nuclear weapons: "It has been my constant effort that our countries be spared the horror of a nuclear war. Only a desire for collective suicide can prompt us to take such a step. I have no such intention. I believe Prime Minister Vajpayee has no such intention either."[62] These remarks had the unintended effect, however, of alarming the international community, fueling its perceptions that Kashmir was a "nuclear flashpoint" and thereby precipitating a forceful American involvement in the crisis.

Second, India made a conscious effort not to enlarge the theater of operations beyond the Kargil sector or to attack Pakistani forces, staging posts, and lines of communications across the LOC, despite the fact that this defied military logic and entailed the acceptance of heavier casualties. Its air force had strict orders to avoid attacking targets in Pakistan-administered Kashmir. This restraint was in marked contrast to India's response in the 1965 and 1971 conflicts, when nuclear weapons had not entered the equation and it had not displayed any inhibitions in invading Pakistan. Other reasons were arguably operative, such as the near-universal international support India was receiving; hence it wished to strengthen the impression that it was a responsible actor in the international system by highlighting Pakistan's irresponsibility, but the fact is that Pakistan was also similarly inhibited and did not enlarge the area of conflict beyond the Kargil sector. Pakistan did not use its air force despite the fact that this decision had a demoralizing effect on the intruding forces and increased a sense of isolation in their posts. Instead, "the PAF studiously avoided raising the ante and the IAF continued to enjoy local air superiority throughout the Kargil conflict."[63] The fact is, Pakistan needed to abandon its troops in Kargil to maintain the fiction that it had nothing to do with these intruders; recall that by contrast it had increased its official support to the infiltrators sent into India during the 1948 and 1965 operations when their operations began to fail.

Restraint was thereby met with restraint. America recognized the restraint shown by both sides. While the Indians did not authorize their air force to cross the LOC, the Pakistanis did not use their air force even during the bitter fighting on the peaks, observed an American official involved in the crisis at a retrospective study. Nuclear deterrence thus made it possible to initiate conventional and subconventional conflict, but deterred its escalation, which provides a corollary to the stability-instability paradox. The evidence is strong that the Kargil conflict revealed the limits of nuclear deterrence to demarcate, if not deter, India-Pakistan conflict.

Third, the Bruce Riedel account of the Clinton-Sharif meeting highlighted U.S. intelligence's discovery of "disturbing evidence that the Pakistanis were preparing their nuclear arsenal for possible use.... Clinton asked Sharif if he knew how advanced the threat of nuclear war really was? Did Sharif know his military was preparing their nuclear-tipped missiles? Sharif seemed taken aback and only said that India was probably doing the same."[64]

While most American officials subscribe to the Riedel version of events regarding the movement of nuclear weapons, fewer informed Indians or Pakistanis regard it as credible. Recognizing America's ability to monitor bases via satellites and other technological means, they also believe that the imagery is open to misinterpretation. As one Pakistani interviewed for this book pointed out, the base at Sargodha was very large and some activity always evident. Trucks moving out of Sargodha could have been carrying conventional missiles, not necessarily nuclear-tipped ones. In Pakistan's opinion, the Americans produced no credible evidence that Islamabad was preparing or moving nuclear warheads (of course, such evidence might have been gathered by means that might be compromised by their public release). Furthermore, Americans, conscious of their inability to detect the Indian nuclear tests in 1998, jumped to a premature conclusion regarding Pakistan; such misinformation, Pakistanis argue, seems to have been used to coerce Sharif, who was already apprehensive and unsure about the army's intention, especially after the removal of one army chief.

General V. P. Malik, India's army chief at the time, also complains of exaggeration in the Riedel account: "If the U.S. President had any such information, he would have communicated that to the Indian Prime Minister and we would have known about this."[65] This assertion has been confirmed by Mushahid Hussain, then Pakistan's minister of information.[66] However, General Malik's immediate successor in office, General S. Padmanabhan, has publicly stated that Pakistan "activated one of its nuclear missile bases and had threatened India with a nuclear attack."[67] According to a very senior Indian military officer, India took steps to update its War Book around the end of July 1999, to incorporate the lessons of Kargil.

Fourth, the possession of nuclear weapons played an indirect role as well by bringing renewed attention to the region during the Kargil crisis. By contrast, earlier border clashes or India's LOC crossings in 1972, 1984, or 1988 sparked little international interest. Now that India and Pakistan had become de facto nuclear weapon states, the international community was keen to defuse the situation lest, in their calculation, it led to unthinkable developments.

Miscalculations and Lapses

The lapses of judgment during the Kargil mini-war and crisis were plentiful on both sides. Pakistan's first major miscalculation had to do with the likely Indian response: that is, it failed to understand how a democracy might respond to a military provocation. With midterm elections due in a few months in India, the Bharatiya Janata Party (BJP), having been defeated in parliament in April, had very little to show to attract votes. Given the domestic political problems confronting Prime Minister Vajpayee and his party, it would have been very difficult for them to back down in the face of what they were labeling an aggression.

Whether the Pakistan army had war-gamed the likely reactions of India or the international community to an intrusion across the LOC with any degree of realism is unclear—it probably had not, since the operation was planned in great secrecy. Such a simulation might have predicted Indian furor and a strong reaction from New Delhi but also have shown Pakistan opting for constraint in supporting these covert operations if they ran into difficulties. The recordings of conversations between General Musharraf and the chief of

General Staff, Lieutenant General Mohammed Aziz, indicate an expectation that after the loss of a few aircraft India would panic, not that India would escalate and throw large numbers of troops and artillery into the battle.[68]

Second, Pakistan's timing was unwise—world leaders recognized that the elections in India had delayed the peace process, but they were looking forward to the eventual implementation of the Lahore Declaration and thus did not take kindly to what they saw as actions that would affect the status quo. In fact, Pakistan was completely wrong in its undoubtedly wishful thinking that the intrusion could secure international support to defreeze the Kashmir dispute in its favor. International sentiment was definitely against any action by either India or Pakistan, now nuclear weapon states, that could exacerbate tensions and instabilities in South Asia, let alone precipitate a conflict with the unpredictable potential to approach the nuclear threshold. Pakistan failed to appreciate that the international community of the post–cold war era, after its experience with the disintegration of the erstwhile Soviet Union and Yugoslavia, would view askance any attempts to redraw settled interstate boundaries.

Third, on a tactical level, unconventional forces usually have trouble holding onto territory unless they are reinforced by regular troops and supported by adequate ground and air power. The continued occupation of isolated posts, at heights of 3,000–4,000 meters in inhospitable terrain across the LOC, was untenable unless the intruders were reinforced and replenished, or a diversionary attack was launched elsewhere to draw off the Indian troops concentrated in the zone of conflict. It is unclear how much forethought went into the way these posts would remain occupied, especially in winter, when snowfalls would make it virtually impossible to bring in fresh troops or supplies. Continued logistical support became impossible even during the conflict, leaving the posts isolated and easily overrun by the superior numbers, artillery, and air support available to India. Ironically, by claiming that only mujahiddin and irregulars were involved in the Kargil intrusions, Pakistan surrendered the use of its own air force and had to abandon the intruders when the Indian forces mobilized.

Mistakes on the Indian side, some also serious, occurred largely in the early stages of the crisis, before it became a shooting war. Neither the Indian army nor the intelligence services had any inkling that Pakistan had made extensive but secret preparations to send its forces across the LOC into the Kargil sector. They had become complacent, perhaps lulled by the nine years of peace since the last crisis and the peace dialogue that had produced the Lahore Declaration of February 1999.

However, the Indian security establishment had little reason to join in the public euphoria over the Lahore Declaration, or to lower its guard along the frontiers. In the ensuing blame-game, the relevant agencies endeavored to distance themselves from the patent failure of intelligence by indicting other organizations. Army Headquarters, for example, pointed its finger at local formations and the internal (Intelligence Bureau) and external (Research and Analysis Wing) intelligence agencies, thereby absolving its own higher officials and the government from responsibility for lapses in assessing the available intelligence.

While primarily indicting the intelligence agencies, the Kargil Review Committee (KRC) Report also notes that the local armed forces/paramilitary personnel in the Kargil sector had been slow to acquire tactical intelligence across the LOC and to act upon it with alacrity. The committee did not comment on the larger failure of the political leadership to act on the strategic intelligence concerning the buildup of forces and equipment across the LOC.[69] The dismal work of intelligence on the Indian side accounts in part for the army's confused, and later massive, reaction to the intrusions.

In any case, it seems evident that the intelligence agencies paid inadequate attention to this sensitive sector; moreover, they failed "to use even the equipment and technologies already available to them for aerial surveillance."[70] Yet it is also improbable that they had not detected in the least the extensive preparations in Skardu preceding the intrusions: notably the building up of ammunition stocks, the construction of tracks up to and beyond the LOC, and the transportation of stores to the occupied posts remained undetected. More likely, these activities were not realistically assessed. In other words, intelligence fell short not just at the tactical or local level but also at the strategic or command level. This may have been due in part to the unwillingness to derail the Lahore peace process by taking countermeasures that might have been deemed provocative.

Decisionmaking

One of the stranger aspects of the Kargil crisis is the debate over the degree of calculatedness on the Pakistani side and the extent of Prime Minister Sharif's knowledge about the operation before it was launched. On May 24, an Indian defense officer apparently reckoned the operation "was preceded by considerable planning by the Pakistani army and ISI." Two days later, the Indian Foreign Ministry stated: "This operation was obviously undertaken with the full complicity and support of the Pakistan government."[71] On May

28, however, India's defense minister said he believed that neither Nawaz Sharif nor the ISI was involved in the Kargil operation. A few days later, India's home minister held Sharif responsible for the intrusions, even though the government might not have been "fully informed by its Army about the incursions." In mid-June, a Hong Kong weekly reported: "Pakistan PM Nawaz Sharif" not only "knew about the operation in advance" but was also kept well briefed about its details. According to an intelligence operative, there had been a series of meetings in recent months of a kitchen war cabinet comprising Sharif, top military and intelligence officers, and senior defense and foreign ministry officials.[72] Subsequently, a Pakistani daily reported, "Mr. Sharif has been kept in the broad picture of Pakistan's Kashmir policy, the basic contours of which he himself approved."[73]

If Sharif was briefed, did he understand what he was being told? He (like Rajiv Gandhi) was uninterested in the minutiae of government except in the case of special projects or issues. Five years after the Kargil clashes, Sharif claimed in a widely publicized interview with the news magazine *India Today* that he was never properly briefed by General Musharraf on the true intent of the Kargil intrusion.[74] A few weeks later, this statement was publicly challenged by Chaudhry Shujaat Hussain, briefly prime minister and a former party colleague of Nawaz, who subsequently allied himself with Musharraf. He claimed that Sharif was not telling the truth about not being aware of the Kargil operation until he got a call from Prime Minister A. B. Vajpayee of India.[75] According to Hussain, Sharif was briefed six times on Kargil. Hussain also maintained that during a detailed briefing before Sharif left for Washington, the latter pointed out he was not told about many things. In response to this remark, Musharraf reportedly took out his diary and gave the exact dates on which he had been briefed.[76]

If the Musharraf tapes are any indication, the Pakistan army seems to have been in complete command of the diplomatic and military dimensions of the Kargil operation: one conversation included the two generals discussing the brief that Foreign Minister Sartaj Aziz should carry to New Delhi—mentioning that he should demand demarcation, but "not get into specifics," while refusing a cease-fire that would allow the Indians to resume movement along the road between Dras and Kargil. The tapes also seem to indicate that Sharif was kept uninformed of the purpose and scope of the operation.

One can only speculate as to how much Sharif knew about Operation Badr/Koh Pemah. In our view, he was probably only vaguely familiar with its outlines and had little idea of its details or the possibilities and consequences of its failure. Another relevant question is whether he was made aware of the possible reactions of India and the international community to these intrusions. Probably not, at least not in any clear terms. Similarly, Rajiv Gandhi was only vaguely aware of the implications of the Brasstacks exercise and the likelihood of a strong reaction by Pakistan. In the case of Kargil, however, a small circle of Indian decisionmakers worked very closely together, with Prime Minister Vajpayee at the center receiving important inputs from Minister of Foreign Affairs Jaswant Singh, Deputy Prime Minister (and Home Minister) L. K. Advani, and National Security Adviser Brajesh Mishra.

A Very Public Crisis

Kargil was South Asia's first televised war. The Indian government's initial response to the incursions was slow, but once on its feet it orchestrated a brilliant campaign to highlight Pakistani culpability, dramatize the courageous Indian response, and shape both domestic and international opinion in India's favor. One incident given heavy coverage was the killing and mutilation of the bodies of six captured Indian soldiers, including an officer.[77] Army officers were made freely accessible, trips were organized to the front line (notably the areas near Kargil where Indian artillery pounded Pakistani positions), and a senior foreign ministry official (Ramindar Jassal) gave daily press briefings at the Ministry of Defense.

Pakistan's military moves may have precipitated the crisis, but its press paid little or no attention to Kargil until May 15, 1999, while India's press began its coverage on May 3, which from the beginning was far more intense. As the crisis mounted, however, accounts in the Pakistani press soared (figure 5-1), reaching a peak in the tenth week of the crisis (the week of July 3), when Nawaz Sharif met President Clinton in the White House.

American press coverage of the 1999 crisis was, as in 1990, episodic. Two weeks might go by without any reports even though the crisis lasted nearly three months from beginning to end. However, the U.S. media did carefully cover the post-crisis coup by General Musharraf in October.

Observations and Lessons Learned

Kargil intensified feelings on both sides. An angry India felt it had been "stabbed in the back" by Pakistan. An embarrassed Pakistan fumbled over the contradiction between stated facts and the reality on the ground. Thus

Figure 5-1. *Press Coverage, Kargil Crisis*

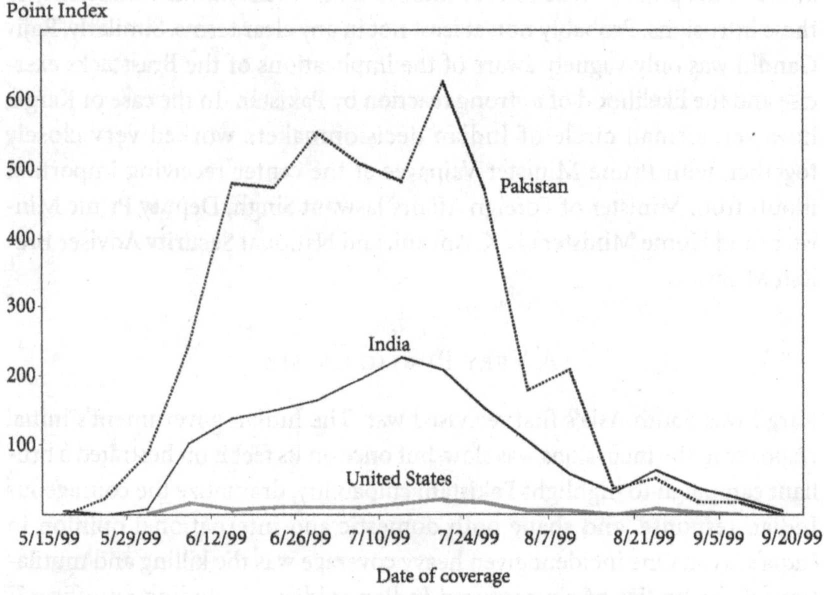

no bilateral agreements of any significance were reached in the wake of the conflict. This was unusual. The Tashkent and Simla Agreements were negotiated soon after the India-Pakistan wars of 1965 and 1971, and a slew of military CBMs were negotiated after the Brasstacks Exercise of 1986–87 and the Kashmir-related compound crisis of 1990.[78] The first serious engagement between the two countries did not occur until two years later, in July 2001, at the abortive Agra summit, by which time General Musharraf had become President Musharraf. With the failure of the Agra summit, discussed in chapter 6, tensions between the two states immediately escalated and paved the way for the 2001–02 border crisis.

Heeding one lesson of their earlier conflicts, India and Pakistan did keep communications between the two leaderships open during the 1999 war. On May 24 Prime Minister Vajpayee conveyed a telephone warning to his counterpart in Pakistan that "all possible steps" would be taken to "clear our territory" of all intrusions in the Kargil sector.[79] Similarly, Prime Minster Sharif had a telephone conversation with his Indian counterpart on May 28 expressing concern over the unfortunate turn of events and suggesting that Pakistan send its foreign minister for talks. Both these events occurred during the height of the crisis. The prime ministers had also established a back-channel communication route, involving Niaz Naik and R. K. Mishra. This channel remained open during a good part of the Kargil conflict but was terminated at the end of June when its existence became public.[80]

During the ensuing crisis negotiations, the American team was also scrupulous in informing both India and Pakistan of conversations with the other side. For example, Clinton told Vajpayee of the results of the crucial July 4 meeting in Washington, when Sharif promised to withdraw his forces from their forward position.[81] Inadvertently, this did not play well in Pakistan, because Sharif and the army were trying to "save face" after the Kargil fiasco—the last thing either needed was to have their embarrassment shared with their chief enemy, India. Both the army and Sharif tried to pin the responsibility for the American role on each other.

However, the open communications were offset by belligerent statements and provocative actions, including missile deployment and troop movements closer to the border. It can be argued that the transition from sub-conventional to conventional conflict along the continuum of violence did "bring in [its] wake the potential for escalation both horizontally and vertically and, as a result, challenged stability in a way that sub-conventional violence and unconventional violence often do not."[82] The Kargil conflict could therefore have escalated beyond the conventional to the nuclear level since nuclear-capable missiles were deployed and the rhetoric had heated up.

Nonetheless, Kargil taught both sides something about doctrine and war. Pakistan learned that it needed to mount a conventional response to a conventional threat, and that limited war was still possible even though the region had gone nuclear. India learned a strategic lesson in that the army immediately began searching for a doctrine that would enable it to fight a limited war under conditions of nuclear stalemate. This doctrinal shift, traceable to Kargil, made the subsequent crisis of 2001–02 even more alarming.

In addition, the Kargil episode demonstrated the importance of third parties. While India has consistently tried to avoid the involvement of a third party, in this case it did not object to the American role at all. In fact, it urged the great powers to exercise their influence over the Pakistanis. In the final analysis, it was American dialogue that accelerated the pace of developments leading to the conclusion of the crisis.

The crisis showed too that the presence of nuclear weapons could both exacerbate and contain conflict. Pakistan could launch a proxy war in Kashmir in 1989 because it was in a relationship of "nonweaponized" deterrence with India. This was followed by the 1990 Kashmir-related crisis. The Kargil conflict closely followed the reciprocal nuclear tests, and exemplified what is recognized as the "stability-instability" paradox. This thesis holds that "lowering the probability that a conventional war will escalate to a nuclear war, along preemptive and other lines, reduces the danger of starting a conventional war; thus, this low likelihood of escalation, referred to here as 'stability,' makes conventional war less dangerous, and possibly, as a result, more likely."[83] In other words, the stability of a bilateral nuclear deterrent relationship can be eroded by the instability induced by the greater viability of conventional war. Kargil demonstrated this clearly. Pakistan could test the limits of its newly minted deterrent relationship with India by insulating its intrusions across the LOC from the threat of a wider conventional and nuclear conflagration.

Finally, as a result of Kargil, the LOC came to be treated as an inviolable boundary between the two countries. The United States made this clear in the short Clinton-Sharif joint statement, which emphasized throughout that "it was vital for the peace of South Asia that the Line of Control in Kashmir be respected by both parties," and that "concrete steps are taken for the restoration of the Line of Control in accordance with the Simla Agreement."[84] Significantly, the three-paragraph statement refers to the fact that the LOC would be "respected" as would its "sanctity," and that steps would be taken toward its "restoration." Furthermore, the Simla Agreement creating the LOC is mentioned twice in this agreement.[85] The juridical value of the LOC was thereby strengthened, which should discourage future attempts to alter its contours. Also, the circumspection shown by both countries in not extending the Kargil conflict to other areas for various reasons underlined, inadvertently perhaps, the sanctity of the LOC and cast doubt on Pakistan's argument that it was a temporary border that could be redrawn.

CHAPTER SIX

The 2001–02 Border Confrontation

On December 13, 2001, at around 11:40 a.m., as the Indian parliament was in an uproar over a report on emergency purchases undertaken for the Kargil operations, shots rang out in the Parliament House complex. The standoff that ensued between the Indian security forces and those who had attacked the complex was broadcast in real time on major television stations. It involved multiple explosions and the exchange of hundreds of rounds of fire, and left twelve dead.

Once the government of India concluded that Pakistan-based terrorist groups were responsible and Pakistan refused to take action against them (Islamabad claimed that the allegations lacked evidence), it ordered a full-scale mobilization of its armed forces and deployed them along the entire India-Pakistan border. Pakistan was asked to cease cross-border terrorism immediately and to hand over some twenty criminals wanted in India, to whom, the Indian government alleged, refuge had been provided in Pakistan. India snapped communications between the two countries, as well as bus and train services and flights of Pakistani aircraft over Indian territory. It also withdrew its high commissioner from Islamabad. Pakistan initiated a counterdeployment, and there was a palpable sense that war was imminent. This was especially the case on two occasions after the attack on the Indian parliament: in early January 2002 and in mid-May 2002. On both occasions the United States intervened to defuse the situation. At Washington's urging, Pakistani president Pervez Musharraf issued statements on both occasions pledging to stop cross-border infiltration into India and disband the jihadi organizations that were sponsoring this activity.

This became the longest-lasting crisis in South Asia as the Indian and Pakistani militaries faced off on the border for almost a year. This eyeball-to-eyeball confrontation between two of the largest armies in the world had the clear potential to drift into war either by deliberate design or by accident, misperception, miscalculation, or leadership irrationality. Widespread and alarmist press coverage lasted for many months, as did high-level international (especially American) efforts to defuse the growing tensions. The confrontation continued until October 2002, when India unilaterally decided to withdraw its troops from their advanced positions along the international border and the Line of Control (LOC) in Kashmir.

The 2001–02 crisis raised new questions and had important consequences. Why did India undertake its military buildup? Why did it threaten and then halt its planned offensive? Did India succeed in its attempt at coercive diplomacy, forcing Islamabad to back away from its support for terrorists and separatists? As for consequences, the border crisis brought increased American involvement into South Asian affairs and may have had a significant impact on how India shaped its future nuclear and military doctrine. It was also followed by the most sustained peace process in many decades, raising the natural question of whether this might be the last India-Pakistan crisis.

The Crisis

The months following the Kargil mini-war in 1999 were filled with turbulent events and dashed hopes. Two results of that crisis were deep anger in India and political turmoil in Pakistan, climaxed by a coup in which Prime Minister Nawaz Sharif was ousted after trying to remove the army chief, Pervez Musharraf. There was a brief flicker of hope that bilateral relations would improve when both sides agreed to hold a summit meeting in Agra between President Musharraf and Prime Minister Atal Bihari Vajpayee in August 2001. However, the Agra summit was a fiasco, largely because of inadequate preparation (the talks did not even have a settled agenda) and the private skepticism of key policymakers on both sides.

This diplomatic failure was followed by another period of coolness and a new spurt in cross-border terrorist activities, culminating in a spectacular act of terrorism: an attack on the Jammu and Kashmir legislative assembly in Srinagar. On October 1, 2001, a truck filled with explosives rammed into the main gate of the assembly, killing thirty-eight people. One militant was immediately killed, and later security forces killed two of his accomplices during a long encounter in a nearby building. The militant group Jaish-e-Mohammed initially claimed responsibility for this attack but later denied any involvement.

The attack two months later on the Indian parliament, in which five militants and seven security personnel were killed, sent the region into full crisis mode. Pakistan immediately condemned the attack, as did the Kashmiri Muslim group, the All-Parties Hurriyat Conference (APHC), and sought an inquiry into the incident to discover who was responsible. The Muttahida Jihad Council (an alliance of Pakistan-based Kashmiri mujahiddin) quickly denied any connection and went so far as to state that Indian intelligence agencies were to blame.

The Indian View: A Necessary Response to Terrorism

The Indian leadership portrayed the attack as an attempt to kill or take hostage senior politicians and portrayed it as an assault upon the very foundations of Indian democracy, a view shared by many informed Indians. It could have wiped out many of the legislators present in Parliament House. This view was widely shared by much of the international community. Indians of all political persuasions compared it in its symbolism to the 9/11 terrorist attacks in the United States. Prime Minister Vajpayee stated that it constituted an attack on the Indian nation, which had been battling against terrorism for more than two decades. Echoing the statements of leaders like British prime minister Tony Blair and U.S. president George W. Bush, he declared in a "Message to the Nation": "Our fight is now reaching the last stage, and a decisive battle would have to take place."[1]

The Indian public and leadership were in an uproar and the government was pressured to take early action against those responsible. Its investigation quickly pointed to the hand of the Pakistan-based groups Lashkar-e-Toiba (LET) and the Jaish-e-Mohammed (JEM) in the incident.[2] The modus operandi was similar to that employed in other fedayeen (suicide) attacks launched by these two organizations in Kashmir, notably the assault on the legislative assembly building in October 2001. As in the earlier incidents, the terrorists made calls from their cell phones to Karachi (where JEM has its offices) shortly before the explosions (in which they too lost their lives), and their grenades and detonators bore the markings of an armaments company that had a subsidiary unit in Pakistan. A large quantity of dried fruit and prepaid phone cards were also recovered from their bodies, along with a wireless set, cash, and five cell phones, all of which suggested that they had planned for a prolonged stay inside Parliament House. This is consistent with the hypothesis that an alternate plan of the terrorists was to hold the parliamentarians hostage and bargain with the Indian government for their release.

Many in Pakistan were not persuaded, however. They found the cell phone calls to Karachi too neat a coincidence: Was it possible that they were planted? One year after the attack, the Indian courts meted out sentences of capital punishment to the three Indians convicted of masterminding the attack with the help of Pakistan-based militant groups. Much has been made of the acquittal of the four accused conspirators by the Delhi High Court after their conviction by the trial court. The charge against them was that they had conspired with the terrorists to launch the attack on Parliament House. Conspiracy, difficult to establish in Indian law, was ruled not proved against the accused, which is different from saying they were innocent. The question of whether Pakistan was involved in the matter was not an issue for adjudication by the trial and High Court; its concern was whether a conspiracy between the terrorists and the accused could be proved against the latter.[3] A lingering question for some Pakistanis and Indians was how did these Indian conspirators amass so much influence as to employ militants from Pakistan to carry out their plan?

Telephone numbers stored in the cell phones led to the arrest of several Indians. About $20,000 in Indian currency was recovered from two suspects in Srinagar along with a laptop containing images of the Indian parliament and Home Ministry stickers used by the terrorists to gain entry into Parliament House. Further investigation revealed that the attack was planned by Ghazi Baba, the supreme commander of the JEM in India, who had previously been involved in the hijacking to Kandahar of Indian Airlines flight IC-814 in December 1999. He met his death in a clash with the Indian Border Security Force in 2003.

An Indian spokesperson confirmed that evidence indicating the attackers were Pakistanis consisted of "firstly, information . . . provided by their co-conspirators to this effect, and secondly [the fact that] they had made phone calls to their families in Karachi on December 12, on the eve of the attack." Furthermore, "the evidence of involvement of these terrorist groups in the December 13 attack had been shared with the Governments of USA, UK, France, Germany and Japan . . . [and] with Russia too."[4]

The Indian government demanded that Pakistan end the activities of these two terrorist groups, take their leaders into custody, and freeze their financial assets, implicitly accusing Pakistan of fomenting their militancy. In what Indian officials saw as more than a coincidence, both the spokesman of the LET and the director-general of Pakistan's Inter-Services Public Relations Department, Major General Rashid Qureshi, had made identical statements accusing the Indian intelligence agencies of having stage-managed the attack on the Indian parliament.[5]

President Musharraf rejected these demands, stating that India's proof of their complicity was inadequate. On December 19 the Pakistani Foreign Office echoed this line, noting that India had failed to agree to Pakistan's suggestion for an impartial inquiry or to respond to Pakistan's request for evidence. India then issued a demand for the extradition of some twenty criminals on its wanted list who had been given asylum in Pakistan. This list was handed over to Pakistan's deputy high commissioner on January 1, 2002. Significantly, it included five Sikh terrorists who had been living in Pakistan for years and were believed to be plotting the revival of militancy in Punjab. The list also included notorious criminals charge-sheeted in the Bombay blasts case, notably Dawood Ibrahim, Chhota Shakeel, and Tiger Memon; LET founder chief, Hafiz Mohammad Sayeed; JEM founder chief, Maulana Masood Azhar; chairman of the United Jehad Council, Syed Salahuddin; the five hijackers of flight IC-814; and some Kashmiri terrorists. Pakistanis refused to consider handing them over to India and instead asked for evidence so that they could be tried in Pakistan.[6]

With that, India cut many communications and diplomatic links with Pakistan and mobilized its armed forces.[7] Responding to the Indian troop concentration on its borders, Pakistan placed its troops on heightened military alert.

Operation Parakram

On December 18, 2001, India launched Operation Parakram (Valor), deploying strike formations comprising tanks and heavy artillery closer to the border. Some of the troops were from Central India and Ambala, where two of India's three strike corps were headquartered. The force eventually consisted of an estimated 800,000 troops, including its three strike corps, positioned along the India-Pakistan border. Indian air force units and satellite airfields were activated, and the Eastern Fleet was shifted from the Bay of Bengal to the northern Arabian Sea to join the Western Fleet in a blockade of Pakistan. Mines were laid and troops deployed with their full wartime complement of equipment and ammunition.

Under increasing public pressure, the Vajpayee government had decided to show its outrage after the attack on parliament. As in Kargil, extensive television coverage only fueled the public's anger over the attack on parliament, already at a high pitch because of the spurt in cross-border terrorism after the Agra summit and attacks on the Kashmir assembly. The prevailing sentiment, especially that of the political establishment, seemed to be that Pakistan's provocations had reached intolerable proportions and called for a suitable response—namely, a massive mobilization.

Similarly, the official rationale for Operation Parakram, as stated by India's Ministry of Defense, was that "Pakistani provocation reached a dangerous point with the December 13 attack on the Parliament. A more forceful response became necessary. Additional troops were moved along the Line of Control (LOC) and the International Boundary in a state of readiness, inter alia to prevent further infiltration of terrorists into India."[8]

India's initial plan was to make multiple thrusts across the LOC to seize territory in Pakistan-held Kashmir, retaining the option of occupying areas of military significance, such as the Lipa Valley and the Hajipir Pass.[9] A major commando operation in January 2002, to "hit and seal off major terrorist launching pads in Pakistan Occupied [Azad] Kashmir," was apparently called off at the last moment.[10] At the same time, the commander of Two Corps (a strike corps) was peremptorily removed from his post, ostensibly for exceeding his orders and deploying his troops in their battlefield locations.[11] While the press speculated on the reasons for his removal, this incident managed to convey the impression that the Vajpayee government was not serious about going to war and that the momentum underlying the military mobilization was weakening, which, unintentionally, greatly reassured Pakistan.

India's war strategy changed after the Kaluchak incident on May 14, 2002, in which the families of Indian soldiers were massacred. India's modified plan was to concentrate its three strike corps in the Rajasthan sector, so as to draw Pakistan's two strike corps into desert terrain and inflict heavy attrition losses on them. Although plans were well advanced, the Indian government did not give the order to attack. Several commentators have suggested that New Delhi was inhibited by the state of nuclear deterrence, the conventions that had been established during the Kargil conflict, and American pressure. These explanations for India's non-action are assessed later in the chapter.

Several other war scenarios were also considered at this time, but in the end all were rejected. These included an attack across the Cholistan desert to excise Sindh from Pakistan and a plan to place Lahore under siege to force the surrender of Pakistan-held Kashmir. There was also talk of cross-border raids by helicopter-borne special forces to destroy terrorist camps and conduct punitive attacks on Pakistan's regular forces. On the economic front, India considered imposing financial pressure on Pakistan by prolonging the deployment of its troops. Of course, this would have affected the Indian economy as well. As for military moves, even though inferior to India in gross numbers, Pakistan was not without its own options.

The Indians had stressed that the aim of Operation Parakram was "to put Pakistan on notice and to signal how seriously the country viewed the attack on its Parliament" and "to tell the world that India's patience was running out."[12] Their intention had clearly been to compel Pakistan to end what India perceived as its policy of promoting terrorism in Kashmir, return to India the twenty individuals wanted for criminal or terrorist activity, and to initiate hostilities if that did not happen. Moreover, by threatening war, India had wanted to compel the United States to pressure Pakistan, its new ally in the war on terrorism. Until the advent of the current crisis, remarked senior Indian journalist C. Raja Mohan, Pakistan had been the one seeking to manipulate the risks of a nuclear confrontation for political objectives. In the latest crisis, however, India was the one subtly using the threat of nuclear war to mobilize the international community against Pakistan.[13]

Compellence, as the strategy is widely called, has its inherent risks.[14] As analyst Rajesh Basrur has pointed out, the problem of compellence is that the opponent can always reverse his behavior. Once the threat was withdrawn, what was to prevent Pakistan from reverting to behavior that was just altered? On the other hand, compellence had some attraction for democratic India. Democracies, it is widely thought, are more effective at compellence than non-democracies: they can point to a public that will punish them if they do not act upon the threat of military force.

Pakistan's View: Coercive Diplomacy

Pakistan's response to the Indian buildup and threatening statements was to mount large-scale counterdeployments of its forces in a manner reminiscent of the Brasstacks exercise of 1987. Pakistan analysts said India's maneuvers smacked of "coercive diplomacy," a strategy of threatening to use force and simultaneously practicing diplomacy to achieve a particular objective. In this "very dangerous game of brinkmanship," noted Pakistan's high commissioner to London, "India needs to come back to the negotiating table, just like every other country in the world has when it has problems to resolve with another country."[15] According to another eminent Pakistani, India's tactics amounted to policies of "try-and-see" and "the gradual turning of the screw."[16]

Bent on countering India's efforts to persuade Americans to pressure Pakistan, Islamabad consistently argued that India's military mobilization was detrimental to the new international objective: the U.S.-backed "war on terrorism." India's massive mobilization therefore needed to be met with a redeployment of Pakistan's forces from its western borders and operations in the Tora Bora Mountains to its eastern borders. This view resonated in Washington, which was now in the invidious position of not being able to tell India that it should not proceed in this manner in its own war against terrorism.

The U.S. response to the events of September 11, 2001, had been to form an international coalition to combat terrorism—a coalition joined by both India and Pakistan. Whereas Pakistan had supposedly joined the coalition to combat terrorism as a victim of terrorist activities and had played a crucial role in this war on terrorism, India, according to most Pakistanis, had joined the coalition merely to portray as terrorism what it considered to be the Kashmiri freedom struggle.

During this confrontation, Prime Minister Vajpayee reportedly told the three Indian service chiefs to prepare for war with Pakistan.[17] According to one Pakistani scholar, the Indian leadership had developed a "dangerous strategic psychosis," convincing themselves that a limited conventional war was feasible and had begun to think that Pakistan's alleged threat to use nuclear weapons was merely a bluff.[18] While Pakistan believed that it was being very cautious and had scrupulously refrained from issuing irresponsible statements, it felt that Indian utterances clearly indicated a deliberate attempt to raise the temperature.

From Pakistan's vantage point, India's leadership had turned to coercive diplomacy partly because of domestic political pressures (several state elections were approaching, including one in Kashmir itself). But it also needed to cover up the government's inability to prevent attacks on two legislatures (in Srinagar and New Delhi) and address Indian concerns about the growing U.S.-Pakistan rapprochement. The Indian government, said Pakistani strategists, wanted both to channel popular anger away from itself by blaming Pakistan and to establish a link between al-Qaeda and what it considered the freedom struggle in Kashmir.[19]

Pakistan felt that it had done its bit. Musharraf had suddenly extended a hand to a surprised Vajpayee on the conference dais during the inaugural session of the Eleventh South Asian Association for Regional Cooperation

(SAARC) summit in Kathmandu on January 5, 2002. However, the subsequent Indian response was cool, and the situation worsened. Then on January 12 the Pakistani president delivered a strong speech on national television highlighting the stark choice facing Pakistan—lawlessness and destructive religious extremism, on the one hand, and his vision of a tolerant, educated, law-abiding, strong, and progressive Islamic society, on the other.[20] Although the speech was directed at the people of Pakistan, it was also addressed to an American and international audience.

With regard to the twenty suspected terrorists, whose extradition some Indian writers have said could have ended the stalemate, Musharraf had pledged that no Pakistani would be extradited to India, yet he had also banned five Pakistan-based militant organizations, arrested their leaders, frozen their assets, and locked up their offices. He asserted, moreover, that no organization would be allowed to give itself militant names such as Jaish (army), Lashkar (volunteer force), or Sipah (soldier) or would be allowed to indulge in terrorism in the name of Kashmir. At the same time, he made clear that Pakistan would not abandon its stand on the Kashmiri right to self-determination, as enshrined in the UN resolutions. In addition, Musharraf again called on India's prime minister to "bring an end to Indian state terrorism" and to enter into a dialogue over the ongoing Kashmir dispute, "on the basis of the aspirations of the Kashmiri people."[21]

Throughout the confrontation, Pakistan questioned Indian figures on infiltration and terrorism, complaining that no neutral organizations were permitted to operate in what it officially termed "Held Kashmir" (the Indian-administered part of the state) to monitor cross-border terrorism. India, it said, was playing the roles of judge, prosecutor, and jury. Furthermore, while Pakistan regarded India's accusations as a form of intimidation, India itself frequently issued contradictory statements, as pointed out by Pakistani officials and others, some saying that cross-border terrorism had decreased, others that it had not. Pakistan denied that it was encouraging militant organizations and stressed that no cross-border militant activity was occurring on the Line of Control, especially after President Musharraf's speech on January 12.[22] It openly and frequently acknowledged, however, that a determined Kashmiri "freedom fighter" could still cross over despite Islamabad's tight vigilance and control. So could ordinary Kashmiris, who had families and property on both sides of the LOC.

Countering criticism of their own policies, many Pakistanis noted that India's behavior in general and throughout this crisis was largely governed by the domestic political calculations of the Bharatiya Janata Party (BJP), the largest component of the coalition National Democratic Alliance (NDA). They charged that India-Pakistan hostility, though promoted by vested interests on both sides, further deteriorated when Hindu nationalists, epitomized by the BJP and its affiliates, came to power in India. Their determination to make India a Hindu state, the Pakistanis alleged, triggered the events in which Indian citizens were killed, the property of the Muslim minority was damaged, and mosques were desecrated. This not only struck a blow to India's reputation as a secular state but also heightened violence in a country renowned for its nonviolence.[23]

In 2002 the BJP was facing increased criticism from human rights groups, international observers, and (privately) from some of its NDA coalition members. The Gujarat communal riots in the spring of 2002 had repudiated the BJP's claims that no communal killings had taken place during its rule. The party's role in the Ayodhya episode of 1993, which triggered large-scale religious violence, coupled with the attempt of the affiliated militant Hindu group (Vishwa Hindu Parishad) to defy the central government on the issue, took a heavy toll on the BJP's image.[24] Unable to show much for its years in government except for five nuclear tests and two crises, the BJP seemed, from a Pakistani perspective, to have decided to indulge in a hate campaign against Muslims in general and Pakistan in particular. Although the BJP thought this anti-Pakistanism would pay rich dividends, especially in Uttar Pradesh, it lost the assembly elections in almost every state except Goa, and even in Uttar Pradesh local issues seemed to have been far more important to voters.[25] Anti-Pakistanism did appear to pay some dividends in Gujarat, however, where the BJP comfortably won the December 2002 elections.

Pakistanis also envisioned an economic explanation for India's continued troop concentration. India, they surmised, may have felt its large economy could sustain periodic burdens of increased military expenditure, whereas Pakistan's would collapse in the case of a prolonged confrontation. Some in Pakistan also believed that as the prospect of hostilities grew more remote, it would become more difficult for Indian army officers to maintain the morale of their troops and convince them of the necessity to remain deployed against Pakistan. As Indian sources point out, however, boredom, rather than low morale, was the problem.

Building Up to a Withdrawal

The irrelevance of the border confrontation became evident with the passing weeks, especially after India failed to follow through on its planned offensives in January and May 2002. This indecisiveness appeared to result from Washington's pressure and its assurance that Pakistan would be prevailed upon to cease cross-border terrorism and bring its jihadi organizations under control. Indeed, President Musharraf had made key statements on January 12 and May 27, 2002, committing himself to serious action in this regard. A crackdown on the jihadi organizations did take place in January, but with some backsliding in April; then it was resumed in May/June, again with some backsliding. India felt Musharraf's failure in this regard may have been due to domestic political imperatives or to the influence of key stakeholders in the army and the Directorate of Inter-Services Intelligence.

The effectiveness of the massive Indian troop deployment became questionable as cross-border terrorism from Pakistan continued. Indeed, as army troops left their counterinsurgency positions to redeploy in their battle locations, infiltration increased. In simplified terms, battle locations in a war situation are positioned along mountain ridges to take advantage of the high ground, while counterinsurgency operations require them to be located in the valleys to interdict infiltration. As a result, counterinsurgency operations in Kashmir were left to be handled by the paramilitary forces, which were not as effective in this role as the regular army. India did not even pull its troops back after June 2002, despite the fact that the monsoons made offensive operations militarily infeasible; by the end of June, elements of India's leadership had also recognized that the political and economic cost of the military buildup was exceeding any possible political or strategic gain. The buildup continued, nonetheless, owing to organizational imperatives and the desire to ensure that the approaching assembly elections in Kashmir would take place successfully and securely.[26] This latter explanation can be challenged, however, as the Kashmir elections, though successful, were still surrounded by considerable violence.

Cross-border terrorism seemed to continue unabated in the run-up to the Kashmir elections, from June to October 2002.[27] While General Ved Malik estimated a 53 percent reduction in cross-border terrorism after June, other informed observers show that terrorist movement, both foreign and indigenous, across the LOC, continued as before. Indeed, attacks on the security forces and political workers increased in the June-September period, as did casualties. Thus the official explanation for the continued troop deployment (that it was designed to prevent massive terrorist infiltration from disrupting the Jammu and Kashmir election in October 2002) was probably an attempt at post hoc rationalization of Vajpayee's indecisiveness and the paralysis caused by nuclear deterrence. At least one Indian civilian official intimately involved in this crisis has acknowledged that New Delhi permitted it to go on much longer than necessary—given that the decision to actually fight was never made.

As a grand strategy, India's policy created an impasse since New Delhi had refused to withdraw its troops until cross-border terrorism ceased, shunned a bilateral dialogue unless this occurred, and refused to accept external mediation to achieve these objectives. All this seemed to suggest that resolution was only possible through conflict. However, notes one analyst, "escalation generally becomes less and less likely the longer confrontation lasts. As the crisis continues each state becomes increasingly confident that it is facing a resolute adversary."[28] In this case, the crisis ended following Deputy Secretary of State Richard Armitage's visit to the region in early June 2002. By then the political leadership had recognized that further provocations would be risky and made ready for the actual drawdown, in October 2002.

The Withdrawal

In announcing a gradual "strategic relocation from the border," the military's euphemism for stand-down, India explained the reason for doing so was that "the Armed Forces were deemed to have achieved the immediate objectives assigned to them."[29] Though some gains might have been made, India did not achieve its primary objectives: it had not ensured an end to cross-border terrorism or obtained the extradition of wanted criminals from Pakistan. Nevertheless, New Delhi claimed that it had succeeded in forcing President Musharraf to acknowledge that Pakistan had been supporting cross-border terrorism and to agree to restrain fundamentalist Islamic organizations in Pakistan. Meanwhile, Indian officials including the ministers of defense and foreign affairs continued issuing tough statements even after the decision had been made to withdraw forces from the border—a decision that sprang from some combination of the risks inherent in a war with a nuclear-armed Pakistan and the potential opprobrium that India would face if seen to have used military force first with its dangerous escalatory potential, whatever the provocation might have been.

The international community's pressure on India was perhaps a crucial factor. A travel advisory and warning were issued by the U.S. government in late May, followed soon thereafter by similar cautionary statements from the United Kingdom, Canada, and Japan, among others, which seemed to have influenced the Indian decision to pull back. The warnings severely affected the travel and tourism industry, lowered business confidence, and conveyed an implied threat that further sanctions could be imposed in the event of an attack. The travel and hotel industry reportedly pressured the Indian government to heed these warnings and defuse tensions along the border, although key policymakers on the Indian side deny this was a factor. In Pakistan's view, India decided to withdraw its troops from the border because of the needless financial cost of the border operation and its effect on the fighting abilities of the forces, as well as the continuous pressure of the international community. Pakistani officials responded promptly and positively, stressing that they would swiftly reciprocate.[30]

Consequences

The crisis taught Pakistan few lessons to speak of, primarily because India had initiated the troop movements and Pakistan was in a reactive mode. The Karachi *Dawn,* for one, concluded that "all along these nerve-racking months, Pakistan maintained a dignified posture of restraint, condemning terrorism, repeatedly offering talks to New Delhi for resolving all disputes, including Kashmir, and a phased withdrawal of troops by both sides."[31] Most Pakistanis were satisfied with the way in which the nation's military capabilities—including its nuclear assets—seemed to have deterred India from attacking, or even from launching limited probes. Whatever it was that had "worked"—the existence of nuclear weapons, Pakistan's conventional capabilities, or Indian reluctance to risk a wider war—Pakistani policymakers, especially in the army, felt that the 2001–02 crisis had been managed well from the perspective of strategy and outcome. This is not to say that the army had no alarming moments, especially early in the crisis when it saw the extent of Indian preparations, but from a military perspective the crisis seemed well handled, and the management of it aroused no criticism within the armed forces. One significant lesson Islamabad did take away was that a military approach is unlikely to pay dividends. This renewed the government's interest in dialogue and led it to embark on a peace offensive of sorts, marked by repeated expressions of its willingness to start the dialogue anytime and anywhere. These efforts eventually seemed to bear fruit, for in 2003 Prime Minister Vajpayee offered to enter into talks on Kashmir, and Prime Minister Zafarullah Khan Jamali proposed a unilateral cease-fire along the LOC. Diplomatic relations were also upgraded (the ambassadors, who had earlier been withdrawn during the Kargil conflict, were recalled to their posts during the crisis) and efforts were made to restore communication and transportation. In addition, many new CBMs were seriously considered concerning travel and visas, humanitarian cooperation, sports activities, and the disposition of detained fishermen.

From an Indian perspective, gains and losses fell into several categories: military, financial, and political. Militarily, the armed forces learned the importance of assessing the problems involved in the large-scale movement of troops and of integrating formations such as the strike corps, which included infantry, mechanized infantry, artillery, and armor elements in a joint exercise. This allowed New Delhi to identify and rectify weaknesses and also to recognize the need for a shift in tactical doctrine from a defensive to an offensive posture, leading to significant changes in Indian army doctrine.

At the same time, despite the absence of hostilities, there were significant fatalities on the Indian side. These were the result of de-mining operations, accidents, psychological stress (read suicide), or harsh weather conditions. While field commanders had difficulty in explaining to their men the government's decision to mobilize and deploy, and then not fight, the claim that troop morale had deteriorated is not accurate. Officers and jawans got extra pay and their families received extra rations during this prolonged deployment.[32]

The enterprise was costly: $2 billion seems a reasonable estimate of the additional outlays that the mass mobilization imposed on the defense budget.[33] They do not include the indirect costs due to the loss of freight and passenger traffic by the railways, the diversion of trains for the transport of troops and equipment, and losses in the tourism and civil aviation industries because of the travel advisories issued by Western governments. Indian strategists comforted themselves with the thought that the mobilization was also costly for Pakistan, which a few years earlier had been bankrupt. However, Pakistan's macroeconomic situation had improved after 9/11, and it had begun receiving substantial economic assistance from the United States. There is no evidence that any economic crisis led Pakistan to negotiate a settlement.

Strategically, it is hard to draw a balance sheet of Indian gains and losses. India certainly did not meet its original objectives. Despite Musharraf's public pledge to stem the flow of terrorists into Kashmir, cross-border terrorism continued, and Pakistan did not dismantle its terrorist infrastructure. The twenty criminals granted asylum in Pakistan were not extradited. Judged as an exercise in coercive diplomacy by India, Operation Parakram was an obvious failure. President Musharraf, in fact, claimed later that his armed forces had succeeded in "defeating the enemy without fighting a war."[34]

The exercise revealed that "neither India nor the international community could generate sufficient pressure to force [Pakistan] to compromise on Kashmir. India did not have the option of going to war, and the international community needed Pakistan in the campaign against terrorism."[35] In a way reminiscent of Pakistan's Kargil misadventure, India, too, misjudged the international support it could attract before attempting coercive diplomacy. Apart from the possibility of initiating conventional operations, which was fraught with the danger of escalation, India "had no options up its sleeves to meet sub-conventional threats through sub-conventional means."[36] Indeed, after it had mobilized its forces, India had few options left other than to open hostilities. With the passage of time, this option, too, became unavailable since India failed to appreciate the fuller implications of 9/11—namely, that India would need to go it alone in dealing with Pakistan, now an American ally in the war on terrorism. India's motives thereafter focused on pressuring the United States to prevail upon Pakistan to cease cross-border terrorism, although Vajpayee's style was serendipitous: he preferred to defer decisions in the belief that the passage of time would yield a solution.

Perhaps most important to India, President Musharraf had been compelled to admit that Pakistan was sponsoring cross-border terrorism in Kashmir, an admission that eroded Pakistan's standing in the international community. In his address to the Pakistani people on January 12, 2002, Musharraf had announced a ban on five militant outfits, promising that no organization would be allowed to indulge in terrorism in the name of Kashmir. On May 27, 2002, he reaffirmed his "assurance that no infiltration is taking place across the Line of Control. . . . Pakistan will never allow the export of terrorism anywhere in the world from within Pakistan."[37] And on June 6, 2002, Musharraf told visiting Deputy Secretary of State Richard Armitage that cross-border infiltration of terrorists would "visibly and permanently" cease, and this "would be followed by other activities that had to do with the dismantling of the camps that led to the capacity to conduct these kinds of operations."[38] The public admission of Pakistan's involvement was a diplomatic victory for India. These statements also further sanctified the inviolability of the LOC.

As far as domestic politics were concerned, the Indian leadership could, and did, claim that elections to the Jammu and Kashmir legislative assembly were successfully conducted in September-October 2002, with a voter turnout of 44.62 percent, despite the strenuous efforts of militant groups to disrupt them. The government touted this as quite an achievement, "keeping in view the fact that all Pak-based outfits had issued threat calls and separatist outfits had openly canvassed for boycott of polls."[39] Observers universally judged the elections to have been free and fair, despite a few minor aberrations.

American Activism

Many countries, including Germany, Russia, France, Japan, Iran, Saudi Arabia, and Turkey, advised Pakistan to restrain terrorist groups operating from its side of the LOC and simultaneously urged India to cease its military buildup. There was also an intense American-British effort to prevail on India and Pakistan to refrain from escalation. Both countries coordinated their policies very closely, even if they saw the crisis in different ways.

The India-Pakistan crisis of 2001–02 was the first test of the Bush administration's conscious decision to maintain good relations with both India and Pakistan in the post-9/11 context. Both were partners in its "war on terrorism." In Pakistan's case, the situation was complicated because Islamabad was part of the solution as well as part of the problem. The United States could not conduct military operations in Afghanistan without Pakistani support, but it possessed incontrovertible evidence that Islamabad had strong ties to the Taliban and that its support for Islamic extremists operating in Kashmir and even India was undiminished. Washington had been prepared to overlook these past ties because Pakistani cooperation was essential, but the attacks on the Kashmir assembly and Indian parliament took the Bush administration by surprise. It had assumed that India-Pakistan relations had made progress, and that even the failed Agra summit had served to engage the two countries (at the time, there was no U.S. ambassador in either India or Pakistan).

Hence the U.S. role in the management of this crisis did not come about simply because the Indian and Pakistani governments were playing to an American audience. Washington itself had important interests at stake—and ultimately these helped bring the crisis to an end.

First, Washington feared a potential war, possibly a nuclear war, in the subcontinent. Such hostilities could interfere with the Pakistan-based American operations in Afghanistan. Washington repeatedly called on both countries to exercise restraint, concerned that its own troops not be targeted during the chaos of an India-Pakistan war.[40] Second, the Pakistanis had threatened to move their forces from the Afghan to the Indian borders, which could have weakened the hunt for al-Qaeda and Taliban remnants.

Eventually its exasperation with both sides—notably India—might have been what prompted Washington to withdraw nonessential personnel from the American embassy and issue a related warning to its citizens, although as discussed shortly, there were real grounds for concern regarding a war. This action had the desired effect of showing New Delhi that there were limits to America's willingness to pressure Pakistan on behalf of India, and that Washington's war on terrorism, which necessitated cooperation with Pakistan, was more important to it than was New Delhi's war on terrorism. A signal failure of the Indian establishment lay in its miscalculation of the milieu, which had radically changed after 9/11. Pakistan had become crucial to the United States for waging its war against terrorism in Afghanistan. In a sense, India miscalculated outside sentiments in much the same way that Pakistan did when it assumed its Kargil intrusions would internationalize the Kashmir dispute to its advantage.

In 2001–02, however, American policy was torn between two logics in a more striking way than during earlier crises. One was the logic of the American-Indian entente, which presupposed that India was a rising power of considerable strategic potential and that the U.S.-India relationship was the new cornerstone of American policy toward South Asia. This logic dictated sympathy for India as the victim of terrorist attacks, the expansion of military exercises as fast as possible, the sale to India of as much sensitive technology as the nonproliferation lobby in Washington would permit, and the cultivation of Indian elites. Since India was a prospective strategic ally, the Bush administration gave New Delhi the benefit of several doubts, including evidence that it was preparing to initiate a war, albeit for quite justifiable reasons.

On the other hand, U.S. policy could not ignore the logic of the revived relationship with Pakistan. This was a marriage of convenience between former allies, requiring the U.S. partner to accommodate Pakistan's nuclear program (which indirectly benefited India since its program would then have to be accommodated as well). In honoring the relationship, the United States also felt it had to keep silent about Pakistan's assistance to separatists and extremists in Indian-administered Kashmir and provide uncritical support for the still-weak Pakistan government, including its military head, General Musharraf.

Throughout the crisis, American policymakers had to keep an eye on these imperatives: the possibility of Indian attack, the need to respond to Indian pressure regarding Pakistan's support for terrorists and extremists, and the threat that the Indian buildup posed to America's own war on terrorism. To further complicate the American position, Washington wanted to develop stronger ties with New Delhi and was worried about Pakistan's domestic stability and the reconstruction of Afghanistan, all the while looking westward in anticipation of a prospective war in Iraq.

An entirely new team of American officials dealt with the 2002 crisis. Preeminent among them was Ambassador Robert W. Blackwill, who served as Bush's ambassador to New Delhi from 2001 to 2003.[41] Blackwill was strongly persuaded that Pakistan was up to no good in Kashmir, and before he left New Delhi, he publicly criticized the government of Pakistan on several occasions for supporting terrorists. However, according to one American official who observed the crisis from the vantage point of the U.S. embassy in Islamabad, Blackwill failed to see that Pakistan had become the first priority for the United States and tended to exaggerate India's role as part of the war on terrorism.

Otherwise, the Department of State, notably Deputy Secretary Richard Armitage, dominated American policy during the 2001–02 crisis, in large part because after 9/11 relations with Pakistan were intimately tied to relations with the Taliban and Afghanistan. Armitage had been part of the senior policy team in earlier Republican administrations and was familiar with regional personalities and events. After 9/11, the White House was preoccupied with al-Qaeda and, increasingly, Iraq. The Department of Defense had divided interests in the region: on the one hand, it had acquired bases in Pakistan for operations under way in Afghanistan; on the other hand, it was moving forward with a series of joint military exercises with the Indian armed forces that were unprecedented, even though they were quite limited in scope.

Crisis Response

From the U.S. perspective, events in South Asia seemed to be moving toward war on two occasions, with serious implications for American global and regional interests and possibly American lives. The threat certainly seemed real following the attack on the Indian parliament on December 13, to which the United States responded at several diplomatic levels. President Bush had called Vajpayee on that day, expressing sympathy and offering the assistance of counterterrorism experts "if so desired." Secretary of State Colin Powell also called Foreign Minister Jaswant Singh. On the day after the attack, Ambassador Blackwill visited the Indian parliament, afterwards stating that the assault was "no different in its objective from the terror attacks in the U.S. on September 11" and expressing solidarity with the Indian government: the

United States and India, he emphasized, were "together" in the struggle against terrorism. He offered condolences and repeated President Bush's offer of FBI and other assistance. Blackwill later met with Jaswant Singh and Defense Minister George Fernandes, reiterating that the U.S. offer of FBI assistance was "open-ended."

The embassy's position on the crisis was clear from the start. Blackwill and his team saw the Indian military buildup as a direct and understandable response to the terrorist attack in Srinagar and on the Indian parliament. Although it was important to bring an end to the buildup and the heightened risk of war, the Indians did have, in the words of one U.S. official, "moral parity" with the United States when it came to the war on terrorism. If the crisis was triggered by Pakistani-supported terrorism, then it had to be resolved by putting an end to that support. Second, Blackwill saw the crisis as an opportunity to show India that the United States no longer hyphenated its relationships with India and Pakistan. He argued publicly and privately that Washington should have been given an opportunity to further strengthen America's strategic relationship with New Delhi. One year after the crisis, Blackwill called on the speaker of India's lower house of parliament, the Lok Sabha, to stress the American government's continuing condemnation of that "brutal attack on the heart of Indian democracy," which the Bush administration considered "an attack on all democracies as well as an attempt to undermine the efforts of those seeking regional peace and security."[42]

Yet Washington was somewhat reluctant to publicly criticize Pakistan, which by then was vital to U.S. operations in Afghanistan and an important locus of Islamic radicals in its North-West Frontier Province and Baluchistan. On December 14, the State Department spokesman indicated that it would be "premature" for the United States to start reacting to attacks in India until the Indian government completed its own investigation; a few days later, on December 17, the White House urged both India and Pakistan to share information, work with each other, and take no action that would in any way hinder the war against terrorism. The ongoing operations in Tora Bora were of paramount importance to the United States at this time. Officials publicly reiterated the importance of waiting until an investigation established who was responsible for the attack, and privately, American officials were frantically urging restraint on New Delhi.

The tug-of-war between the embassy and Washington continued, but in the end the latter came around. Blackwill managed to persuade senior Washington policymakers that the "war on terrorism" was indivisible, that India and the United States were on the same side; and that Pakistan was a source of terrorism and had to be restrained. Despite much tugging back and forth, Blackwill had forced the issue with his first speech before the Indian parliament, and everything the United States did after that—its pressure on Musharraf, efforts to persuade Pakistan to ban the LET and JEM and other groups, and the public assertion that Pakistan had to be responsible for terrorism beyond its borders, especially in India and Afghanistan—flowed from an assumption of Pakistani complicity in supporting terrorist activities. In a sense, the Bush administration shared the view held by the Clinton administration during the Kargil crisis that Pakistan was the irresponsible state in South Asia, even though it was the Indian military buildup that precipitated the crisis.

On December 18, in response to Indian assertions that Pakistan was responsible for the attack, American officials repeatedly expressed the hope that no action would be taken that could "make more difficult the fight against terrorism in the region."[43] A couple of days later the State Department indicated that Secretary Powell had spoken to Musharraf on the importance of Pakistan's curbing extremists; it also emphasized that India and Pakistan needed to take steps against the terrorists, and that this was not a time "for them to take action against each other."[44]

One week after the attack, on December 20, President Bush announced that LET would be added to the list of terrorist groups, remarking that the attack on the Indian parliament had been preceded by an attack on the Jammu and Kashmir assembly in October. The next day it was announced that the assets of two more terrorist organizations, including the LET, would be blocked. Blackwill met with senior BJP leaders to dispel their apprehensions about American policy, stating that Washington viewed the attack on the Indian parliament as the handiwork of the same terrorists responsible for 9/11.

On December 27 Secretary Powell officially announced that JEM and LET were foreign terrorist organizations, thus putting even more pressure on Pakistan to ban them, and a week later stated that Pakistan had done a great deal since the crisis started, notably in arresting LET and JEM leaders, among others. Again, he and other American officials publicly and privately pleaded with India to exercise restraint, and with Pakistan to limit its countermobilization. Powell shared with India's home minister L. K. Advani (on a visit to Washington) the news that Musharraf had taken "some steps" regarding terrorism, but that the United States was looking "to see what additional action he has taken."[45] While Pakistan soon banned the LET and JEM, and Powell praised Musharraf's "bold and principled" stand against terrorism and extremism "both in Pakistan and outside of Pakistan," this period marked the first peak in what has been called the Twin Peaks Crisis.[46]

The crisis then seemed to wane, until a terrorist attack on the army camp at Kaluchak on May 14 raised the possibility again of an Indian retaliatory strike. Further complicating American policy, and perhaps Indian calculations, was the approaching monsoon, which ruled out any significant ground and air operations thereafter. The Kaluchak attack, which targeted the families of soldiers, brought high-level statements of sympathy and caution. On May 15, President Bush called Prime Minister Vajpayee to express his condemnation of the "terrible and outrageous" attacks on the camp. In a press conference in New Delhi, Assistant Secretary of State Christina Rocca asserted that India and Pakistan were dangerously close to war and subsequently met with Kashmiri Hurriyat leaders in India. She had to face stiff questioning from both sides of the political divide regarding the release of Bruce Riedel's study of the Kargil crisis. Tensions in the subcontinent were at their peak, and Indians and Pakistanis alike immediately attacked the Riedel paper, especially the inference that Pakistan had weaponized at the height of the Kargil crisis; there was widespread (but inaccurate) speculation that the study was released to influence Indian policymakers, and that Riedel was given special access to classified material for the study.

On May 24, the *Washington Post* reported Indian plans to attack across the LOC in Kashmir, and the crisis deepened. Senior American officials such as Powell, Armitage, and Secretary of Defense Donald Rumsfeld kept up the stream of cautionary advice and high-level visits to South Asia while simultaneously planning the evacuation of Americans from South Asia. American officials also had talks with the Indian military about providing its forces with advanced-technology special-force equipment—unmanned aerial vehicles and ground sensors—which would have strengthened India's counterterrorism capabilities. On June 5, President Bush spoke with both Musharraf and Vajpayee, issuing a statement that urged the easing of tensions and, significantly, suggested an American willingness to resolve the "many underlying issues" dividing India and Pakistan. In its wording, the statement could simultaneously be read in New Delhi as an expression of American support against Pakistani-sponsored terrorism and in Islamabad as one of American support for a dialogue on Kashmir. Later Secretary of State Powell publicly urged Pakistan to carry out its pledge to restrain militants but called on

India to further deescalate and resume talks with Pakistan on "all issues," especially Kashmir.

The Travel Advisories

On May 31, 2002, the United States warned its citizens to defer travel to India and Pakistan and urged nonessential personnel to actually *leave,* an extraordinary precaution.[47] Its travel advisory stated: "Conditions along India's border with Pakistan and in the state of Jammu & Kashmir have deteriorated. Tensions have risen to serious levels and the risk of intensified military hostilities between India and Pakistan cannot be ruled out. As a result of these concerns, the Department has authorized the departure of all U.S. Government personnel in non-emergency positions and family members in India." It added that Americans should defer travel to India and that American citizens currently in India should leave the country. The British government, coordinating its policies closely with those of Washington, issued an almost identical statement.

These warnings were followed by similar advisories from Japan, France, Germany, Israel, and other countries and are widely thought to have brought the crisis to a conclusion, but that was not the case. While important, the American advisory was not intended to pressure the Indian government nor was it decisive in forcing New Delhi to pull back from a confrontational position. According to American officials interviewed for this study, it was part of normal departmental procedure with inputs from both the embassies and the State Department, which made the final decision to issue the notice. A new crisis had clearly started; the Indians had mobilized their forces, nuclear threats were being exchanged, and no India-Pakistan dialogue appeared to be taking place. The Department of Defense, officials say, began to calculate potential radiation plumes and medical treatment in case of a nuclear exchange, while the U.S. military expressed strong concern about having to operate in a nuclear environment, even for the withdrawal of American civilians. Conceivably, the travel advisory was also intended to balance the private and public warnings issued by Washington's interlocutors to Pakistan, urging it to take meaningful steps to curb the flow of terrorists into Kashmir from its territory.

Upon receiving word of the advisory, some prospective visitors and tourists canceled their travel plans and hotel bookings. Indian firms, notably those in the software, airline, and travel industries, appealed to the government to help stem the losses related to the advisory. Their pleas were at the center of a *New York Times* column by Thomas Friedman, who wrote that the Indian government was under "another new, and fascinating set of pressures" that made nuclear war, from its side, unthinkable.[48] By pressures, Friedman was referring to contacts between India's software and information technology industry and perhaps American companies, which "essentially told the nationalist Indian government to cool it."[49] In a later version of these events, Friedman toned down the language somewhat.[50] However, the initial columns contributed in part to the popular understanding of the crisis: which is that economic pressures from American and Indian companies were the major factor in ending the crisis.

For their part, American companies deny that they applied such pressure, while American officials are firm in their belief that this had nothing to do with the Indian government's decision to back off. In the words of one American close to the shaping of American policy, "this was a matter of high policy, not one of a few dollars—even a few million dollars—the travel advisory was issued because the conditions at the time warranted it, not to pressure the Indian government."[51]

At the same time, there is some evidence that the warning affected Indian calculations. At one point, a senior Indian official asked an American official, "What American national interest was served by the warning?" To Americans, this suggested that some Indians were furious at having been pressured. Was this anger feigned? Others believe the travel warning provided the pretext for the Indian leadership to justify the drawdown to its own military establishment. Yet another interpretation (appearing in an Indian retrospective study) is that the army was furious when told there would be no war.[52] This use of the advisory was, according to informed American officials, completely unforeseen.

After the crisis subsided, the American assessment was that war had been in the offing but that the United States had helped its "two friends" to avert a crisis. In October, Assistant Secretary Rocca reflected that regional tensions had almost reached the breaking point in the spring of 2002, but with the help of the United States, Britain, and others, war was averted. Subsequently, the U.S. administration and its supporters claimed the U.S. management of the crisis was one of the major foreign policy successes of the Bush administration. In Washington's assessment, Indian and American pressure on Pakistan succeeded at least in part: Islamabad did reduce infiltration, although the infrastructure supporting it was left untouched and the euphemistic "terrorist training camps" were not disbanded.

Role of Other Countries

More than in any other recent crisis and, as in dealing with the 1962 India-China war alongside the United States, Great Britain played an important role in the 2002 crisis. While Washington was clearly the "heavyweight" political power, British diplomacy was no less active, and in some cases visits by senior British officials (there were at least a dozen) prepared the groundwork for an American visit. Overall, a joint strategy was developed to "keep the pitch covered," and senior emissaries from either the United States or United Kingdom were always available to be dispatched if the temperature started rising.

The United Kingdom, according to informed British sources, was the first to be concerned about the risk of nuclear war (regarded as being greater than zero and, by some, as being much higher), as the United States was preoccupied with Operation Enduring Freedom (OEF), the war in Afghanistan. The British calculated that the risks of a nuclear war were greater than the possible negative implications for OEF. In the words of one British official, a nuclear war could have left behind two or three million dead, thirty million casualties, and untold economic costs.

The role of other countries was insignificant, largely because they did not have comparable access to the players and information. There is no evidence of serious Chinese involvement, even with its regional ally, Pakistan. Japan, which has a considerable economic role in both India and Pakistan, was almost totally consumed by the problem of evacuating Japanese citizens from the region and let the Americans and British do the heavy lifting in terms of a strategy of persuasion. Yet Japan also was worried about an escalation, particularly one that would involve nuclear weapons, and even diverted one of its few civilian aircraft equipped with the self-identification technology suitable for flights into a war zone.[53]

Nuclear Weapons and Escalation

India and Pakistan may have come very close to fighting a large-scale war in 2002, and such a war could have escalated uncontrollably. The readiness of the Indian armed forces to launch a conventional assault on Pakistan highlights their belief that such hostilities would not provoke Pakistan to threaten or use its nuclear weapons and their hope that, in extremis, the Indian leadership would not blink. As it turned out, the second assumption proved wrong, hence the first assumption could not be tested.

The state of nuclear deterrence explains in large part India's caution in not launching operations into Pakistan, especially after it became clear that cross-border terrorism had declined only temporarily and episodically, despite President Musharraf's strong statements. Other than suggesting caution, the precise degree to which nuclear weapons entered the calculus of the decisionmaking elites during this crisis, especially in India, is unclear. Key political and military actors from both countries responded to our questions about this in two ways: they simply denied any nuclear thinking or refused to reply on grounds of national interests.

As in the Kargil conflict, the potential for escalation and even the use of nuclear weapons were factors in the border confrontation crisis, despite the denials that this was so (or the studied silence) of many Indian policymakers interviewed for this project. Despite the lack of concrete evidence, it would not be unreasonable to assume that the relevant military and nuclear establishments were on heightened alert during the 2001–02 crisis; given the timing of missile tests, it may be that test missiles were kept ready for use during a politically opportune moment.

Both countries undertook provocative actions and issued incendiary statements, which aggravated international fears of an impending disaster. India deployed its Prithvi missiles along the Punjab border at the beginning of the crisis. When asked about this, George Fernandes confirmed that India's "missile systems are in position."[54] Pakistan also moved its short-range Hatf-I and Hatf-II missiles along the India-Pakistan border as part of its military buildup. It is unclear whether these missiles were armed with nuclear or only conventional warheads.

During this crisis, as in others, Pakistan and India also undertook provocative missile tests. To allay the anxieties of the international community, each country typically issued reassuring statements that the tests were routine and part of their ongoing missile development programs. These tests, in the middle of crisis situations, however, highlight the influence of the nuclear/defense scientists and the military in India and Pakistan, who constitute powerful vested interests propelling their missile programs.

For example, in the last week of January 2002, in the midst of the crisis, India test-fired its nuclear-capable Agni-II surface-to-surface missile up to a distance of 420 miles. This missile test was reportedly scheduled for the middle of December but postponed to the end of January to avoid adding to existing tensions.[55] For his part, George Fernandes described the test as "flawless"; other officials downplayed it as part of India's long-term military plans, unrelated to the standoff between the two countries.[56] Pakistan, not surprisingly, condemned the test as provocative and destabilizing.[57] India then tested its BrahMos supersonic cruise missile, developed in collaboration with Russia; Pakistan again expressed concern, noting that "introduction of this new weapon system will aggravate the existing balance in the region and further encourage India's hegemonic designs."[58]

Pakistan test-fired its nuclear-capable Ghauri-I (Hatf V), Ghazni (Hatf-III), Abdali (Hatf-II), and Shaheen (Hatf-IV) missiles in rapid succession between May and October 2002. The Ghauri-I test, it claimed, was "part of the research and development of Pakistan's indigenous missile programme, which is an essential element of Pakistan's policy of maintaining minimum deterrence in the interest of our security."[59]

Missile tests and statements about nuclear war may be a way for the leadership to demonstrate that it has the political will and military means to escalate a crisis, even up to the level of nuclear war. Yet because of international sensitivities, leaders also take care to downplay tests and deny that their rhetoric is meant to be provocative. It is hard to tell which statements and tests were "signals" and which were just a bit of chest-thumping. Even if they were supposed to be signals, were they intended for domestic audiences, the British and Americans, or the other side? Because of their profusion, it is difficult to determine what messages one side or the other might have wanted to send to any audience. Indeed, if there was signaling, we have not been able to piece together evidence as to whether the intended party "received" it. To further complicate matters, India and Pakistan often engaged in simultaneously ameliorative and contrary actions such as downplaying in the media the fact that their unmanned aerial vehicles (UAVs) had been shot down by the other during January 2002, which had potentially dangerous escalatory possibilities.[60]

The Impact on Military Doctrine

In India the 2001–02 crisis heightened the ongoing debate within the armed forces, especially the army, on how to translate India's superior conventional forces into a military and political advantage over Pakistan, given the existing state of bilateral nuclear deterrence. This question is discussed at length in chapter 7, but for now suffice it to say that the crisis made clear that mobilization, per se, heightens the risk of war by placing a premium on advertent or inadvertent escalation. These risks would multiply if contact with the nuclear forces of the adversary were established, which would lead to "heightened preparations for nuclear operations, including the loosening of central civilian control over nuclear weapons and the dissemination of launch authority to military commanders. Among small nuclear powers this could be particularly dangerous, since their early warning and command and control apparatuses are likely to be less redundant and resilient."[61] Yet another point to consider is the likelihood of nuclear assets, especially short-range missiles armed with nuclear warheads, being either captured or destroyed in border engagements; this would engender a major crisis that could rapidly escalate to dangerous levels.

After the 2002 crisis, the Indian military further refined its new doctrine of limited war, developed in 2000 after the Kargil crisis, calling the new version Cold Start. Its purpose was to reduce the time interval required to mobilize and deploy troops since the military's attempt at a quick offensive into Pakistan had faltered because of the long period of mobilization and deployment from peacetime stations. India therefore could not have achieved the element of surprise needed for such a strike, if that had been part of its strategy. Under Cold Start, Indian forces capable of undertaking offensive operations on short notice were to be established along the LOC and the international border and the Indian military was to restructure to increase the number of strike formations while reducing their size. This would presumably enable India to respond to hair-trigger situations such as the ones that developed during this crisis. The strategy would also place Pakistan on the defensive and could erode its policy, safeguarded by the state of nuclear deterrence, of using cross-border terrorism and proxy war as political instruments.

This deployment pattern would also instill a sense of greater responsibility in the Indian political leadership before it decided to order a general mobilization of the troops.[62] An unstated consequence of the new military doctrine, however, could be to make it difficult for the leadership to reconsider such orders once issued. The doctrine therefore has possible serious repercussions, because without continued political intervention, future crises could be more vulnerable to escalation pressures. An India-Pakistan conflict could also arise in these circumstances by design, accident, or unauthorized behavior. This new doctrine would magnify the dangers of instability and would blur the differences between design, accident, and unauthorized behavior. Thus the distinction between pursuing a no-first-use policy, officially sanctioned by the Indian government, and the first-use policy favored by Pakistan would also be obscured.

DECISIONMAKING

Formally, India had entrusted the Cabinet Committee on Security (CCS) with taking the major decisions in the border confrontation crisis. The CCS includes the ministers of external affairs, home, finance, and defense and is headed by the prime minister. It was routinely supplemented by the national security adviser and, when required for advice or information, by the service chiefs and senior civilian bureaucrats. The CCS was serviced by the cabinet secretary, who is the head of India's civilian bureaucracy. The manner in which the CCS functioned during the border confrontation crisis has come under some criticism.[63] Apparently, it often took major decisions in an ad hoc manner without the benefit of well-considered papers drawn up by the ministries concerned, which is the usual procedure followed in the government of India. As a result, several with a direct interest in the decision were excluded, even in the case of an emergency.

Despite the CCS's formal role, important decisions during the 2001–02 crisis were made by five individuals, only to be ratified later by the committee. They were Prime Minister Vajpayee, Finance Minister Jaswant Singh (he and Yashwant Sinha traded ministries in July 2002), National Security Adviser Brajesh Mishra, Foreign Minister Yashwant Sinha, and Home Minister Advani. Significantly, all were members of the Bharatiya Janata Party, the dominant member of the ruling National Democratic Alliance coalition government. Unusually, the defense minister, George Fernandes, was not part of this inner circle.

Conversations with several of the key players during the 2001–02 crisis indicate that one person had the power to make war and peace decisions, and that was Prime Minister Vajpayee. He received advice from Mishra and Jaswant Singh, as in the Kargil crisis, but his party colleague, and sometimes political rival, L. K. Advani also played an important role, especially regarding internal security issues. All of these key advisers deferred to Vajpayee, and in the end he decided against using force. According to several of Vajpayee's key advisers, political authorities discussed the idea of attacking Pakistan with the Chiefs of Staff Committee, but there was no evidence that the presence of nuclear weapons was a restraining factor at this time; in fact, it was widely believed that redlines had already been crossed. For one full day in early January, the option of crossing the LOC was discussed, but no decision was ever reached, probably because of Vajpayee's view of the crisis; speculatively, he may not have wanted to go down in history as the man who provoked a nuclear war. More likely, he saw any war as undoing his earlier efforts to reconcile with Pakistan. Some of his closest advisers, interviewed for this project, are still not certain about Vajpayee's real motives.

The personality and professional predilections of the Indian army chief during this crisis are also relevant. General S. Padmanabhan was to some degree cut in the Sundarji mold and favored aggressive, offensive tactics. He was also quite critical of America, and in a thinly veiled fictional account written after the crisis, he developed scenarios in which the United States and India find themselves on a hostile course.[64] However, there is no evidence that either Padmanabhan's strategic orientation or his views on America had a determinative influence on Indian decisions during the crisis.

Regarding the decision to withdraw the troops from the border, the manner in which it was taken has been considered cavalier. The National Security Advisory Board was convened on October 16 and after hearing from former army chief General Malik recommended the pullback. Within hours of this meeting, the government simply announced that Operation Parakram was over and that the army was directed to undertake a "strategic relocation" of its forces. For that matter, the executive failed to offer the armed forces an explanation of its political objective even when the mobilization was first ordered.[65]

Compared with Kargil and the 1990 crisis, the border confrontation was managed in a relatively straightforward way in Pakistan, closely resembling the approach of Zia and Arif during the 1987 Brasstacks crisis. President Musharraf was at the center of the decisionmaking process, in consultation with key military and civilian advisers, notably the directors-general of the Inter-Services Intelligence (DGISI) and military operations (DGMO), and one of his close personal advisers, the civilian Tariq Aziz. The Foreign Ministry played a role, as did a few of the corps commanders. To our knowledge, no opposition politicians were consulted; the National Security Council was not established until two years later, in April 2004.

Public Opinion and the Media War

Public opinion in both countries was irrelevant to decisionmaking during this crisis, yet the authorities worked hard to garner support for their decisions. The Indian government used public outrage over the terrorist attack on parliament to sway opinion on behalf of the move to confront Pakistan along the border. This official sensitivity to public opinion is evident in a bellicose statement by General Padmanabhan, then chief of the army staff, on January 11, 2002.[66] Made under official direction, the statement was designed both to warn Pakistan and shore up public support. It is unusual in Indian politics for a service chief to make such a declaration. The BJP, however, did occasionally use the service chiefs to serve their political ends. Immediately after the Kargil conflict, for example, they decorated their election rallies with portraits of the service chiefs to capture public support.

After its deployment of the armed forces, the government made little effort to explain their short or long-term mission. The contradictory statements issued on the fluctuations in terrorist violence in Kashmir and the role of cross-border terrorism in promoting this phenomenon only served to confuse public opinion to the point where it became indifferent to the statements issued by the government news agencies.

On Pakistan's side, the 2001–02 crisis was hardly a priority for the press—which was seized by the question of Musharraf's political fortunes, internal violence in Pakistan, the murder of Daniel Pearl, the killing of a busload of French military technicians, an attack on the American consulate (also in Karachi), the collapse of the Taliban, and so forth. The crisis was a peripheral concern for the Pakistani public, and there is little evidence that Pakistan took India's alarm signals seriously. Although nuclear signaling was evident (nuclear forces were mobilized as part of the general mobilization), panic did not ensue, as it had in Kargil; once the initial crisis of December passed, there was no panic in Pakistan over the movement of nuclear forces. As usual, the vernacular (Urdu) media were very bellicose about Kashmir and relations with India.

Over time, Pakistan's policy of differentiating the terrorism in the West mounted by al-Qaeda from that in the East surrounding the Kashmir issue became harder to justify, yet President Musharraf felt caught between the two. Under American pressure, he publicly stated on January 12 and May 27, 2002, that Pakistan would not support terrorist activities from its soil and that it would curb jihadi organizations within the country. Musharraf felt compelled to satisfy America by apprehending the Taliban and al-Qaeda elements from their hideouts in Pakistan and by taking steps to reform the educational system that was giving birth to fundamentalism. However, he also had an obligation to his domestic stakeholders. He could not offend either the rightist parties that were his own creation or the religious parties that he had propped up to prevent prominent political leaders such as Nawaz Sharif and Benazir Bhutto from returning home from exile.

As the border confrontation crisis revealed, inflammatory statements, missile tests, and provocative actions had become part of the political landscape. While not uniquely South Asian, the level of rhetoric between these two states during crises had steadily grown. Several audiences were targeted: the domestic population, the opposing country, and the international community. By 2002 the latter had become convinced that South Asia was a "nuclear flashpoint." Both India and Pakistan manipulated the nuclear fears for political advantage; Pakistan routinely linked the Kashmir dispute to the nuclear-flashpoint hypothesis, and the entire purpose of India's troop mobilization along the India-Pakistan border was ostensibly to frighten Pakistan into stopping cross-border terrorism and producing the twenty wanted criminals, but in reality the pressure was aimed at the United States, in the hope that it would prevail on Pakistan to deliver on these demands.

The Press Coverage Escalates

This was South Asia's longest-ever crisis. It did not lead to war, but it commanded intense and escalating press coverage over its duration, although there were peaks and valleys (figure 6-1). Particularly intense, Indian press coverage increased fivefold from the coverage of 1990. American press coverage more than tripled in intensity over the same period, and more than quadrupled at its highest point. Concern over a nuclear war may not have been the only reason for American interest. American policymakers, the press, and the informed public were undoubtedly more sensitized to events in South Asia after the 9/11 attacks, with terrorism a central theme as America engaged the world and its troops battled in Afghanistan. American television crisis coverage peaked during the week of May 27–31, one of the rare periods when South Asian affairs (other than the invasion and removal of the Taliban government in Afghanistan) dominated news stories.[67] As for Pakistan, press coverage there was remarkably subdued compared with previous crises, but when India mobilized its forces in midsummer, Pakistan's press coverage was nearly as intense as it had been during the Kargil crisis.

Coverage reached a double peak in India and the United States. One surge came after the December 13, 2001, attack on the parliament; coverage remained high over the next seven weeks but then declined until about the sixteenth week of the crisis (around mid-March). The next peak occurred about the twenty-third week of the crisis, six months after it had started, as India engaged in threatening moves and Pakistan began to shift forces from the Afghan border. Press coverage continued at reduced intensity until the forty-third week of the crisis, but even this level was comparable to that of the Brasstacks crisis. Coverage in Pakistan was subdued at first, with head-

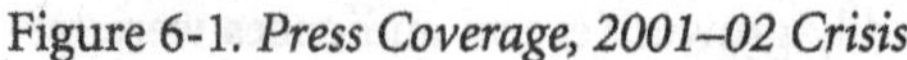

Figure 6-1. *Press Coverage, 2001–02 Crisis*

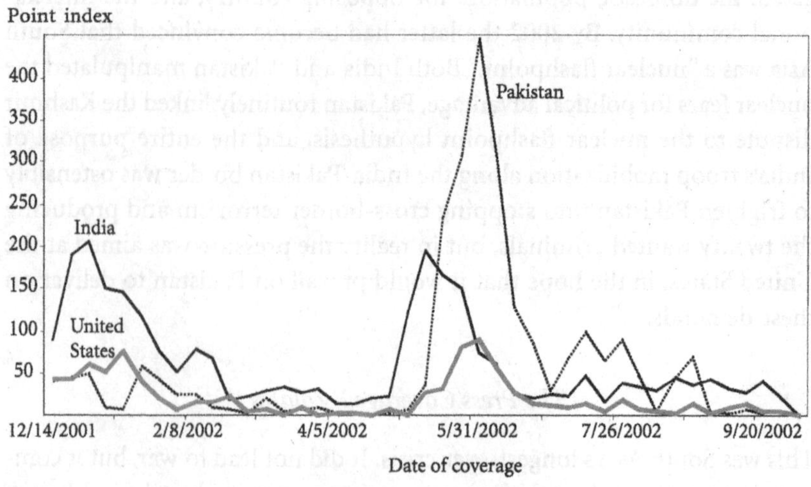

lines dismissing India's "explosive rhetoric" and suggesting that this was a "drama" somehow manufactured by the Indian government. It peaked during the twenty-fourth week, on about June 6. When the coverage of the three countries is compared, India's press gave the first peak greater and more intense attention than the second; the American press gave the mid-June and initial buildup comparable attention, but the two Pakistani newspapers barely covered the December crisis.

Observations and Lessons Learned

The striking feature of the 2001–02 crisis was that it contained the seeds of a major war and, as in Kargil, foreign intervention played a significant role as each side attempted to influence the other side through the good offices of outsiders, notably the United States. We draw six major lessons from this crisis.

First, what did not happen in this crisis is as important as what did. India did not cross the LOC. It was prepared for war militarily, its army was eager to press ahead, but in the end it did not move. The reason, according to some in Pakistan, is that India was effectively deterred, whereas Indians believe that the Indian government lost its nerve. In our view, the crisis did not slip into all-out war for at least four reasons:

—As time passed, Pakistan's preparations reached a level that would have prevented India from achieving an easy military victory. Even in the window in which it could have attacked, India would have taken eleven to fourteen days to mobilize, but Pakistan only four.[68]

—Indian leaders did consider, and some were concerned about, the possibility of the conflict escalating to nuclear war.

—There was also some concern about American disapproval should India precipitate a conflict.

—Despite the army's enthusiasm, civilian politicians, notably Vajpayee, had reservations about the massive use of force.

Second, although there was no absolute proof linking the terrorist attacks to Pakistan, the Indian leadership decided to act as if Islamabad had been responsible, if only by looking the other way. In the words of a key Indian decisionmaker, "We were aware of—we recognized—the Musharraf/Pakistan line that they were not in control of militants, and we therefore accepted Musharraf's remark that a crackdown on militants might lead to lawlessness on the streets. It was difficult for both of us to make these kinds of decisions." While some in India wanted to attack Pakistan, in the end the civilian leadership was content to come away with a half-victory, in that Pakistan made a promise (partly fulfilled) to cease support for cross-border extremists. India thus decided to work with the Pakistani leadership, though it was not the leadership it might have desired. This willingness led to the revival of the "composite dialogue," or peace process, the following year.

Third, the crisis demonstrated that coercive diplomacy requires the threat of force to remain credible as an instrument of national policy. India twice backed away from initiating hostilities during Operation Parakram, giving the impression on both occasions that it had succumbed to American pressure. Indeed, Vajpayee later admitted that the time for military action had been in the immediate aftermath of the attack on parliament in December 2001 as Indian forces were deployed along the border in the first week of January 2002. He acknowledged, moreover, that his government was dissuaded from taking such action by the United States. This hesitation occurred again in May 2002 after the Kaluchak massacre when American pressure, reinforced by the travel advisories issued by the Western countries, seemed to have persuaded India to desist from opening hostilities. Yet the possibility remains that the Indian leadership welcomed such pressure because this enabled it to shift the blame for its own inaction to the Americans.

Furthermore, India lowered the sense of urgency, with some effect on Pakistan's perception of its intent, when it failed to specify a time frame for Pakistan to comply with its demands. This perception was further reinforced when India shifted its military objectives from attacking Pakistan-administered Kashmir across the LOC, the locus of terrorist training camps and a support infrastructure for militants, to drawing Pakistan's strike forces into the Thar desert, where Indian armor divisions were waiting to wage a war of attrition against the smaller Pakistani forces. India thus created the impression that its demands were flexible, which made bargaining difficult. It offended a basic principle of bargaining: that demands should not be increased, for otherwise the other side would lose faith in the bargaining process. Indeed, negotiations had become impossible because no forum was available to discuss the compromises that would have allowed both countries to achieve their objectives. The two ambassadors could have taken on this task, but they had been withdrawn. India's ambassador was withdrawn at the beginning of this crisis, and India asked that Pakistan's ambassador to New Delhi be withdrawn following the Kaluchak incident. Moreover, Pakistan had no incentive to accept the Indian demands. Its generals were confident that a state of nuclear deterrence had been established during the Kargil conflict; therefore it was not especially concerned about the Indian mobilization, although defensive measures were taken.

Fourth, while nuclear weapons were not decisive in either precipitating or resolving this crisis, the fact that both sides had them shaped decisions in Islamabad, New Delhi, and Washington. Both India and Pakistan had come to see that despite major provocations (the attack on the Indian parliament was unprecedented), there was a state of mutual nuclear deterrence between them, and this left no real alternative except some kind of carefully crafted and limited war, the continuation of a political and strategic stalemate, or moves to normalize their adversarial relations. In our judgment, the 2002 crisis was a turning point in regional stability, perhaps the equivalent of the Cuban missile crisis in American-Soviet relations. In December, Islamabad feared that the Indians might attack, for anger in India was running high (and it was considering such an attack). By May, the situation was different: the Indian army had "done its worst" with all three strike corps deployed, yet the twenty wanted criminals were still in Pakistan's hands; at the same time, cross-border infiltration had gone down, but the infrastructure was still in place and, though concerned, India did nothing. By June, Musharraf was publicly asserting that India had been deterred by Pakistani conventional forces. At least some of the senior Indian leadership concluded that further confrontation would produce nothing by way of important concessions, that a war was out of the question, and that the only consideration was when and how India would back down.

Fifth, the "lessons learned" on the Indian side were clearly different. The senior political leadership, notably Prime Minister Vajpayee, felt that coercive diplomacy, military pressure, and nuclear threats had produced only limited results, and he moved to revive India-Pakistan dialogue in April 2003, which was an admission that compellence had its limits as a strategy. Yet the Indian military and some strategists remained staunch in their belief that a limited, controlled conflict with "high-technology long-range 'surgical' accurate strikes" is the only available option to implement a policy of coercive diplomacy when nuclear weapons are present. According to Jasjit Singh, "In the years ahead, air (and missile) power will be the central tool for conventional deterrence, as well as controlled punitive strikes for coercive diplomacy."[69] Whether this would qualify as a limited conflict in Pakistan's view is unclear, especially as it is impossible to imagine India and Pakistan abiding by negotiated norms. Whether limited conflict can be controlled is also unclear, since the losing side would naturally be tempted to reverse its losses and the victorious side tempted to enlarge its objectives. Both these possibilities make escalation more likely than restraint.

Sixth, the United States again played an ambiguous role, being uncertain as to which side to come down on and also being unwilling to mount a long-term strategy of regional conflict resolution. Washington was interested in crisis *management*, not in conflict *prevention* or *resolution*. For the most part, past crises did not trigger enough concern for the United States to move beyond management because it had minimal interests in the region; ironically, in 2002 it had *too many* such interests, notably the active war in Afghanistan and the possibility of a new strategic relationship with New Delhi (which would not, however, include support for an Indian military assault on Pakistan). Although no presidential engagement took place, administration officials privately acknowledged that the pattern of the Clinton administration's intervention in Kargil was something of a model for their own policies in 2001–02. Strobe Talbott correctly pointed out that "the cushion in the bilateral relationship between Washington and New Delhi—and crucially the room to maneuver in the triangular one that included Islamabad—resulted from the buildup in trust between Washington and New Delhi during the previous three years."[70] In the end, Washington's intervention was helpful, but the United States may have missed an opportunity to address the problem of long-term regional instability.

CHAPTER SEVEN

Peace and War in South Asia

Despite some underlying similarities, each of the four crises examined in this book was unique in its story and logic. Together, they highlight several key policy and strategic issues, particularly the changing nature of the rivalry between India and Pakistan, the impact of their different political systems on crisis behavior, the influence of the international community, and the complex relationship between the crises and nuclear weapons.

Patterns of Crisis

Crises are usually defined as short-term events. The Brasstacks, 1990, and Kargil crises took place over a matter of weeks; the 2001–02 crisis lasted almost a year. Yet even the prolonged crisis of 2001–02 shared with the others a sense of impending violence and focused the attention of the international community on the region, mostly to pressure Pakistan to commit itself to a no-interference policy and to urge India to pull back its massed forces from the border. All four crises captured more attention and lasted longer than the threats of the early 1980s, which went largely unnoticed. In other respects, however, they each evolved along different lines.

The Brasstacks crisis featured no exchange of fire and no possibility of crossing a nuclear threshold. In a nutshell, it was precipitated by India's military exercises, became full blown when General Zia ul-Haq and his vice chief of army staff laid out the possibility that Pakistan would counterattack India's vulnerable state of Punjab, and then subsided when India decided not to react to Pakistan's military response. The ultimate motive of those who planned and ran India's Brasstacks exercise still remains unclear. Was it intended as a routine, if bloated, training exercise, or was it an "open-ended" strategic gambit? This crisis was propelled by a very small group of Indian and Pakistani policymakers trying to calculate the moves of the other and prepare a countermove in anticipation. Although Pakistan did engage in some nuclear rhetoric afterward, the crisis itself did not have an overt nuclear component. However, it was conducted in the context of a race to acquire nuclear weapons, and its outcome contributed to the position in both countries that nuclearization was both desirable and inevitable.

The 1990 crisis is distinctive in its motives and purpose. It had no clear strategic objective, only a series of faltering military and political responses to changed circumstances, beginning with India's flawed elections in Kashmir, which led to increased Pakistani support for dissident Kashmiris. Then India misread Pakistani signals, press reports, and public statements (often by politicians who were unsure of their own political standing), which created an aura of crisis, especially after elements of the Indian and Pakistani militaries were put on high alert. Although there was apparently no plan for a calculated escalation, Pakistan used the possibility of escalation as a way of freezing any Indian response. Yet it was unaware that India was misreading its signals. The crisis finally dissipated after dialogue and concerted American intervention made it evident that neither India nor Pakistan was really interested in raising the ante, despite the uncertain situation in Kashmir. Because no single issue drove the crisis, it was easily defused, and the United States could take credit for the stand-down. For the first time, but not the last, outside powers considered the crisis more serious than did either India or Pakistan.

The 1990 crisis brought the first intimation of a nuclear attack, in large part because of the article by journalist Seymour Hersh—but only after the crisis. At that point, regional arsenals had few, if any, nuclear weapons, and there was no evidence to suggest that either country had mobilized its tiny nuclear assets. In both India and Pakistan, however, the crisis strengthened the hand of those who felt that nuclear weapons were essential to their nation's security. Overall, this crisis was compounded by incompetence, opportunism, and missed signals. It serves as a reminder that a combination of domestic political disorder and missed signals can put two states into a crisis mode.

By contrast, the Kargil mini-war of 1999 involved extensive combat, the fear that India might strike beyond the Kargil theater, and the chance that one or both states, already self-declared nuclear weapons powers, might climb several steps up the escalation ladder and be the first to use nuclear weapons. Because the actual crisis situation was so heated and widely publicized—it was South Asia's first TV war—many in the region and abroad feared that the conflict might get out of hand.

This was also the case in 2001–02, even though no actual combat took place during that crisis. India's military preparations for Operation Parakram were so extensive and the provocation so acute that most onlookers took New Delhi's threat of escalation seriously. However, some Pakistanis and a few Indians correctly identified the strategic purpose behind India's buildup and threatening rhetoric, which emanated from a lesson learned during the Kargil conflict: how to coerce the United States to pressure Pakistan and thereby achieve a limited political victory. Pakistan tried this tactic too, claiming that India's pressure along the international border in the east made it difficult to support the U.S. military operation in the west near Afghanistan. After going right up to the edge, India apparently saw no profit in moving forward, yet succeeded in forcing Pakistan to make a number of terrorist-related concessions and then relaunched the much-deferred composite dialogue. Thus India's massive troop deployment along the border may have triggered the subsequent peace process that continues to this day.

The Media and Press Coverage

Since the first of these crises took place, the community of reasonably informed citizens has expanded rapidly through the spread of modern electronic media, including television and the Internet. Private television channels and cable networks have superseded state-controlled media in both countries in both credibility and coverage. Expertise outside the governments is no longer limited: a network of think tanks, independent scholars, nongovernmental organizations, and a better informed political community has arisen to challenge government policy on vital matters. Retired generals in both states play an active public role, and even Pakistan's united front in support of government policy has cracked. Although the government "narrative" still dominates thinking in both states, it does not go unchallenged. Of course, the press does not always play a mature role and may fall short where objectivity is concerned, but public opinion has become more important and is solicited more often (especially in India), as demonstrated in the last two crises.

In situations of crisis, the press, including the elite press, seems to gravitate to the government's position. The press coverage of these four crises in

India and Pakistan certainly showed little, if any disagreement from the line of the government of the day. Several other points can be made about the behavior of the elite press of India, Pakistan, and the United States during the four crises.

—In the crises clearly initiated by one country or another (as in Brasstacks and Kargil) or in which one country was considered culpable (as in 2001–02), the press of the other country did not necessarily hasten to provide more and deeper coverage. The Indian press was slower off the mark than the Pakistani press in 1987, but did not respond any faster in Kargil. However, the Indian press was very active and assertive in 2002; speculatively, this strengthened India's policy of compellence, as the putative threat to initiate a war with Pakistan was made more credible by intense and widespread press coverage.

—In every case, the *New York Times* and the *Washington Post* came to the crisis later, and with less intensity, than did the Indian and Pakistani papers that we have examined.

—We note a clear increase in press coverage from crisis to crisis, especially in the Indian and Pakistani press, and in the American press after 9/11. From 1987 to 2002, each successive crisis received more sustained and intensive coverage, except perhaps in the Indian press from 1990 to 1999. Overall, crisis press coverage in India, the United States, and Pakistan increased eightfold over a period of fifteen years.

—The press itself is an unreliable indicator of the presence or absence of a crisis. During the Brasstacks crisis, American press coverage was practically nonexistent. In the initial stages of the border crisis, coverage was highly asymmetrical. Two leading Pakistani newspapers gave it scant and dismissive coverage. Yet six months later, they gave the mobilization of the Indian army very intensive coverage, while Pakistani officials were themselves somewhat relaxed about the prospect of war. Was the Pakistani press responding to government encouragement, to the strong coverage in the Indian press (evident on radio, television, and satellite TV), or to its own judgment of the risks of war? We have no definitive answer to these questions, or to the broader problem of the relationship of the press to a government under pressure, except to note that governments everywhere try to use the press to mobilize opinion and send "signals" to other states. Finally, in several cases coverage lagged behind real-world events, or peak coverage occurred at different points of time.

American press coverage of the South Asian crises was in general less regular and intense than coverage in India and Pakistan, as to be expected from foreign as opposed to domestic concerns. American coverage increased markedly after 2001—its coverage of the border crisis dwarfed coverage of pre-9/11 Kargil, Kashmir, and Brasstacks crises—indicating a heightened post-9/11 sensitivity to international affairs. Not only were there more prominent news stories, but day-to-day coverage was also more regular.

American press coverage also focused on U.S.-related affairs; for example, U.S. coverage of the 2001–02 crisis spiked around week 26, coinciding with a trip to India by Secretary of State Colin Powell. Meanwhile Indian coverage spiked almost a month earlier in the crisis, around the time of diplomatic talks between India and Pakistan.

It is impossible to say whether the crises were themselves increasingly "important" or whether the press just treated them so. It is also difficult to determine whether press coverage in all three countries was directly related to how senior government officials viewed the crises. When the Indian and Pakistani press downplayed the severity of Brasstacks and Kargil, respectively, were they following the government's lead? Recall that in the 2002 crisis the Indian press was uninhibited, mirroring the strategy of the Indian government. Finally, we have not looked at or tried to measure how the crises were treated in the electronic media, notably television, and how this might have influenced press coverage, or (after 1995) how the crises figured on the Internet or were portrayed in popular culture, notably the Indian cinema. Anecdotally, there was a massive public and media response to the Kargil crisis, which led directly to a number of films about India-Pakistan conflict and war. Bollywood not only produced several patriotic potboilers but also issued a number of films (such as *Veer-Zaara* in 2004) that dealt thoughtfully with India-Pakistan relations. After the peace process began in earnest in 2003, several planned war films were reconfigured to emphasize the importance of India-Pakistan understanding.

Crisis Termination

These four crises were not resolved. They were managed, and then they ended, with the underlying causes still unaddressed. None of the crises concluded with a genuine peace, and none were purging events in which both parties came to see that their differences could be resolved peacefully, or even by a long-enduring process of dialogue and compromise. At best, the composite dialogue that followed the 2001–02 border confrontation is a wary engagement, possibly a temporary truce; at worst, it is the calm before yet another storm.[1] Meanwhile, both India and Pakistan continue to add to their conventional and nuclear arsenals, conduct spectacular missile launches, and engage in major military exercises.

All the crises ended because both sides recognized, although not at the same time or in the same fashion, that further escalation was self-defeating. The dramatic Pakistani counterdeployment of 1987 demonstrated to India that it could not at that point manage a successful war with Pakistan. By the time it could take on Pakistan's conventional forces some ten years later, Pakistan was a declared nuclear weapons state that might have already deployed its nuclear arsenal. The 1990 crisis, which took place in the intervening years, simply petered out, bereft of a guiding strategic idea and of any opportunity for either side to take quick advantage of the other. Indeed, Pakistan was satisfied because it seemed to have calculated that the conditions were ripe for a bleeding operation in Kashmir instead. The Indians, under pressure in Kashmir and led by a cautious government, had no appetite for a wider war.

The 1999 Kargil crisis occurred after India and Pakistan had achieved a rough form of nuclear parity. Although many Indians might have wanted a large-scale conventional war, this made it very risky. India managed to snatch a political victory out of an initial military reverse when it persuaded the United States to help contain Pakistan. The pattern was repeated in the next crisis of 2001–02, without the shooting, although India's political victory is yet to be blessed by a permanent end to Pakistani interference in Kashmir.

If each of these crises were replayed, what is the likelihood that they would escalate to a full scale war or worse? Three of the crises (Brasstacks, Kargil, and 2001–02) might have exploded into open-ended war, although none had a potential for global calamity; only the 1990 crisis seems to have remained well in hand—no strategic purpose or driving ambition lay behind it, and there was not much risk that a miscalculation or misjudgment would have caused a war.

Strategic Objectives and the Crises

How did the crises reflect, advance, or retard India's and Pakistan's essential strategic objectives? During much of the period in which these crises took place, Pakistan sought a major role in Afghanistan and even farther afield in Central Asia, while still challenging India's hold on Kashmir. Pakistan's Kargil gambit was a clever tactic at the wrong moment. It underestimated the international response to a crisis between two nuclear weapons states, miscalculated India's reaction, and misjudged India's capabilities to escalate and threaten a wider war. In the end, Pakistan seemed overextended, not least because of its chaotic domestic politics and its failing economy.

India has sought to emerge as a major power and to play a role on the Asian and global stages. Its "Pakistan problem" stems from the fact that Islamabad often challenges India militarily. India has not been able to figure out a way of dispatching its regional challenger, compromising with it, or ignoring it. The Brasstacks crisis, precipitated by India, might have led to a war that would have crippled Pakistan before it became a nuclear weapons state. India's decision not to escalate the crisis allowed Islamabad to bring its nuclear program to fruition. The 2002 crisis was precipitated by India's response to terrorist attacks on one of its seats of government. As a result, India achieved its more limited objective of forcing Pakistan to reduce its support for separatists and terrorists, although fundamental India-Pakistan differences remained unresolved.

Except in the 1990 episode, strategic ambitions (and fears) were a feature of these crises. There may also have been a desire for vengeance to punish the other side, a driving force in Pakistan's 1990 and 1999 support of separatist forces in India, in retaliation for New Delhi's 1971 intervention in East Pakistan. Thoughts of preemption or preventive war may also have entered the picture, an Indian motive in triggering the Brasstacks crisis. In addition, political leaders may have thought that a crisis could give them a strategic advantage if they played their cards correctly, as the Indian leaders calculated in the latter stages of the Kargil crisis and believed overwhelmingly during the 2001–02 crisis.

The Crises and Perceptions

Perceptions do make a difference—and did make a difference. The difficulty, of course, is not simply in listing the perceptions or the "intentions" of the other side or their likely response; people can string together a series of scenarios and choices, and if they keep at it long enough, they are bound to include the right answer. Rather, the difficulty is in picking the correct scenario and making the right choice. This requires a deeper judgment of how the other side would see both itself and an unfolding crisis. For the most part, neither side in our four crises had a sure grasp of the other's fears and hopes, and at times one or both sides miscalculated the role that outsiders might have played.

The crises clearly contributed to a major change in perceptions, both within and outside the region. As we discuss in the next section, the crises occurred while both India and Pakistan were becoming nuclear weapon states, and by 1990 each came to see the other as such a state. However, it took two more crises for them to comprehend the full implications of being nuclear, and they are still on a learning curve in this regard.

Their attitudes toward each other *as states* also underwent a transformation. With the advent of Pakistan's large-scale support for militants and sensational terrorist attacks in India, particularly bombings in Mumbai, Srinagar, and New Delhi, many Indians came to regard Pakistan with hatred. Furious at these attacks, and unable to reach the infrastructure that supported militants and terrorists, India was forced to turn to others in order to pressure Pakistan, a strategy that was only partly successful. This growing view of Pakistan as an evil state also complicated Indian attempts to negotiate with Islamabad, and it took an act of great statesmanship by Atal Bihari Vajpayee to revive the composite dialogue after 2003. On the Pakistani side, there remained widespread irritation and anger with India for its failure to negotiate seriously on Kashmir, but this was slowly joined by grudging respect for India's rapid economic growth and even its political stability. Many Pakistanis were also embarrassed by the crude attempt to pressure India via the Kargil operation, and by the incoherence of Pakistan's own political system, which fostered widespread sectarian violence and forced the military to once again assume power.

The crises were also important in shaping outside views of India and Pakistan. Once Soviet forces were driven from Afghanistan, South Asia was again seen as a strategic backwater; this view was dramatically altered by the 1990 crisis, and by the Kargil and 2001–02 crises. Yet two other developments spawned different images and have been important in shaping Western (especially American) perceptions: the first was Pakistan's role in the war on terrorism, which led to a forgiving attitude toward General Pervez Musharraf and the military regime; the second was India's spectacular emergence as a leading force in high technology and its potential as a major economic power. On balance, the image of "Crisis South Asia" has been temporarily superseded by "Emerging South Asia," although one more crisis could revive the former.

The Global Environment and America's Role

How did the radical changes in the global environment between 1987 and 2002 affect the onset, duration, and termination of these four crises? For the most part, the world saw the Brasstacks crisis as a sideshow to the war in Afghanistan that was raging at the time. By and large, the world ignored the crisis except when it distracted Pakistan from its support for the mujahiddin in Afghanistan.

A few years later, Afghanistan had been forgotten, and the 1990 crisis was viewed as a relatively minor "regional" event. The world's attention was riveted on the growing crisis in the Persian Gulf and then on the civil wars of Yugoslavia. By then, however, many minds had made the connection between "Kashmir" and "nuclear," especially after the post-crisis revelations about Pakistan's alleged movement of nuclear weapons.

The international community—other South Asian countries, China, Japan, and the major Western powers, notably the United States—treated Kargil and 2001–02 with utmost seriousness, as major crises. Coming after the 1998 nuclear tests, they catapulted South Asia into the headlines around the world, where it remains today. Taken together, the recurrent crises and the tests hardened the perception that Kashmir was the most dangerous place in the world.

The role of the United States in these events increased from crisis to crisis and became more explicit. Its role was peripheral during Brasstacks, largely that of a spectator. Washington's presence was more evident during the 1990 crisis, although its engagement deepened only after the crisis was well on its way to resolution. It was ubiquitous in both 1999 and 2001–02; in Kargil the United States acted as an umpire, calling the shots as it saw them and forcing one side to back down. By 2001-02, Washington had reverted to the role of a "fixer," tilting the balance with the determination to bring the crisis to a rapid and peaceful conclusion. The degree of Washington's involvement has varied across these crises, ranging from the dispatch of a "mission" in 1990 to high-level presidential involvement in 1999 and high-level official visits to both India and Pakistan in 2001–02.

One quality of American engagement in these crises has been its ad hoc, short-term nature. The Reagan administration never took Brasstacks seriously as a crisis, viewing it as a misunderstanding between friends. The first Bush administration saw 1990 as inadvertent and sent a personal emissary to deal with the problem—its team arrived just after the crisis had passed. The Clinton administration did get deeply engaged in the Kargil crisis, but again personal diplomacy was the instrument of choice, beginning with the Zinni visit and ending with Clinton's own meeting with Nawaz Sharif. Finally, in 2001–02 the administration of George W. Bush cobbled together a strategy to cope with India's threat of escalation, a strategy that consisted of a mixture of threats and promises to both Islamabad and New Delhi.

The level and kind of interest the United States has shown have also been affected by Washington's interests in the region. In 1987 Pakistan was working with it to support the mujahiddin in Afghanistan. By 1990 and during the Kargil conflict, America's ties to Pakistan had been greatly diminished, and both crises were treated largely as "regional" affairs, except that in contrast to 1987, there was also a nuclear edge to them. In 2001–02 Washington had strong strategic links with Islamabad, motivated by regional concerns that trumped proliferation and other American interests. It also had a growing relationship with India that it wanted to keep positive.

During these crises both India and Pakistan tried to use Washington to advance their interests, but New Delhi was relatively more successful in this regard. There is evidence that India systematically used the United States to pressure Pakistan during the Kargil crisis and tried to repeat the exercise a year later during the 2001–02 crisis—with somewhat less success. In the case of Kargil, the United States willingly assented—it saw the Pakistanis as culpable and playing a high-risk game that could have led to a nuclear war. In 2002 Washington had a stake in preventing an India-Pakistan war, both because of the nuclear factor and its close working relationship with Islamabad in Afghanistan; any war could have directly weakened its attempt to round up the remnants of al-Qaeda and the Taliban and might have even affected the stability of the Afghanistan government. Thus even though Washington finally came to see the crisis as having been precipitated by Pakistan-sponsored terrorists, it was reluctant to come down hard on Pakistan and instead praised President Musharraf for his "principled" efforts to stop terrorism. This was not exactly an unmitigated success for New Delhi, and its hopes of an uncritically supportive American policy were left unfulfilled.

Pakistan has been somewhat less successful at mobilizing American support, except in the single case of the Brasstacks crisis. Here its relations with America were strengthened and India's weakened, as India was suspected, after the fact, of trying to derail American policy in Afghanistan by threatening a U.S. ally.

Ironically, although India's nuclear tests were intended to enhance New Delhi's international maneuverability, the opposite occurred. In Feroz Hassan Khan's assessment, "the deterrence equation in South Asia now implicitly depends on U.S. intervention. In essence, India's and Pakistan's nuclear policies involve what might be called the 'independence-dependence' paradox."[2] In other words, states pursue nuclear weapons to acquire greater strategic freedom and to deter their adversaries. In reality, they can become even more dependent on outside powers and the international system to secure their national interests, and they often create a domestic expectation of security and strategic advantage that they cannot meet. This was vividly demonstrated during the border confrontation crisis in that both India and Pakistan, in their anxiety to secure U.S. support, mortgaged their freedom of action to the whims of American policymakers who were pursuing their own agenda. All the same, this dependency has not inhibited the two adversaries from initiating or escalating their bilateral crises, which illustrates another dimension of this paradox.

Despite America's greater role in South Asia, this has not led to a sustained analysis of the causes of crisis or a strategy by which future crises might be anticipated and prevented. American engagement in these four major crises was tactical, not strategic, although the consequences for India and Pakistan were strategic, in that they now had to accommodate American concerns as they engaged each other.

Nuclear and Strategic Dimensions

The restraint exhibited by India and Pakistan in successive crises over the 1980s and 1990s increased in tandem with the transparency of their nuclear capabilities. The constraining role of nuclear weapons was nonexistent or at best ambiguous in the Brasstacks and 1990 crises, but it became more explicit in later crises. An authoritative quasi-official Indian review of Kargil notes that during the conflict Pakistani officials and non-officials alike attempted to convey certain implied nuclear threats.[3] Nuclear threats and counterthreats of nuclear retribution were frequent during the border confrontation crisis. Each government also used missile tests to convey warnings and signal its political resolve. India moved its Prithvi missiles closer to the border and also tested its shorter-range Agni missile in January 2002, when an attack on Pakistan was under consideration, which was transparently intended to intimidate Pakistan. For Pakistan's part, when India was contemplating a major operation against it in May 2002, it hastened to conduct a series of short- and long-range missile tests.

The crises have produced a debate over "redlines," a shorthand term for the limits of national tolerance and a signal to an adversary regarding the latter's plans to escalate. The problem is in determining the actual limits, as demonstrated by several fiascoes that occurred as one side or the other attempted to convey its national resolve or the precise parameters of its redlines. In an interview with a group of Italian scientists in 2002, for example, the director of Pakistan's Strategic Plans Division appeared to identify Pakistani redlines in no uncertain terms and then had to retract his remarks as Islamabad did not want to be too specific about its redlines lest the Indians creep right up to them.[4] The Line of Control (LOC) is a particularly important kind of redline. At one time it was not considered a permanent boundary, but the Kargil conflict at least temporarily transformed it into such a boundary. Crossing the international border or the LOC could be a redline, but this might depend on prevailing circumstances, such as the physical presence of American military forces in the vicinity.

India's and Pakistan's declarations of redlines may serve domestic ends but are of questionable strategic value, since full transparency on such operational issues could weaken rather than strengthen the fabric of deterrence, and in any case redlines may change depending upon particular circumstances. India has wisely declined to identify its redlines because any explicit description would indicate the limits of its tolerance, which, if crossed, might require a massive response with nuclear weapons. By identifying these redlines, moreover, India would be bound to act if they were breached, thereby closing other options for responding suitably to provocation. Defining redlines is therefore of greater value to the adversary for planning purposes, as it would be made aware of the limits that could be reached, but not breached, with a relative sense of impunity.

One feature of these crises was a gradual increase in inflammatory statements, with nuclear rhetoric becoming more intense after the 1998 nuclear tests. For example, immediately after India's tests, Home Minister L. K. Advani called on Islamabad "to realize the [consequent] change in the geostrategic situation in the region and the world." The tests had, he noted, "brought about a qualitatively new stage in India-Pakistan relations, particularly in finding a lasting solution to the Kashmir problem," and had made the option of "hot pursuit" available.[5] Later, at the height of the Kargil conflict, Pakistan's foreign secretary warned: "We will not hesitate to use any weapon in our arsenal to defend our territorial integrity."[6] Some months after the 2001–02 border confrontation had ended, President Musharraf disclosed that he would have unleashed an "unconventional war" on India had a single Indian soldier crossed the border. India's feisty defense minister, George Fernandes, in turn assured him that "there would be no Pakistan left" if India used its nuclear weapons in retaliation. Accusing India of "sick war hysteria," Pakistan followed that up by warning India of "an unforgettable reply."[7] These statements were intended primarily for domestic audiences, but their frequency suggests that political leaders in both countries are either unaware of the gravity of the situation and the horrendous damage that would occur in a nuclear exchange or believe that nuclear weapons can be used for war-fighting. It is significant, however, that neither side followed through on its rhetoric, permitting the further assessment that "the rhetoric itself might have had the effect of letting the steam off the heated domestic pressure for action in both countries."[8] None of these explanations is reassuring.

With the passage of time, however, and the realization that nuclear weapons in the hands of an adversary make it difficult to achieve a military solution, such political and military leaders turn into doves, professing peace and reconciliation. One could say that this represents an avian paradox: the morphing over time of hawks into doves during a crisis, without passing through any intermediate stages of owlish wisdom or crowlike cleverness.

As for stability, all new nuclear states tend to explore the limits imposed by their possession of nuclear weapons. They push at the edges before backing off. This was the case in the U.S.-Soviet relationship until the Cuban Missile Crisis, and with China and the Soviet Union until the Ussuri River episode.

What do the crises imply about the two main kinds of stability issues in South Asia—structural and crisis stability? Clearly, the occurrence of four major crises within a twenty-year period indicates a fundamental structural problem. Whether one attributes this primarily to the Kashmir dispute or to other factors, such as India's rise as a major power, South Asia has not been a stable and peaceful region, despite the common cultural and geopolitical heritage of the two states.

As for crisis stability, South Asia's strategists themselves differ sharply on this, some boasting how stable their relations are (the view of many Indians, some Pakistanis), and others how dangerous they are (the view of many Pakistanis and a few Indians). The "we are stable" school usually resents American or foreign interference and also resents the implication that South Asians cannot manage their own affairs; the "we are unstable" school often exaggerates instability because it wishes to draw outsiders into the region or to help make a case blaming the other side for dangerous instability. An interesting perspective is that India-Pakistan "crises do not progress linearly. The level of tension can move up and down, instead of constantly up, as many scenario-builders would have us believe."[9] However, it is also possible that either or both countries might engage in limited aggression in the belief that the other would be deterred from expanding the conflict into a full-scale conventional war that could escalate to a nuclear exchange.[10]

It is evident that the two countries' growing nuclear capabilities have induced both of them to be cautious. South Asia's strategic elites contend that the regional leadership is no less responsible than its counterparts in the nuclear weapon states and is fully cognizant of the horrendous consequences of a nuclear exchange. Their governments, they assert, are not headed by reckless leaders and are fully aware that a nuclear exchange could be as devastating for the "winner" as to the "loser." In fact, they also argue, nuclear weapons states have been led by individuals such as Joseph Stalin, Mao Zedong, and Richard Nixon, who were notorious for their irrationality, fecklessness, and risk-taking. In contrast, they state, Indian and Pakistani leaders have displayed commendable restraint by not enlarging the dimensions of the several wars they have fought against each other, even scrupulously avoiding civilian populations and economic targets. Furthermore, both countries have displayed commendable control over their armed forces in times of crisis. This was especially evident from their restraint in not expanding the Kargil conflict or in not proceeding to conflict in the border confrontation crisis despite the deployment of large forces on either side. Hence, according to this perspective, there is little reason to fear that the two sides will not display moderation with respect to nuclear weapons should a future India-Pakistan conflict erupt.

On the other hand, nuclear weapons have emboldened the states in other ways. Pakistan has become more confident and it has supported dissidents, militancy, and cross-border terrorism in Kashmir with greater impunity. Both countries engaged in brinkmanship in crisis situations, gauging the resolve of their adversary to up the ante. As American analyst Satu Limaye notes, "Both states seek to achieve their ends without war: Pakistan because it might lose, India because it might not win. Neither country has the capabilities or foreign support necessary to engage in a long drawn-out, formal conflict. In using brinkmanship, both India and Pakistan ultimately want to be held back while having the United States push their interests forward."[11]

Since 1990, outsiders, especially American observers, have come to fear a nuclear exchange, and this anxiety has driven American intervention since then. Both Presidents Bill Clinton and George W. Bush and numerous other international leaders have expressed concern, even alarm, at the nuclear rivalry. In June 1998, following the India-Pakistan nuclear tests, the Board of Directors of the *Bulletin of the Atomic Scientists* moved the minute hand of their "Doomsday Clock," the gauge for nuclear danger, from fourteen minutes to midnight to just nine minutes to midnight; in 2002 they moved it up to seven minutes to midnight, asserting that the 2002 crisis was "the closest two states have come to nuclear war since the Cuban Missile Crisis. When the hands of the clock were moved forward in 1998, to nine minutes to midnight, it was in part in anticipation of just this sort of scenario."[12]

The hope that strategic stability would prevail in the subcontinent after the India-Pakistan tests were conducted proved illusory. This is disconcerting but not surprising. The nuclearization of South Asia may have been expected to deter nuclear and large-scale conventional conflict between India and Pakistan. Nuclearization without normalization, however, has merely pushed the adversarial conduct into subterranean channels, epitomized by Pakistan's proxy war in Kashmir, which began in 1989 and which Pakistan eventually pursued with impunity. Indeed, Pakistan's demonstration of its nuclear capability in May 1998 in all likelihood emboldened it to undertake its Kargil adventure and inhibited India from adopting a "hot pursuit" policy. Indian frustration with its inability to convert nuclear capability into political or military advantage seems to have persuaded military circles to think that limited war under the nuclear umbrella remains feasible. This is embodied in the conviction of an Indian general that "strategic space exists between a proxy war and an all out armed conflict, in that there could be a calibrated use of military force below the level of an all out armed conflict. This has led to considerable thought being given to the idea of limited conflict."[13]

Sections of India's strategic community and military leaders continue to believe that India needs to widen the disparity between the conventional forces of the two countries to fight a short and intense war and gain its political objectives. Such a widening gap would involve not just additional air-land capabilities, land-based and air firepower, and mobility, but also, as another general noted, "a restructuring of security instruments to provide versatile and balanced forces, greater induction of technology, greater flexibility in force levels and organizations, and greater inter-services coordination."[14] The serious flaw in this argument is that, after a point, Pakistan might decide that it cannot compete against the larger resource base available to India and might therefore be driven to rely on its nuclear weapons to correct the balance. Speculatively, China could also transfer additional missile technology and conventional arms to Pakistan to restore the present balance.

Overall, the entry of nuclear weapons into the subcontinent, ostensibly to ensure national security, has not made the region more stable or conflict less likely. The Kargil conflict and the year-long border confrontation between the two countries have proven to be exceptions to the accepted wisdom that nuclear weapons stabilize relations, strengthen deterrence, and discourage both conventional and nuclear conflict. Furthermore, nuclear weapons have not reduced the almost routine exchanges of artillery fire across the Line of Control in Kashmir nor mitigated the "proxy war" encouraged by Pakistan that continues in Kashmir. While the deterrent effect of South Asia's nuclear weapons might have reduced the chances of nuclear conflict, it has not made conventional and subconventional conflict less likely. In fact, as we argued several years back, India-Pakistan antagonism has "now entered subterranean channels which is expressing itself in subversive activities and promoting militancy and cross-border terrorism directed against each other.... Nuclear deterrence obviously has no relevance to either preventing or mitigating tensions and instabilities of this nature or the internal security threats they generate in the South Asian context."[15]

The "stability-instability paradox" suggests that the establishment of a nuclear deterrent relationship could induce "stability" between adversarial nations at the nuclear level, but this could be offset by the "instability" ensuing from the greater feasibility of conventional war. In essence, the stability-instability paradox holds that "lowering the probability that a conventional war will escalate to a nuclear war ... reduced the danger of starting a conventional war; thus, this low likelihood of escalation ... makes conventional war less dangerous, and possibly, as a result, more likely."[16]

In our view, no one in the South Asian strategic community seems aware that a state of nuclear deterrence requires it, as Neil Joeck notes, to "rest on a combination of accommodation and reassurance, not on nuclear threats alone ... the relationship must be one of coordination and mutual dependence, not just conflict."[17] Indeed, the obverse situation developed from 1998 (the year of the tests) to 2002. These events make it clear that both countries are still exploring what it means to be a nuclear weapons state.

Historical analogies are always imperfect, but the present nuclear situation in South Asia resembles the U.S.-Soviet competition in many ways. Core or minimal deterrence *seems* to be as robust between India and Pakistan as it was between the two superpowers, but at far lower levels of nuclear capability. Of course, there are also important differences:

> Neither India nor Pakistan seeks to extend nuclear deterrence to a third party; Indo-Pakistani strategic behavior is subject to far more international pressure than U.S. and Soviet nuclear policy was during the Cold War, and this pressure may act as a check on conflict escalation in South Asia. In addition, India and Pakistan maintain small

nuclear arsenals, lacking the large array of tactical and strategic forces that superpowers deployed during the Cold War.[18]

But all four countries knew, after certain levels of nuclear capability were achieved, that any nuclear attack by them could, and might, be met with a retaliatory strike, causing certain and unacceptable damage. However, like the theology of the afterlife, one would only know for certain whether core deterrence can fail when one is dead. When one state deters another, nothing happens. India and Pakistan can claim—probably correctly, but we do not know this for certain—that their respective nuclear forces did "deter" the other side from attacking them. This judgment can only be made, however, when one is certain that the other side really intended to attack and is deterred from doing so by its opponent's capabilities. The case studies provide no certainty on this point.

Less credible than core deterrence is the claim that one's own threat to retaliate with a nuclear strike will deter one side or the other from attacking an ally or a peripheral interest, or from using less-than-total means. The Soviet Union and the United States waged war against each other through proxies for decades. The threat of using nuclear weapons was present in Korea and Vietnam, but in both cases the United States was deterred, not so much by the threat of Soviet retaliation but by concern over the political, moral, and psychological costs of using nuclear weapons, which might not have made a significant military difference in any case. There was also the prospect that such a use might have been met with Soviet pressure elsewhere in Eurasia, Africa, or Latin America. In South Asia, the likelihood of an Indian threat of using nuclear weapons did not deter Pakistan from launching Kargil—this was a classical limited war conducted at a low enough level to make a nuclear response unimaginable, even if it was technically possible.

There was, and remains, enough uncertainty about the level and quality of regional nuclear forces to ask whether either side can achieve "escalation dominance," meaning the capability to match the enemy at the next level of violence and at every successively higher level. Going down this road would have put major high-value targets, notably cities and power-generation facilities, at high risk, and neither India nor Pakistan seems to have found the risk worth taking. As with the United States and the Soviet Union, a low-level skirmish on the periphery was manageable, and even a minor war in Central Europe, but neither side relished the prospect of losing its cities or other major assets for the sake of an ally. Both sides seem to be self-deterred by the prospect of a nuclear war that would destroy critical national assets.

Limited War under the Nuclear Shadow

Both India and Pakistan are slowly coming to an understanding that while nuclear weapons can deter the other side's nuclear weapons, they cannot deter other forms of conventional or subconventional conflict, such as proxy wars, cross-border terrorism, border skirmishes, and punitive strikes by land and air forces, or controlled wars of attrition. In other words, "instability in the nuclear realm encourages instability at lower levels of conflict. In this environment, limited conventional conflict is unlikely to provoke an immediate nuclear confrontation. However, in the event that a limited conventional confrontation subsequently spirals into a full-scale conventional conflict, escalation to the nuclear level becomes a serious possibility. This danger of nuclear escalation allows nuclear powers to engage in limited violence against each other."[19]

In the South Asian crises, especially the last three, Pakistan and India were quite innovative in exploring the options that lie between conventional and nuclear conflict. They showed a willingness to test the methods by which they might escalate without triggering a nuclear response and sometimes heightened the crisis atmosphere by signaling via missile tests and large-scale military exercises. This has required a continuous process of exploration, since each rung of the escalation ladder heralds a new dynamic in which graduated offensive action needs to be countered by an appropriate defensive reaction, so as to ensure that escalation dominance is maintained at all times. But there have been problems with this. In Brasstacks, India miscalculated Pakistan's willingness to escalate, and in Kargil the boot was on the other foot.

The 1998 nuclear tests immunized Pakistan from reprisals by India's larger conventional forces. Pakistan has therefore been able to pursue a low-cost policy of supporting cross-border terrorism, wounding India with "a thousand cuts." Pakistan's confidence in this altered structure of military power was revealed by its launch of the Kargil intrusions and by its claim in the 2001–02 crisis that it "defeated" India's deployed armed forces without engaging them in conflict. Yet this Kargil "victory" came at a high cost for Pakistan, since it triggered a military coup and international opprobrium.

The likelihood of a preemptive strike by either India or Pakistan against each other is very low. Strategists on both sides are aware that without a guarantee that *all* their adversary's nuclear assets would be destroyed in a surprise attack, a preemptive strike would be a very high-risk enterprise.

Concern about an accidental use stemming from a malfunction has led India to emphasize in its nuclear doctrine the need for extraordinary security precautions and safety measures to protect the nuclear stockpile: "India shall develop an appropriate disaster control system capable of handling the unique requirements of potential incidents involving nuclear weapons and materials." Pakistan has provided similar assurances to the world regarding its own command and control system and the security of its nuclear forces and nuclear material.

However, the nuclear doctrines of these two countries could be dangerously mismatched. Although the nuclear doctrines developed by the superpowers during the cold war evolved over a long period of time, significant gaps were later discovered in what each knew about the other side. Do India and Pakistan have any doctrinal or strategic advantage because of their late entry as nuclear weapons states? Theoretically, they could have benefited from the experience of others, but each side has seized upon a segment of the body of nuclear doctrine and adopted that as its own.

Well before 1990, Pakistani strategists were informally discussing the various possible ways of using nuclear weapons as tactical devices against high-value military targets and in city-busting attacks. India's nuclear doctrine, evident in 1990 but subsequently declared openly after the 1998 tests, established that India would await a nuclear attack before using its own weapons in a retaliatory blow. This was the philosophy that underlay Prime Minister Vajpayee's statements and subsequent declarations by Indian officials. They rejected, and in any case did not have the capability for, a first-strike nuclear attack against Pakistan or China.

The likelihood of an India-Pakistan conflict going nuclear arises most credibly from the escalation of a conventional war to a nuclear one. This was simply a matter of intense speculation during the 1990 crisis, but by the Kargil conflict and the border confrontation of 2001–02, escalation was quite conceivable.

How could a limited war that might cross the nuclear threshold be fought? The nuclear doctrines of India and Pakistan do not shed any light on this question. But India's no-first-use policy, in conjunction with the threat of a devastating retaliatory strike, suggests that it would adopt a counter-city strategy. To pursue a limited nuclear war strategy, however, India would need nuclear weapons with relatively low yields for "soft" military targets such as conventional forces, exposed military installations, or logistics centers. Futhermore, these nuclear weapons would have to be used in an air-burst mode to reduce casualties from radioactive fallout in a ground attack against hardened military targets such as missile silos and underground command centers.

Currently, India and Pakistan seem to be relying on first-generation nuclear weapons of uncertain dependability and provenance. While both countries are attempting to arm their missiles, additional testing will be required for them to produce a new generation of reliable nuclear weapons. Whether they are more or less destructive, or presumably safer to store and handle, is another matter. Will India and Pakistan break their commitments not to test? Another crisis would certainly move them in this direction, and a fresh crisis might provide the pretext to further test their arsenals.[20]

What would be the effects of a nuclear war in the region? A number of studies have explored the possible effects on populated centers and on military or economic targets.[21] One such study concluded that "any use of nuclear weapons in the region, even on a small and limited scale, would cause very high civilian casualties and collateral damage and would be likely to cause escalation from a limited nuclear exchange into a major counter-city strike."[22] During the 2001–02 border confrontation, a popular magazine in India described these scenarios for specific cities to convey the chilling message that enormous damage would be likely in any nuclear conflict, especially in the densely populated subcontinent.[23]

Domestic Politics

Domestic political calculations played probably the smallest role in the 1987 Brasstacks event. On the Indian side, Rajiv Gandhi may have used the crisis to make some adjustments in his cabinet structure, but this was a secondary effect. In Pakistan, Zia ul-Haq was secure in his position as military ruler, although Mohammed Khan Junejo, his politically feeble prime minister, had tried to assert himself and was relieved of his post. The crisis was linked to domestic disturbances in India, however, as the insurgency in Punjab was still under way and India suspected a Pakistani hand.

Three years later, in 1990, the political systems of both India and Pakistan were in disarray, with a weak coalition government in New Delhi and an uneasy troika ruling in Pakistan, and domestic politics strongly influenced the behavior of both states. Especially for Benazir Bhutto in Pakistan but also for the United Front alliance in India, mishandling the crisis, or appearing weak, would have been politically damaging.

In the 1999 crisis, politician Nawaz Sharif sought to use the United States to protect himself from his own handpicked army chief, Pervez Musharraf. The attempt failed, and Nawaz was pushed out in a coup shortly after the crisis ended. On the Indian side, the BJP government was itself concerned about looking weak and fought the war as a great patriotic effort, the result of Pakistani treachery, not Indian incompetence. This message was only strengthened by the semiofficial Kargil Report, which found fault everywhere except in the army high command and political leadership. The way in which crisis was managed at Kargil—as a patriotic war, but with a very small circle of decisionmakers—did not change much in the 2002 crisis. This was also a national crusade, in response to a dastardly act of terrorism, and the BJP coalition government had no trouble in keeping its political opposition in line. Ironically, the BJP's subsequent boasting about its strategic triumph, plus its campaign about "Shining India," did not go down well in many parts of the country, and the party was voted out of office in 2004.

As for decisionmaking in each of these crises, this task was in the hands of a very small circle of the decisionmaking elite. During Brasstacks, decisions came down from no more than three or four people in India, perhaps three in Pakistan. In 1990 the circle was a bit wider in both countries, but then there was no real crisis, only the illusion of one. In Kargil and the 2002 border confrontation, the group responsible for policy was again very small, and in Pakistan's case, the lack of expertise among civilians (Nawaz Sharif particularly) ensured the continued dominance of the army in strategic policy.

Could It Happen Again?

A natural question to ask is whether any (or several) of the crises examined in this book could occur again. As each case illustrates, this would depend on many factors.

BRASSTACKS. The evidence is still vague as to the degree of willfulness behind the Brasstacks crisis and whether it was intended to eliminate Pakistan's nuclear program before the latter produced a device. If that was the case, then the closest analogy would have to be an Indian (or a Pakistani) decision to "take out" enough of the other side's nuclear force so as to eliminate the possibility, or reduce the cost, of a second-strike retaliation. Whether this could happen is a function of many calculations: the number and dispersal of nuclear forces, either side's ability to target such forces with conventional or nuclear weapons, their toleration of a retaliatory strike, and the certainty of their intelligence about the intentions and overall capabilities of the other. Given the enormous stakes involved, we believe that such an "out-of-the-blue" strike against the other side is very unlikely.

1990. This kind of accidental or unintended crisis is without doubt the most difficult to predict. Characterized by weakened governments on both sides and dramatic events in Kashmir, a rerun could take place were there to be a violent separatist upsurge in Pakistan, or even a domestic crisis in India.

KARGIL. Would Pakistan attempt another line-straightening operation along the Line of Control in Jammu and Kashmir, or might India attempt the same thing? This certainly would be an option, probably a very unwise one, should the present process of normalization break down and one side or the other come to the conclusion that a little pressure might go a long way in getting the attention of the international community and the adversary.

2001–02. Another terrorist outrage could easily trigger an Indian response like the one that brought New Delhi and Islamabad to the edge of an all-out war. Indeed, Indian forces are now configured for such a response. This scenario, coupled with domestic political disorder (as in the 1990 crisis), might be the most powerful recipe for another major crisis. It is all the more frightening since such terrorist acts are impossible to predict and it may be difficult to assign responsibility for them.

One thing for certain is that the next crisis will be unique. We believe that it will be embedded in its own historical framework and will work itself through according to its own logic. But it will also share the earlier elements of surprise and danger and may escalate to something worse than occurred in all the preceding crises in South Asia and elsewhere in the world.

It is possible that the experience of previous crises might help India and Pakistan (and the international community) better predict, manage, and perhaps mitigate a future crisis. However, while both countries have recently demonstrated a new maturity in their relationship, they enjoyed a similar association during the seventeen years that followed the initial Kashmir war. In 1947 India and Pakistan were more closely linked economically than afterward, travel and trade were easier (real restrictions were only imposed after the 1965 war), and the leaders on both sides of the international border and cease-fire line knew each other well.

Cease-fire or Peace Process?

The four crises described in this book were interspersed with numerous attempts at diplomacy. Most of these turned out to be false starts, but as the level of crisis grew, so did the frequency with which both sides engaged each other. There was also a parallel growth of nonofficial dialogue, and from 1990 onward a whole string of private meetings (and a few with official blessings) discussed the military balance, Kashmir, confidence-building measures (CBMs), and other measures to reduce tension and reach agreement on contentious issues.

The 2003–06 dialogue between India and Pakistan had its roots in the exchange of "non-papers" between Benazir Bhutto and P. V. Narasimha Rao's governments in 1994. These non-papers recognized the importance of Kashmir and identified ways to reduce the level of tensions in Kashmir and ensure peace along the Line of Control and on the Siachen Glacier. This exchange was suspended upon Pakistan's insistence that a plebiscite be held in Kashmir—a UN-approved idea that was totally unacceptable to India.[24]

The dialogue process was further refined in 1997 when, during a meeting on the sidelines of the South Asian Association for Regional Cooperation (SAARC) summit in Male, Prime Ministers Inder K. Gujral and Nawaz Sharif agreed on the need for an "integrated approach" and decided to initiate a "composite dialogue." Follow-up talks between the two foreign secretaries led to the formation of joint working groups to discuss eight issues: Kashmir, peace and security, Siachen, Wullar Barrage, Sir Creek, terrorism and drug trafficking, economic cooperation, and promotion of friendly exchanges.[25]

The May 1998 nuclear tests were followed by a tense period between the two countries. A few months later, on September 23, 1998, Prime Ministers Vajpayee and Sharif met in New York and agreed to restart the dialogue, but apart from a few meetings there was little progress. Then in February 1999, Vajpayee embarked on his "bus diplomacy" trip to Lahore in an attempt at reconciliation. This trip was preceded by intensive diplomatic engagement between the two foreign secretaries during which they laid out their national proposals in the form of non-papers that were not made public but have been pieced together on the basis of interviews with anonymous officials.[26] These proposals provided a blueprint for future negotiations and were designed to increase restraint and reduce the risks emerging from India's and Pakistan's possession of nuclear weapons.[27]

Vajpayee's visit to Lahore by bus across the India-Pakistan border was followed by the opening up of road traffic disrupted after the 1965 war. It was a visit steeped in symbolism. Vajpayee made it a point to visit the Minar-e-Pakistan, a memorial pillar erected to commemorate the Lahore Resolution of 1940, which called for the creation of Pakistan.[28]

In our view, the most important aspect of this declaration was its accompanying Memorandum of Understanding (MoU), which set forth a number of CBMs regarding ballistic missile tests; accidental, unauthorized, or unexplained incidents; and communications and trade between the two countries. This MoU established the foundations for subsequent CBM negotiations; several closely resemble the measures negotiated by the United States and the Soviet Union during the cold war.

Dialogue after Kargil

The Kargil conflict was followed by an abortive summit meeting in Agra and then the 2001–02 crisis. It was not until April 2003, when Prime Minister Vajpayee extended a "hand of friendship" to Pakistan in Srinagar—imbuing his offer with enormous symbolism—that the peace process was resuscitated. Both countries again appointed high commissioners to each other's capitals, expanded their staffs, and after intense negotiations managed to restore air, rail, and bus links. The attempt at normalization was facilitated by the visits of delegations of parliamentarians, journalists, businesspersons, academics, and others. These measures helped to reestablish the situation that existed before the attack on the Indian parliament in 2001 and the border confrontation crisis.

Prime Minister Zafarullah Khan Jamali's proposal in November 2003 to establish a cease-fire along the LOC and his banning of three militant outfits in Pakistan further strengthened the peace process. The cease-fire was thereafter extended to the Siachen Glacier and is still in effect. Transportation and communication links were restored, and sports teams began to visit each other's countries. The cricket matches played by the Indian team in Pakistan were of special significance because they led to a large flow of ordinary citizens from India to witness them and established warm personal ties between citizens of both countries.

Framed against the backdrop of steadily improving bilateral relations, India and Pakistan concluded a number of CBMs. Matters improved rapidly in 2004, following a successful SAARC summit in Islamabad, and a joint statement by President Musharraf and Prime Minister Vajpayee on January 6 condemning terrorism, welcoming further CBMs, and agreeing to the resumption of the composite dialogue. This effort gained further momentum in June 2004 after a Congress-led coalition government came to power.

The Composite Dialogue

Undoubtedly the most important aspect of the composite dialogue revolves around the ongoing Kashmir dispute. A "detailed exchange of views on Jammu & Kashmir" between the two foreign secretaries took place in New Delhi on June 27–28, 2004.[29] Following the talks, conducted in a "cordial and constructive atmosphere," both sides expressed "satisfaction over the ongoing process of dialogue" and "agreed to continue the sustained and serious dialogue to find a peaceful negotiated final settlement."[30] This was the first time since January 1994 that the Kashmir dispute was the subject of a serious dialogue.[31]

The next round of talks focused on water-related issues, of special importance to Pakistan, the lower riparian. More successful were talks between the culture secretaries of India and Pakistan to explore possibilities to improve and encourage people-to-people contacts.

Talks on the two tough territorial issues, Siachen and Sir Creek, were held on August 5–6, 2004. The issue in contention is whether the current ground position of the Indian and Pakistani troops in Siachen should be recorded in maps or on the ground before their withdrawal is effected. India argues that unless the ground situation is demarcated, this territory could be seized by Pakistan, whereas the latter holds that demarcation would legitimize India's "illegal" seizure of this territory in violation of the Simla Agreement. A resolution of the Siachen dispute is important and would firmly anchor the Line of Control at its northern end. Talks over Sir Creek failed to yield any concrete results, each side holding to established positions, although by 2005 a joint survey of the region had been carried out.

Despite the vastly improved atmosphere and these talks, bilateral trade, though it has increased (during April to November 2004 two-way trade touched $340 million—an increase of 150 percent), still remains at an unimpressive level. Hence a joint study group at the level of commerce secretaries has been formed to increase trade five times during the next couple of years by removing bottlenecks.

In June 2004 a meeting of experts on nuclear CBMs was held in Delhi. Although the joint statement released subsequently included some points already agreed upon in the Lahore MoU—such as the continuation of bilateral consultations on security and nonproliferation issues—the agreed clauses and subsequent agreements allowed for expanded dialogues on nuclear and security-related issues, the upgrading of hotlines between the two directors-general of military operations (DGMOs) and introduction of another hotline between the two foreign secretaries, an "agreement with technical parameters on prenotification of flight testing of missiles" (since concluded), and a reaffirmation of the moratorium on conducting further nuclear explosions, except "in exercise of national sovereignty" if one of the countries decided that extraordinary events have jeopardized its supreme interests.[32] In a new agreement signed on February 21, 2007, both sides assumed the responsibility of notifying each other in case of accidents relating to nuclear weapons or material.

New Ideas on Kashmir

In October 2004 President Musharraf made a substantial change in Pakistan's Kashmir policy, no longer insisting on a plebiscite (as called for in early UN resolutions) or on a resolution of the Kashmir issue as a prerequisite for progress on other issues. Pakistan has also provided assurances that it will not allow its territory to be used for cross-LOC infiltration, although Indian observers question whether it can or is willing to control the militants. Currently Pakistan stresses that it will consent to whatever is acceptable to the Kashmiris.

Perhaps the most important aspect of Musharraf's initiative is that a debate regarding the possible solution began within Pakistan. His address was apparently aimed at attaining some form of consensus. For obvious reasons, a national consensus would facilitate forward movement.

Initially, India's response was cool, though its leadership gave some thought to a nine-point strategy (in November 2004) that included initiating a dialogue with all groups in Jammu and Kashmir (especially those who had shunned violence); promoting interaction with Pakistanis; working toward the opening of the Jammu-Sialkot, Uri-Muzaffarabad, and Kargil-Skardu roads; promoting culture; working to decrease unemployment; tackling public grievances; accelerating economic development; avoiding human rights violations by Indian security forces; and involving the media in helping reconstruct the state.[33] Prime Minister Manmohan Singh has also proposed "self-rule" and an "open border" as options and has committed to considering pre-1953 autonomy. While Prime Minister Singh has opposed redrawing the Kashmir map, India no longer holds that Kashmir's accession to the Indian Union must be final, that there is nothing to discuss except

Pakistan's illegal occupation of part of the state, or that cross-border terrorism must cease before a dialogue on Kashmir could begin.

Both countries are inching toward getting their people and the Kashmiris on both sides of the LOC used to the idea of a division of the state, even though the Pakistani leadership holds that the existing partition based on the LOC is unacceptable. A solution suggested via media is to convert the LOC into a soft border. This arrangement gained currency following the opening of the Muzaffarabad-Srinagar road to bus and truck traffic. More road links are under consideration, such as the Jammu-Sialkot and Poonch-Rawalakot roads, which could also serve as meeting points along the LOC for separated families to socialize with each other. These measures would reduce the salience of the LOC as a disputed issue between India and Pakistan. It would also isolate the separatists within the Valley, since the population on both sides of the LOC is enthusiastic about the renewal of long-severed contacts.

The devastating earthquake that ravaged both parts of Kashmir in September 2005 united both countries in a joint effort to provide relief to the affected populations. India sent trainloads of relief material to Pakistan, and its troops were permitted to cross the LOC to conduct relief operations on the Pakistani side. Five border crossings were also opened as a humanitarian measure to allow separated families to socialize with each other, and a new rail link opened in 2006. Despite significant terrorist attacks in Indian cities, notably at the prestigious Indian Institute of Science in Bangalore, and the train bombings in Mumbai, the very popular cricket matches were resumed in January 2006, with the Indian team making a month-long tour of Pakistan.

The one project that would link India and Pakistan but that has failed to materialize is a $4 billion dollar pipeline for transporting Iranian gas to India via Pakistan. The project has been held up because of security concerns about the pipeline as it passes through Pakistan's Baluchistan Province, India's potential energy dependence on Pakistan, the project's cost, the problem of acquiring insurance, and American opposition to the entire deal because of its Iranian links.

An Enduring Peace Process?

The overall atmosphere of India-Pakistan relations has gradually improved since 2003, despite political turmoil in Pakistan and a new government in India. These talks have incorporated discussions on peace and security, confidence-building measures, and Kashmir. Each round has concluded with a cautiously worded communiqué describing the talks as "friendly," "frank and candid," held in a "cordial and constructive atmosphere," and "in the spirit of goodwill and cooperation." Despite the clichés, the important fact is that the dialogues are very popular on both sides.

The talks and the composite dialogue represent an achievement of sorts in that they have taken place after a very long interval in which nothing moved forward. The great concern is that although both sides are making a sincere effort to find effective and practical answers, they still seem unwilling to engage in real compromise. While pessimism may not be in order, we do believe that the underlying suspicion and genuine disagreement on issues of substance could still spawn a new crisis.

It is hard to say whether this reigning suspicion is a product of the crises explored in this book, or whether a future crisis will be fed from the same pool of distrust and rivalry that prevents the two states from reaching agreement on areas where they seemingly have a common interest. There has not been much progress on issues of substantive dispute, such as Sir Creek, Siachen, trade, oil and gas pipelines, water issues, and Kashmir, let alone serious discussion about containing the regional conventional and nuclear arms races. Several of these disputes are undoubtedly ripe for settlement, but any movement in that direction will depend on a basic change of mind-sets and consistent demonstration of political will by the leaderships of India and Pakistan.

Is the current peace process likely to endure? Until recently, India-Pakistan relations ran on a roller-coaster of highs and lows, with an undercurrent of hostility. Are they now entering a temporary and evanescent stage on a path toward normalcy, before inherent factors might supervene and the relationship reverts to more familiar patterns of tension, crisis, and conflict? Both sides of this proposition can be and are being debated.

On the optimistic side, Vajpayee's initiation of a peace process obviously stemmed from his deep personal commitment to normalization with Pakistan, a goal that he pursued in the face of opposition from within his own party. Other Indian prime ministers were at least intermittently committed to normalization. Further reasons to be optimistic could be India's desire to reach out to the people of Pakistan over the heads of its ruling elite, just as President Musharraf tried to appeal to the Indian people over the heads of the Indian government during his visit to India for the Agra talks. Finally, the continuing strategic ties between both India and Pakistan and the United States, and their growing interdependence with regions beyond South Asia, require at least the appearance of normalization.

Strategically, the Kargil conflict and the border confrontation crisis have taught both countries that they cannot gain their political objectives—including a resolution of the long-enduring Kashmir dispute—by force of arms. The state of nuclear deterrence now existing between them as a result of their nuclear tests effectively foreclosed the military option. Moreover, the international community recognizes the danger of any conflict between India and Pakistan escalating, looks askance upon attempts by them to alter the status quo, and would intervene to halt any future conflict lest it cross the nuclear threshold. Although such fears might be deemed excessive, India and Pakistan have to configure these anxieties into their regional strategy if they wish to abide by international norms. In these circumstances, negotiating a way through their bilateral problems seems the only practical option available.

On the pessimistic side, the current peace process is arguably brittle and ephemeral, if the past history of India-Pakistan relations is any guide. A single dramatic act of violence like an attack on a high-value economic or political target, especially if it evokes strong emotional sentiments, could derail the process. So could the assassination of a prominent political leader in circumstances suggesting that it was masterminded from across the border. Some credence should also be given to a change in leadership in either India or Pakistan. The defeat of the BJP-led National Democratic Alliance government in India's general elections of May 2004 and the ascendancy of the Congress-led United Progressive Alliance (UPA) government was of genuine concern in Pakistan, which suspected the UPA would be less than enthusiastic about a peace process bearing the stamp of Prime Minister Vajpayee. This fear was by no means unfounded given the plebiscitary nature of South Asian politics, not to mention Pakistan's clear memory of the aggressive policies of Indira Gandhi, which led to the breakup of Pakistan in 1971. Moreover, some security, intelligence, and foreign policy elites in both countries favor a state of no-war, no-peace, since it enables them to maintain their centrality in the decisionmaking process for both personal and institutional gain. They are unlikely to look kindly on any normalization process lest it impinge adversely on their fortunes.

Key Policy Concerns

The India-Pakistan crises examined in this book form only part of a record of tension and instability spanning more than half a century, punctuated by occasional full-blown wars and, since 2003, a peace process characterized by doubts and uncertainties. Furthermore, both India and Pakistan must manage their policies in the context of a transformed international system. Both states were affected by the decline of the Soviet Union (and the subsequent lack of interest of the major powers in South Asia), and then, paradoxically, by the dramatic increase in American and Chinese regional engagement following the rise of radical Islamic terrorism, especially after 9/11, which centered on Afghanistan but spilled over into Pakistan and India.

This situation suggests several areas in which the policy community needs to do some hard thinking—at the minimum, to prevent the next crisis from escalating to utterly unacceptable levels, or to ensure that a crisis does not even begin, or, ideally, to address the underlying cause(s) of these crises. It would do well to focus its search on policies of the good, the better, and the best.

Kashmir Remains Important

While the deeper causes of these crises are many and complex (the power disparity between India and Pakistan, their clashing national identities, the role of extremists in both states), it cannot be denied that Kashmir is a very important one. It was central in the 1990 and Kargil crises and lurked in the background in the other two.

Kashmir is strikingly similar to Palestine. Both issues are baffling in their complexity and have an internal component relevant to domestic politics but also an external component. The international community views these problems with considerable apprehension, and they both dominate foreign relations in their respective regions: South Asia and the Middle East. Kashmir has been either the chief theater of India-Pakistan conflicts or the main cause of their bilateral crises over the years. Since 1989, a proxy war has been under way in Kashmir. Pakistan has been confident that it can promote cross-border militancy and terrorism there and, thanks to its growing nuclear capabilities, prevent India from expanding the conflict into Pakistan.

India, in its eagerness to portray militancy in Kashmir as being supported from abroad, downplays the indigenous roots of the conflict, which include long-standing misgovernance of the state and the denial of democratic rights to its citizens. Pakistan has made Kashmir the central focus of its relations with India, to the point where it has neglected its own political and economic development. A cease-fire is currently in place as part of the composite dialogue/peace process, and several of the CBMs being negotiated within this framework—including those for Siachen and the Wullar Barrage/Tulbul Navigation Project, the Baglihar dam, and proposals to reestablish road communications across the LOC, as well as general talks about avoiding military incidents across the LOC—address the Kashmir problem. We believe that the realization has dawned on all the parties to the Kashmir imbroglio that they have to make compromises, and that maximalist rhetoric, addressed to domestic audiences, is counterproductive. The dilemma for Indian and Pakistani policymakers is how to make concessions (which all privately agree will be necessary) and still be able to claim "victory." Getting both sides to "win" is a task that seems to have been beyond the grasp of policymakers for the past two generations.

Nuclear Weapons Avert War but Do Not Make Peace

India and Pakistan are in the midst of a transition from being non-nuclear states to being full-fledged nuclear powers. The crises show that nuclear weapons did deter escalation but did not prevent a mini-war in Kargil. The threat of nuclear war also brings in outside powers, and of course, the more nuclear weapons there are, the greater the risk of accident, and the greater the devastation if they are used.

Deterrence now seems to be firmly in place, with a de facto situation of mutual nuclear deterrence, as both states have the ability to wreak unacceptable damage on each other. The International Institute for Strategic Studies estimates that India and Pakistan each have at least forty-plus nuclear weapons.[34] If half of these were dropped on major urban targets, the post-attack recovery time would be incalculable, especially if these targets included Mumbai, Karachi, Delhi, Lahore, and so forth.

Neither the Pakistani intrusion across the Line of Control during Kargil nor the provocative attack on the Indian parliament, the most visible symbol of its democracy, breached Indian redlines, indicating that they are deeply recessed now and implying that both countries have raised their nuclear thresholds to high levels. Thus while Indian strategists have often raised rhetorical questions about Western concepts of nuclear deterrence, they seem to have faithfully adhered to its precepts in practice. It would seem unlikely that either protagonist would employ a nuclear riposte to defend itself against a conventional war except as a last resort, when vital interests are perceived to be in jeopardy.

What these vital national interests are, however, is largely based on the perceptions of a small number of elites in India and an even smaller number in Pakistan. It is unclear to what extent the restraint sometimes observed in their crisis behavior is informed by enlightened self-interest, to what extent it derives from the mediation of the United States, and to what extent it arises from incompetence, a lack of resolution, or an absence of foresight. However, there is little to suggest that this pattern of risk-taking and crisis resolution is informed by an understanding of the nature and consequences of nuclear war and the imperative that nuclear deterrence never break down; if it had been so informed, these crises may not have been generated or would have been brought under control bilaterally, without the intercession of the United States and the international community.

Our examination of these four crises suggests that a policy of deterrence is easier to pursue than a policy of compellence. The status quo is always easier to preserve.[35] In 1987 India was deterred by the conventional Pakistan threat, whereas in 1990 both sides were reluctant to escalate because of the prevailing uncertainty and confusion. The dissuasive power of a nuclear deterrent was responsible for the containment of the Kargil conflict because the two sides reversed their roles as attacker and defender midway in the war but felt constrained from enlarging the dimensions of this limited conflict. The same thing happened in the border confrontation crisis: India sought to alter the status quo by threatening an attack on Pakistan and risking a nuclear riposte; Pakistan, on the other hand, played the easier role as the defender of the status quo. However, neither country was interested in pursuing activist and adventurous strategies. Therefore judgments by the authorities charging that one or the other country was reactionary or inclined toward the status quo are wholly misplaced. Both countries have demonstrated a willingness at different times to explore the space for initiating crises. Whether they will continue to do so in the future is an open question.

India's introduction of such doctrines as limited war and Cold Start seem to contradict its implicit policy of massive retaliation, in that they invite Pakistan to use nuclear weapons first if conventional defense fails. This problem will be exacerbated in years to come, as India builds up its conventional capabilities and Pakistan improves its nuclear ones. These trends could make future India-Pakistan relations very unstable once they have reached the crisis stage.

Clearly, the military and political leaderships of both countries have learned little from past crises and nothing from the crises of other states; indeed, they underplay the seriousness of these past events in order to preserve an image of bravery and resoluteness, primarily to impress domestic audiences, despite the significant pressures of a crisis with nuclear overtones. They also do so to justify large additions to the defense budget and the acquisition of more sophisticated weapon systems, ostensibly to meet the external threats to national security.

Rhetoric and Decisionmaking

The reassuring thesis that nuclear weapons bring an era of stability is partly offset by the readiness of leaders in both countries to indulge in rhetoric, by the concentration of power in the area of national security and foreign policy, and by the absence of checks and balances in the decisionmaking processes of both states. As in many other parts of the world, Indian and Pakistani leaders address very different audiences: those at home, across the border, and abroad, particularly in Washington, D.C. This often results in verbal pyrotechnics, and it requires a nuanced understanding of the context of such rhetoric to recognize which audience is the target. As the American strategist Michael Krepon has noted, "It is very hard to convey consistent messages to all three audiences in a severe crisis. This can lead to mixed signals and confusion."[36]

If existing dialogues are still weak, the risk of recurring crises remains on the horizon. While his own country is hardly free of aberrant decisionmaking, one American official interviewed for this project and involved in one of the crises noted that in the absence of a culture of debate and discussion, states (that is, the officials responsible for making policy) may pursue immoderate and unyielding policies until faced with an unwanted crisis.

The Indian and Pakistani decisionmaking processes relating to strategic and nuclear issues are mirror images of each other. The military dominates the process in Pakistan, since the country's Kashmir, nuclear, and defense policies fall within its exclusive purview even under civilian governments. At the present juncture, there is little doubt that the military is responsible for nuclear decisionmaking, or that the nuclear scientific establishment functions under its command. The capacity of the Pakistani military for risk-taking is part of the history of India-Pakistan relations. Until there is a change of the military mind-set—a matter of great debate and discussion in both India and Pakistan—a major change in policy in Islamabad is doubtful.

One might presume that the process of nuclear decisionmaking in India is more widely dispersed through its defense and foreign affairs bureaucracies, its armed forces, scientific establishment, and the cabinet. Nothing could be further from reality. Nuclear decisionmaking in India has been centralized in the prime minister's office and a very small circle of officials. This group took the crucial decisions regarding Pokharan I (approved by Prime Minister Indira Gandhi) and Pokharan II (approved by a BJP-led coalition), despite the great differences in the political complexion of the two governments. This centralized decisionmaking process precludes wider consultation on major nuclear weapon–related decisions and also insulates core decisionmakers from the collective memory of important government departments and ministries. The lack of institutional structures and the narrowness of the present arrangements in both countries for decisions related to nuclear security do not bode well for crisis stability if the present dialogue should falter. On this count, the prospective reorganization of India's nuclear establishment, which would split its civilian and military elements into two separate organizations and provide greater public and parliamentary supervision over both, may provide a reality check that has hitherto been lacking.

The United States and China

The enlarged role of the United States in South Asian crises is apparent, especially since India and Pakistan have established themselves as overt nuclear weapon states. China can also be expected to play a larger role in regional affairs. The sometimes heavy presence of the Americans (albeit now and then uninformed) has given rise to a paradox: the very country that is *now* relied upon to intervene and prevent a crisis from escalating out of control is the power that is also viewed warily as a threat to the nuclear programs of India and Pakistan. During the cold war, the peace movement and states like India tried to restrain the superpower arms race; now, a superpower is counted on to restrain the excesses of competing new nuclear powers and discourage them from entering an arms race.

America continues to urge caution upon India and Pakistan and enjoins them to normalize their relations, continue the peace process, negotiate measures for reducing nuclear risk, and refrain from deploying their nuclear arsenals. The United States has also been at great pains to demonstrate that it does not view its relations with the two antagonists as a zero-sum game. The problem is that both countries seek its support against the other, making it difficult for the United States to hold the balance even in its bilateral relations with the two countries. This role will continue in the foreseeable future as long as the United States maintains a physical presence in Pakistan and Afghanistan and raises its profile elsewhere in South Asia, especially in

India, which it seeks as a strategic ally. Presumably, Washington will view askance efforts by either India or Pakistan to embark on any future adventurism. The U.S. pressure on Pakistan to undertake a humiliating withdrawal of its troops from Kargil and on India to pull back its troops during the border confrontation crisis are useful pointers to its likely tactics to defuse future crises.

The United States was drawn into South Asian crises because of its antiproliferation policies, but also because of its larger geostrategic interests in the region. There are several paradoxes in this situation. During the cold war years, India had vigorously opposed any outside intervention in the affairs of the subcontinent; indeed, the fetish of bilateralism was pursued with almost religious fervor, while Pakistan had no such inhibitions in seeking the countervailing power of the United States or China to checkmate India. During the Kargil and border confrontation crises, both India and Pakistan had not merely accepted but actively sought American support for their respective positions.

The ironies do not cease here. Both countries view with deep suspicion the possibility that the United States might intervene in regional crises by applying diplomatic pressure or even taking overt action against their nuclear programs. At this level, America is considered inimical to their interests. Both countries are comfortable, however, with the suggestion that the United States should intervene to guarantee that the other conforms to a desired pattern of conduct. A further irony is that India was in the forefront of the global disarmament movement and the pressure imposed on the two superpowers to end their arms race. Now India has embarked upon a path of arms acquisitions and military technological development that is likely to spur a conventional and nuclear arms race in South Asia.

These considerations do not detract from our main thesis, that the United States will remain deeply involved in the subcontinent. Washington has an abiding interest in preventing crises between New Delhi and Islamabad. As the Council on Foreign Relations has urged, "The goal of U.S. diplomacy should be to help India and Pakistan to develop a framework that will enable them to address more constructively than they have in the past issues such as nuclear confidence-building measures (CBMs), de-escalation along the LOC and the Siachen glacier, expanded trade relations, easing movement of people, and reducing hate propaganda."[37] These issues are being discussed within the peace process initiated by India and Pakistan, and U.S. encouragement is obviously propelling them forward. However, would it become more overt and take the form of pressure if the current peace process should break down and war again threaten the region?

Finally, the United States may be overconfident that its diplomacy can defuse a crisis. This danger is made worse by the post-crisis gloating of various U.S. participants claiming to have saved the region from war, notably Robert Gates, Bill Clinton, Colin Powell, and Richard Armitage.

China's growing interest in the region is also evident. Now that India and Pakistan are nuclearized and each has a special relationship with China, the India-Pakistan and India-China nuclear pairs are inextricably linked, which raises complicated issues pertaining to a trilateral nuclear and strategic structure. The international system has little experience in dealing with such situations. Many accounts of international crises draw upon the analogy of the cold war, especially the specific case of the Cuban missile crisis. However, as each new nuclear state explored how far it could go in using force, especially against a nuclear rival, this generated not just the Cuban missile crisis, but also crises between the Soviet Union and China.

China can also be expected to play a role in future India-Pakistan crises. Although there is little to suggest that China presents an immediate military or nuclear threat to India, some in India's security establishment perceive such a potential threat, even though India's relations with China have steadily improved over the past two decades. Significantly, China did not encourage or support Pakistan in its Kargil adventure and joined with the United States in urging caution in 2001–02. That said, China's overt and clandestine cooperation with Pakistan's nuclear and missile program is a matter of grave concern to India. The triangular nuclear relationship that is developing between India, Pakistan, and China complicates defense planning in all three countries.

Understandings, such as the India-Pakistan agreement not to attack each other's nuclear installations and facilities, could also be negotiated between India and China in the future in order to formulate nuclear CBMs and risk-reduction measures similar to those being discussed in the India-Pakistan context. Likewise, the proposals in the memorandum of understanding attached to the Lahore Declaration have application to the Sino-Indian relationship. That relationship could also be expanded to include measures such as bilateral consultations on security concepts and nuclear doctrines; the mutual provision of advance information on ballistic missile flight tests; and notification should an accidental, unauthorized, or unexplained nuclear incident occur, in order to mitigate the effects of fallout and to prevent misinterpretations. Designated emissaries could discuss these issues within the forum established by India and China for mutual consultations on security issues.

The Larger View: Still Troubling

It would be premature to assume that the composite dialogue/peace process will result in peace, and not another crisis or even a war. From a broader perspective, the situation in South Asia remains troubling. It is an open question whether the crises of the past add up to a turning point in history, the equivalent of a regional Cuban missile crisis. Can India and Pakistan follow the path of cooperation and enhance regional stability, while still developing their own mutual balance of terror? The half-decade after their nuclear tests included the Kargil conflict and the border confrontation crisis; this was perhaps the most dangerous period in their tangled history. The perils of those years lead one to seriously question both India's belief that conventional war, limited or otherwise, is possible under the nuclear shadow and Pakistan's conviction that subconventional conflict can be pursued under the aegis of nuclear deterrence.

India is developing a military doctrine that would enable it to launch conventional operations against Pakistan. The doctrine is rooted in the change from a defensive (Kargil conflict) to a compellence (border confrontation crisis) strategy, and in the belief that a Kargil-in-reverse should also be possible if the strategic balance in South Asia remains stable. Influential sections of Pakistan's ruling elite are convinced that proxy war waged through dissident elements in Kashmir still remains a viable option. Meanwhile, India has become confident since 9/11 that it is on the right side of history as the long-suffering victim of cross-border terrorism, first in the Punjab and now in Kashmir, and has placed itself on the same side as the United States and the major Western powers. For its part, Pakistan has found it necessary to undertake a painful adjustment of its earlier policies to support religious fundamentalism within its borders and jihad elsewhere in the world.

There are powerful systemic factors favoring the success of the peace process. Pakistan's perilous economic situation and the influence of jihad and Islamic fundamentalism on its internal polity are matched by Delhi's growing realization that relations with Pakistan will have to be normalized if India wishes to play a larger role on the world stage and proceed with its ambition to rival China's economic growth. The wisdom has also dawned on the two leaderships that, in the terms of Bernard Brodie's magisterial injunction, the chief purpose of those military establishments in possession of nuclear weapons is no longer to win wars, but to avert them.[38] Above all, the international milieu and the presence of the United States in the region will not favor the constant alarms that India and Pakistan are prone to raise every few years.

Although recent events do not bode well for the future, it is hard to ignore South Asia's overall success in maintaining a modicum of democracy while undertaking radical economic and social reforms. When all is said and done, we remain optimistic that India and Pakistan will learn not only from the mistakes of others but, more important, from their own mistakes and successes.

Appendix: Methodological Note

The press index was built by assessing the level of press coverage in the elite English-language newspapers in India, Pakistan, and the United States. These papers are not, of course, representative, but they are influential, especially among English-speaking elites in India and Pakistan (where they often influence the coverage given to news by the vernacular press). A single coder in each country culled through two separate newspapers for each of the four crises: the *Hindu* and *Times of India* in India; the *Nation* and *Dawn* in Pakistan; and the *New York Times* and *Washington Post* in the United States. Each crisis story was scored on the basis of its location in the paper, the type of article, and the day of the week. Any mention of the crisis in an article merited inclusion. Note that this approach is not "content analysis," as classically understood, but an attempt to measure comparatively the weight given to the story by three different national presses.

News stories were tabulated as follows:

News item	*Points*	*Notes on field*
News story: banner headline, super size	5	Headline in extra large type, extends across several columns
News story: lead story	3	Front page, above or below the fold
News story: medium prominent	2	Prominent within a subsection
News story: least prominent	1	Small subsection story
Other non-story coverage (for example, maps and graphs)	1	News coverage without text (for example, a map or a table)

Opinion items, including op-ed pieces, were also tabulated, according to the following scale:

Opinion item	*Points*	*Notes on field*
Op-ed by outside author: prominent author	2	Judgment of author's prominence is subjective, so the author's name has been provided
Op-ed by outside author	1	Opinion piece with a byline (not representing the newspaper's staff)
Opinion articles appearing in a Sunday newspaper with unusual coverage or special articles	2	
Masthead editorial	2	The lead editorial in the op-ed page
Letters to the editor	1	

Notes

Chapter One

1. President Clinton stated: "The most dangerous place in the world today, I think you could argue, is the Indian subcontinent and the line of control in Kashmir." See "Remarks by the President on One America Initiative Religious Community Call to Action," March 9, 2000 (http://clinton6.nara.gov/2000/03/2000-03-09-remarks-of-the-president-at-one-america-event.html [December 15, 2005]). The influential Indian strategist Bharat Karnad thinks it wrong to characterize South Asia as a crisis-prone region. See his "South Asia: The Irrelevance of Classical Nuclear Deterrence Theory," *India Review* 4 (April 2005): 173–213.

2. See Sumit Ganguly and Devin T. Hagerty, *Fearful Symmetry: India-Pakistan Crises in the Shadow of Nuclear Weapons* (Oxford University Press, 2005). Peter Lavoy of the U.S. Navy Post-Graduate School Monterey has developed two separate projects on the Kargil and 2002 crises, and he and his colleagues have graciously shared their work with us.

3. The studies were as follows: on the Brasstacks crisis, Kanti P. Bajpai, P. R. Chari, Pervaiz Iqbal Cheema, Stephen P. Cohen, and Sumit Ganguly, *Brasstacks and Beyond: Perception and Management of Crisis in South Asia* (New Delhi: Manohar, 1995); on the 1990 crisis, P. R. Chari, Pervaiz Iqbal Cheema, and Stephen Philip Cohen, *Perception, Politics and Security in South Asia: The Compound Crisis of 1990* (London: Routledge-Curzon, 2003); and on the Kargil and 2001–02 crises, P. R. Chari, Pervaiz Iqbal Cheema, and Stephen Philip Cohen, "Limited War under the Nuclear Shadow in South Asia: The Kashmir Crises of 1999 and 2001–2002," presentation by Chari and Cohen at the U.S. Institute of Peace, Washington, June 23, 2004 (for an audio transcript, see www.usip.org/events/2004/0623_wkssasia.html [October 14, 2005]).

4. See Wendy D. Roth and Jal D. Mehta, "The *Rashomon* Effect: Combining Positivist and Interpretivist Approaches in the Analysis of Contested Events," *Sociological Methods and Research* 31 (November 2002): 131–73.

5. Glenn H. Snyder and Paul Diesing, *Conflict among Nations: Bargaining, Decision Making, and System Structure in International Crises* (Princeton University Press, 1977), p. 7.

6. Craig Calhoun, "A World of Emergencies: Fear, Intervention, and the Limits of Cosmopolitan Order," *Canadian Review of Sociology and Anthropology* 41 (November 2004): 373.

7. Drawn from the summary of crisis and conflict in Richard N. Lebow, *Between Peace and War: The Nature of International Crises* (Johns Hopkins University Press, 1981), pp. 7–12.

8. Charles F. Hermann, "Some Issues in the Study of International Crises," in *International Crises: Insight from Behavioral Research,* edited by Hermann (New York: Free Press, 1972), p. 6.

9. Ibid., p. 10.

10. Michael Brecher and Jonathan Wilkenfeld, *A Study of Crisis* (University of Michigan Press, 1997), p. 3.

11. Michael Brecher, *Crises in World Politics: Theory and Reality* (New York: Pergamon, 1993).

12. Yehezkal Dror, *Policymaking under Adversity* (New Brunswick, N.J.: Transaction, 1986).

13. Carnes Lord, "Crisis Management: A Primer," Institute for Advanced Strategic and Political Studies, Washington, 1998, p. 16.

14. Patrick James, "A Case Study of the International Crisis Behavior Project," Philosophy of the Social Sciences, September 2004 (www.icbnet.org/Info/project_information.html).

15. See http://pss.la.psu.edu/MID_DATA.HTM.

16. The Project for Excellence in Journalism at Columbia University has a discussion of different methodologies for doing content analysis (www.stateofthenewsmedia.org/index.asp).

17. Scott Sagan, *The Limits of Safety: Organizations, Accidents and Nuclear Weapons* (Princeton University Press, 1993), pp. 44–45. For a comprehensive discussion of complex systems in politics, see Robert Jervis, *System Effects* (Princeton University Press, 1997).

18. On Kashmiri ethnicity, see Navnita Chadha Behera, *Demystifying Kashmir* (Brookings, 2006); for a general overview, see Sumit Ganguly, *The Crisis in Kashmir* (Washington: Woodrow Wilson Center Press, 1997).

19. George Fernandes, "Opening Address," in *Asia's New Dawn: The Challenges to Peace and Security,* edited by Jasjit Singh (New Delhi: Knowledge World, 2000), p. xvii.

Chapter Two

1. For detailed analysis, see Pervaiz Iqbal Cheema, *Sanctuary and War* (Quaid-i-Azam University Press, 1978), pp. 25–32.

2. For details, see S. M. Burke, *Pakistan's Foreign Policy: An Historical Analysis* (Oxford University Press, 1973), pp. 323–26.

3. The following draws from Dennis Kux, *Estranged Democracies: India and the United States 1941–1991* (London: Sage, 1993), pp. 233–35.

4. For detailed analysis, see Pervaiz Iqbal Cheema, "India-Pakistani Relations," in *India and Her Asian Neighbours*, edited by Bertram Bastiampillai (Colombo: Bandaranaike Centre for International Studies, Bandaranaike National Memorial Foundation, 1992), pp. 37–65.

5. Robert G. Wirsing, "The Kashmir Conflict," *Current History* 95 (April 1996): 171–76.

6. Robert G. Wirsing, "The Siachen Glacier Dispute II: The Strategic Dimension," *Strategic Studies* (Islamabad) 12 (Autumn 1988). See also Wirsing, *Pakistan's Security under Zia 1977–88: The Policy Imperatives of a Peripheral Asian State* (New York: St. Martin's Press, 1991), pp. 143–94.

7. Lieutenant General M. L. Chibber, "Siachen—The Untold Story (A Personal Account)," *Indian Defence Review*, January 1990, pp. 89–95. See also Raspal S. Khosa, "Siachen Glacier Dispute: Imbroglio on the Roof of the World," *Contemporary South Asia* 8, no. 2 (1999): 187–209; and Lieutenant-General V. R. Raghavan (Ret.), *Siachen: Conflict without End* (New Delhi: Viking, 2002), pp. 47–57, which details the opening moves of the conflict.

8. For a list of CMC reports, see www.cmc.sandia.gov/regional-southasia.htm (October 20, 2005).

9. Sumit Ganguly and Devin T. Hagerty, *Fearful Symmetry: India-Pakistan Crises in the Shadow of Nuclear Weapons* (Oxford University Press, 2005).

10. Milton R. Benjamin, "India Said to Eye Raid on Pakistani A-Plants," *Washington Post*, December 20, 1982.

11. See Karen Elliot House and Peter R. Kann, "Zia Says Pakistan Has No Plans for Nuclear Bomb," *Wall Street Journal*, July 10, 1984.

12. John Elliott, "Pakistan Invasion of Kashmir Forecast by Rajiv Gandhi," *Financial Times*, London, February 6, 1984.

13. See "India–Pakistan Tension Causes Concern to U.S.," *New York Times*, September 15, 1984; and William K. Stevens, "India Worried by U.S. Links to Pakistanis," *New York Times*, October 21, 1984, which summarized the preemptive strike story.

14. Based on interviews with a senior Pakistani military official.

15. See "Pakistani Cites Nuclear Advance," *New York Times*, February 10, 1984; and *Times of India*, September 15, 1984, citing Pakistani press coverage.

16. For a discussion of Indian plans to attack Kahuta, based on interviews with a number of Indian political and military leaders, see George Perkovich, *India's Nuclear Bomb: The Impact on Global Proliferation* (University of California Press, Berkeley, 1999), pp. 240–41, 258, 283.

17. The phrase was first used in Ravi Rikhye, *The War That Never Was: The Story of India's Strategic Failures* (Delhi: Chanakya, 1988).

18. To further strengthen its diplomatic position, especially in relation to Wash-

ington, Pakistan officials also pursued a strategy of turning South Asia into a denuclearized zone, a proposal that India was unwilling to consider.

19. There are different American and Pakistani versions of how these contacts came about and who was involved.

20. This accusation was made by the Indian delegations to the Inter-Parliamentary Union, which was holding its meeting in New Delhi. *Economic Times,* April 17, 1993.

21. John M. Goshko and Don Oberdorfer, "U.S. Moved Quickly to Calm Pakistan and India after Bombay Bombings," *Washington Post,* April 15, 1993, p. A22.

22. These are 2001 figures. See Kashmir Study Group, "Kashmir: A Way Forward," Larchmont, N.Y., 2005.

23. C. Dasgupta, *War and Diplomacy in Kashmir: 1947–48* (New Delhi: Sage, 2002).

24. For the Pakistani perspective, see Pervaiz Iqbal Cheema, "Pakistan, India and Kashmir: A Historical Review," in *Perspectives on Kashmir: The Roots of Conflict in South Asia,* edited by Raju G. C. Thomas (Boulder, Colo.: Westview Press, 1992).

25. Ministry of Home Affairs, *Annual Report, 2004–2005,* annexure II, p. 164.

26. See www.satp.org/satporgtp/countries/india/states/jandk/data_she.

27. Human Rights Watch, *Behind the Kashmir Conflict: Abuses by Indian Security Forces and Militant Groups* (New York, 1999), pp. 1–3.

28. See Ashley J. Tellis, "Stability in South Asia," DB-185-A (Santa Monica, Calif.: Rand, 1997), pp. 30–33.

Chapter Three

1. This chapter is based in part on Kanti P. Bajpai and others, *Brasstacks and Beyond: Perception and Management of Crisis in South Asia* (New Delhi: Manohar, 1995), plus additional interviews with Americans, Indians, and Pakistanis involved in these events.

2. See "Agreement on Military Exercises, Manoeuvres and Troop Movements" (April 6, 1991). The text of the agreement may be seen in Michael Krepon and Amit Sevak, eds., *Crisis Prevention, Confidence Building and Reconciliation in South Asia* (New Delhi: Manohar, 1996), pp. 255–57.

3. Based on interviews, New Delhi, 1993–94. Another criticism was that apart from the "waste of money that any country can ill afford," it should be noted that "every [military] vehicle has a mileage life after which 1st, 2nd, 3rd Echelon repairs are carried out. After that the vehicles are discarded. The mileage done by all vehicles were [*sic*] so high that for three years after Brass Tacks the Indian army was unfit for war." Lieutenant General P. N. Hoon (Ret.), *Unmasking Secrets of Turbulence: Midnight Freedom to a Nuclear Dawn* (New Delhi: Manas Publications, 2000), p. 112.

4. See K. Sundarji, *The Blind Men of Hindoostan: Indo-Pak Nuclear War* (New Delhi: UBS Publishers' Distributors, 1993).

5. Keith Flory, "Getting Closer to Brasstacks," *Statesman,* March 7, 1987. These technical details were explained to the press corps during a field visit arranged for them by Generals Sundarji and Hoon, the western army commander. The following draws from interviews with several Indian officers serving at the time.

6. Manoj Joshi, "From Maps to the Field," *Hindu*, March 29, 1987.

7. Ravi Rikhye, *The War That Never Was: The Story of India's Strategic Failures* (Delhi: Chanakya, 1988).

8. Bajpai and others, *Brasstacks and Beyond*, p. 35, and interviews with officers who served at that time.

9. This characterization of Pakistani concerns was provided by General K. M. Arif, the de facto commander of the Pakistan army, who devotes a full chapter to the crisis in his memoirs. See General K. M. Arif, *Khaki Shadows: Pakistan 1947–1997* (Oxford University Press, 2001), chap. 6, "Exercise Brass Tacks."

10. Major Khalid Mehmud, "Strategic Dimensions of 'Brass Tacks,'" *Pakistan Army Journal* 30 (March 1989): 10.

11. This section and the following draw heavily on interviews shortly after the crisis with senior Pakistani civilian and military officials.

12. Interview with a very senior military official.

13. ISI is the premier Pakistani intelligence organization, dominated by the armed forces.

14. Interview with a very senior Pakistani military official who claimed that the Indian DGMO did not provide the requisite information. Later, a very senior Indian military official explained that live ammunition was taken to dumps close to the actual exercises.

15. This was apparently stated by the army commander in a BBC interview at that time. See Hoon, *Unmasking Secrets of Turbulence*, p. 109. Hoon also mentions that the exercise was originally set in an east-to-west configuration because General Sundarji wanted the setting to be "as realistic as possible" (p. 104); it was changed to a south-to-north configuration after January 20 in the light of other developments in New Delhi.

16. See the account of Humayun Khan in *Diplomatic Divide: Cross-Border Talks*, edited by David Page (New Delhi: Roli Books), p. 50. This also contains the account of India's High Commissioner to Pakistan, G. Parthasarathy.

17. Ibid., p. 51.

18. Based on interviews with a senior Pakistani military official.

19. Based on interviews with former American officials.

20. Based on an unpublished article by a serving army officer. See also Mehmud, "Strategic Dimensions of 'Brass Tacks.'"

21. See Bajpai and others, *Brasstacks and Beyond*.

22. Ibid., pp. 32, 37.

23. Ibid. This is also based on an interview with a very senior military official. General Sundarji gave an alarming briefing to Indian editors on January 18, characterizing the Pakistan army's movement as menacing and aggressive.

24. Khan in *Diplomatic Divide*, pp. 54–55.

25. See *Muslim* (Islamabad), January 28, 1987.

26. The following is based on an interview with a very senior foreign ministry official and on official logs of the period.

27. *Nation*, February 6, 1987.

28. *Hindu*, January 30, 1987.

29. Jaswant Singh, "Brass Tacks to Brass Flaps," *Illustrated Weekly of India*, March 1, 1987, pp. 22–23.

30. Interview with several senior Pakistani military officials.

31. Humayun Khan's reflections in *Diplomatic Divide* indicate that he was kept completely out of the picture and only learned of the crisis when he was summoned by Natwar Singh to be given a "stern" message.

32. See Hoon, *Unmasking Secrets of Turbulence*, p. 104.

33. Ibid., p. 109.

34. In an attempt to measure the intensity and duration of press coverage, we examined six newspapers, two each from Pakistan, India, and the United States. Each crisis was scored using a protocol that measured the location, number and type of coverage for each story in each newspaper, and the time period during which the paper covered the story. Interstate comparisons are limited by the fact that the newspapers were coded by three different individuals in the United States, India, and Pakistan and by the fact that each newspaper has its own style and format. The two Indian papers were the *Times of India* and the *Hindu;* the two Pakistani papers were *Dawn* and the *Nation;* and the two American papers were the *Washington Post* and the *New York Times.* Both Indian papers covered in this project are well-regarded national dailies, with no strong ideological bent, and both at that time had strong ties with the Indian government. In Pakistan, *Dawn* is regarded as the closest there is to a "paper of record" and is centrist-establishment in its outlook, while the *Nation* is somewhat more nationalist and anti-Indian in its outlook. The *Washington Post* and *New York Times* are the two most important centrist-liberal papers in the U.S. foreign policy establishment.

35. *Telegraph* (Calcutta), January 19, 1987.

36. *Pakistan Times*, January 24, 1987.

37. Khan in *Diplomatic Divide*, p. 55.

38. In conversations with one of the authors, New Delhi, 1993.

39. William R. Doerner, "Knocking at the Nuclear Door," *Time* Magazine, March 30, 1987, p. 42.

40. They took a similar view during the minor India-China border confrontation growing out of Exercise Checkerboard in 1987, when China was still seen as a major ally against the Soviet Union.

41. Indeed, the American propensity to encourage dialogue between regional adversaries was one reason why Pakistan provoked a Kashmir conflict with India in 1965: it was less sure of U.S. support, but hopeful of assistance from China.

42. In the parallel India-China dispute (Checkerboard), hardly any U.S. officials were aware of the origins of the conflict, and most of the relevant records had long since been shipped to storage. This bureaucratic fact of life has its comical side, as when American officials have to be briefed by foreign governments about the history of their own position on a particular issue or problem.

43. A number of key members of the House and Senate were not afraid to challenge the administration's nonproliferation policy publicly and vigorously. Perhaps the most dramatic challenge came from Senator Alan Cranston, who, in lengthy and widely publicized testimony to a Senate committee on June 12, 1984, provided a number of details concerning the Pakistani nuclear program.

44. He did this on March 4, 1986, in an appearance on an Indian television news program, "Janvani," in response to a question.

Chapter Four

1. See Benazir Bhutto, *Daughter of the East* (London: Hamish Hamilton, 1988).

2. W. H. Morris-Jones, "India after Indira: A Tale of Two Legacies," *Third World Quarterly*, April 7, 1985, p. 248.

3. Robert Wirsing, *India, Pakistan and the Kashmir Dispute* (New York: St. Martin's Press, 1994), pp. 128–29.

4. Asia Watch, *Kashmir under Siege: Human Rights in India* (New York: Human Rights Watch, May 1991), p. 13.

5. Interview with a very senior Pakistani general.

6. Salamat Ali, "The Counter-Punch," *Far Eastern Economic Review*, October 26, 1989, p. 25.

7. Michael Krepon and Mishi Faruqee, eds., "Conflict Prevention and Confidence-Building Measures in South Asia: The 1990 Crisis," Occasional Paper 17 (Washington: Henry L. Stimson Center, April 1994), p. 5. This is the transcript of a meeting convened by the Stimson Center to discuss the 1990 crisis. Participants included the U.S. ambassadors to New Delhi and Islamabad in 1990 and several South Asian diplomats and military officers.

8. *India Today*, June 30, 1990, p. 71.

9. Jagmohan Malhotra, *My Frozen Turbulence in Kashmir* (New Delhi: Allied, 1991).

10. Shirin Tahir-Kheli, "Lessons for the Future: The Gates Mission to India and Pakistan," unpublished manuscript, n.d., p. 6.

11. See "The Enemy Within," editorial, *India Today*, March 31, 1990, p. 11; Sumit Ganguly, "Avoiding War in Kashmir," *Foreign Affairs* 74 (Winter 1990–91): 63–65; M. J. Akbar, *Kashmir: Behind the Vale* (New Delhi: Viking, 1991), p. 215; "Crossfire: Kashmir," *India Today*, August 13, 1991, pp. 77–81; George Fernandes, "India's Policies in Kashmir: An Assessment and Discourse," and Jagat Mehta, "Resolving Kashmir in International Context of 1990s," both in *Perspectives on Kashmir: The Roots of Conflict in South Asia*, edited by Raju G. C. Thomas (Boulder, Colo.: Westview, 1992), pp. 286, 394–95; Alastair Lamb, *Kashmir: A Disputed Legacy 1946–1990* (Oxford University Press, 1993), pp. 332–40.

12. Lamb, *Kashmir*, p. 59.

13. According to Robert Oakley, the popular uprising in Kashmir was primarily spontaneous, but once the movement gained momentum Pakistan began to take an interest in it and groups like the Jamaat-i-Islami and ISI became active. See Krepon

and Faruqee, "Conflict Prevention and Confidence-Building Measures in South Asia," p. 6.

14. *The Nation* (Lahore), January 12, 1990.

15. *Frontier Post,* January 29, 1990.

16. Sikander Hayat, "Vigilant Eyes on Kashmir Control Line," *Frontier Post,* January 29, 1990.

17. S. Viswam and Salamat Ali, "Vale of Tears," *Far Eastern Economic Review,* February 8, 1990, pp. 19–21.

18. Raja Asghar, "Bhutto Predicts Victory for Kashmir Independence Campaign," Reuters Library Report, March 13, 1990.

19. Mark Fineman, "Attacks Spark War Fears between India, Pakistan," *Toronto Star,* April 15, 1990.

20. Steve Coll, "Assault on Pakistan Gains Favor in India," *Washington Post,* April 15, 1990.

21. "Separatists Seized in Kashmir, *New York Times,* April 16, 1990.

22. The following is based on interviews with General Beg.

23. "Indian Threats Demand Vigilance," *Dawn* (Karachi), April 12, 1990.

24. General V. N. Sharma (Ret.), "It's All Bluff and Bluster," *Economic Times* (Bombay), May 18, 1993.

25. In the terminology of both the Indian and Pakistan armies, a "corps" consists of one infantry division and one armor division, or two infantry divisions supplemented by an armor brigade. But the number of divisions is flexible and could be augmented for operational purposes.

26. B. G. Deshmukh, *A Cabinet Secretary Looks Around* (Mumbai: Bharatiya Vidya Bhavan, 1998), p. 64. Deshmukh was Indian cabinet secretary during the crisis.

27. Steve Coll, "Indian Troops, Separatist Violence Aggravate Kashmir Crisis," *Washington Post,* April 13, 1990.

28. Interview with a very senior Pakistani military official.

29. Mark Fineman, "India's Leader Warns of an Attack by Pakistan," *Los Angeles Times,* April 15, 1990, p. 7.

30. Reuters Library Report, April 19, 1990.

31. "If Pushed beyond a Point by Pakistan, We Will Retaliate," *India Today,* April 30, 1990, p. 76.

32. *India Today,* May 15, 1990.

33. Interview with members of the mission. See also Robert M. Gates, "Preventive Diplomacy: Concepts and Reality," excerpts from a speech to the Conference on Preventive Diplomacy, Taipei, Taiwan, August 29, 1996.

34. "Administration Concerned over Possible India-Pakistan Conflict," Associated Press, March 6, 1990.

35. Al Kamen, "U.S. Voices Concern over Kashmir; State Dept. Cautions India and Pakistan," *Washington Post,* April 19, 1990.

36. M. Ziauddin, "U.S. Envoy Holds Talks on Kashmir," United Press International, May 20, 1990.

37. P. R. Chari, Pervaiz Iqbal Cheema, and Stephen Philip Cohen, *Perception, Politics and Security in South Asia: The Compound Crisis of 1990* (London: Taylor and Francis, 2003), p. 102.

38. Interview with a senior American official.

39. Gates, "Preventive Diplomacy: Concepts and Reality."

40. Seymour Hersh, "On the Nuclear Edge," *New Yorker*, March 29, 1993, pp. 56–67.

41. Josef Korbel, *Danger in Kashmir* (Princeton University Press, 1966).

42. George Perkovich, *India's Nuclear Bomb: The Impact on Global Proliferation* (University of California Press, 1999), p. 293.

43. See Deshmukh, *A Cabinet Secretary Looks Around*, p. 70.

44. Raj Chengappa, *Weapons of Peace* (New Delhi: HarperCollins, 2000), p. 357.

45. Ibid., pp. 118–19.

46. Based on an interview with a former senior air force officer.

47. "Indian Prime Minister on His Country's Nuclear Policy," Xinhua General Overseas News Service, February 21, 1990.

48. *Far Eastern Economic Review*, May 17, 1990, p. 11.

49. "Indian Prime Minister on His Country's Nuclear Policy."

50. David Housego and Zafar Meraj, "Indian Premier Warns of Danger of Kashmir War," *Financial Times*, April 11, 1990; Coomi Kapoor, "Indian Threat of Armed Reprisals," *Times* (London), April 11, 1990; Tony Allen-Mills, "India Ready for War after Hostages Are Executed," *Independent* (London), April 12, 1990; Mark Fineman, "India's Leader Warns of an Attack by Pakistan," *Los Angeles Times*, April 15, 1990; "VP Urges Nation to Be Ready as Pak Troops Move to Border," *Times of India*, April 11, 1990.

51. *Muslim*, May 18, 1990. Almost ten years later, after India conducted a series of nuclear weapons tests, Advani, then minister for home affairs, repeated the threat. Various interpretations have been put upon the latter, one being that the Indian government was trying to pressure Pakistan to test and that Advani's threat was calculated to produce this result.

52. Ramanna was brought into the V. P. Singh government because of Singh's desire to include a number of scientists and technocrats. He was also associated with the earlier (1974) nuclear test. Reuters Library Report, May 17, 1990.

53. Sundarji, quoted in "If Pushed beyond a Point by Pakistan," *India Today*, p. 76.

54. Sharma, "It's All Bluff and Bluster."

55. Hersh, "On the Nuclear Edge," pp. 56–57.

56. James Adams, "Pakistan 'Nuclear War Threat,'" *Sunday Times*, May 27, 1990.

57. Hamish McDonald, "Destroyer of Worlds," *Far Eastern Economic Review*, April 30, 1992, p. 24.

58. See Krepon and Faruqee, "Conflict Prevention and Confidence-Building Measures in South Asia."

59. Hersh, "On the Nuclear Edge," p. 65.

60. Krepon and Faruqee, "Conflict Prevention and Confidence-Building Measures in South Asia."

61. William Burrows and Robert Windrem, *Critical Mass* (New York: Simon and Shuster, 1994), p. 85.

62. James Woolsey, Hearing before the Senate Government Affairs Committee (February 24, 1993). Woolsey spoke long after the crisis, but his remarks, presumably prepared by his service, reflect the dominant opinion within the American intelligence community at the time.

63. Chari and others, *Perception, Politics and Security in South Asia*, p. 133.

64. Shekhar Gupta, "Benazir Bhutto: Playing with Fire," *India Today*, May 31, 1990.

65. J. N. Dixit, *Anatomy of a Flawed Inheritance: Indo-Pak Relations, 1970–1994* (Delhi: Konarak, 1995), pp. 124–25.

66. *Dawn*, January 21, 1990.

67. Ibid.

68. "Crush Pak Camps: BJP," *Times of India*, April 8, 1990.

69. David Housego, "India Urged to Attack Camps in Pakistan over Strife in Kashmir," *Financial Times*, April 9, 1990.

70. Stephen P. Cohen, *The Pakistan Army* (Oxford University Press, 1992), p. 146.

71. *Nation*, February 7, 1990.

Chapter Five

1. Musharraf devotes an entire chapter to Kargil and discusses it in other sections of his memoir, *In the Line of Fire* (New York: Free Press, 2006).

2. India's minister of external affairs (and sometimes minister of finance and defense), Jaswant Singh, has devoted a chapter to Kargil in his memoir, *A Call to Honour: In Service of Emergent India* (New Delhi: Rupa, 2006).

3. Strobe Talbott, *Engaging India: Diplomacy, Democracy, and the Bomb* (Brookings, 2004).

4. The text of the Lahore Declaration was published in the *News* (Lahore), on February 22, 1999.

5. "Pak Bid to Capture Siachen Post Foiled (UNI News Report)," *Indian Express*, October 28, 1998 (www.indianexpress.com/res/web/pIe/ie/daily/19981028/30150424.html [January 15, 2007]).

6. Musharraf, *In the Line of Fire*, pp. 87–98.

7. There is a very large Indian literature on this crisis. See, in particular, General Ved K. Malik, *Kargil: From Surprise to Victory* (New Delhi: HarperCollins, 2006). See also the massive battle history by Lieutenant General Y. M. Bammi (Ret.), *Kargil 1999: The Impregnable Conquered* (Noida: Gorkha, 2002); and Major General Ashok Krishna (Ret.), AVSM, and P. R. Chari, *Kargil: The Tables Turned* (New Delhi: Manohar, 2001). One very thoughtful American account is Colonel John H. Gill (Ret.), *Military Operations during the Kargil Conflict*, rev. ed. (National Defense University, Near East-South Asia Center for Strategic Studies, April 11, 2003).

8. See *Keesing's Record of World Events 1999*, vol. 45, no. 5 (May 1999), p. 42936. See also *SIPRI Yearbook 2000* (Oxford University Press, 2000), p. 21.

9. See "Soldier's Hour," *India Today*, July 26, 1999, p. 13.

10. Musharraf, *In the Line of Fire*, p. 90.

11. Major General Ashok Krishna, "The Kargil War," in *Kargil: The Tables Turned*, edited by Krishna and Chari, p. 108.

12. Two divisions were relocated in the Kargil area alone. See Malik, *Kargil: From Surprise to Victory*, pp. 129–30.

13. For brief details of the role played by the Indian air force and the navy in the Kargil conflict, see Krishna and Chari, eds., *Kargil: The Tables Turned*, pp. 132–37.

14. For details, see Sartaj Aziz's interview with Indian lawyer/journalist A. G. Noorani, "The Truth about Lahore Summit," *Frontline* Magazine, February 16–March 1, 2002.

15. Suzanne Goldenberg, "India's Balancing Act on Kashmir," *Guardian*, London, June 1, 1999.

16. See "Agreement Fails to Halt Kashmir Fighting," *CNN*, July 5, 1999 (www.cnn.com/ WORLD/asiapcf/9907/05/kashmir.02).

17. Musharraf, *In the Line of Fire*, pp. 89–90.

18. Shireen M. Mazari, *The Kargil Conflict 1999: Separating Fact from Fiction* (Islamabad: Institute of Strategic Studies, 2003), p. 24. This view was strongly endorsed by at least one senior Pakistani army officer directly involved in the planning for Kargil interviewed for this project.

19. Musharraf, *In the Line of Fire*, p. 90.

20. See Sartaj Aziz's interview in Noorani, "The Truth about Lahore Summit." Also, senior Pakistani military officers interviewed for this project stressed India's continuous interdiction in the Neelam Valley as a factor shaping Pakistani military planning.

21. Mazari, *The Kargil Conflict 1999*, pp. 29–30.

22. The FCNA gave a detailed briefing at Gilgit on January 12, 2003, presented by a senior serving military officer and subsequently referred to as *Gilgit Briefing 2003*. One of the authors was also invited to attend. For detailed discussion of some of the points raised at the briefing and for a detailed analysis, see Mazari, *The Kargil Conflict 1999*, pp. 42–62.

23. Mazari, *The Kargil Conflict 1999*, pp. 15–16.

24. Musharraf, *In the Line of Fire*, p. 90.

25. Ibid., p. 98.

26. General Jehangir Karamat (Ret.), "Learning from Kargil," *News* (Lahore), August 5, 1999.

27. Brigadier Shaukat Qadir (Ret.), "An Analysis of the Kargil Conflict, 1999," *Journal of the Royal United Services Institution*, April 2002, pp. 24–30.

28. See Asad Durrani, *An Unhistoric Verdict* (Lahore: Jang, 2001), esp. part 4, "Kargil," pp. 183–218. This is a compilation of newspaper articles, several of them written at the time of the Kargil operation.

29. See President Musharraf's website (www.presidentofpakistan.gov.pk/ FromThePresidentsDesk.aspx).

30. Musharraf, *In the Line of Fire*, p. 95.

31. Nasir's views seem to reflect those of Aslam Beg, a former army chief, who faults Benazir Bhutto for failing to accept Beg's original plan to move across the LOC at Kargil. See Lieutenant General Javed Nasir (Ret.), "Kargil—The Bitter Hard Facts," *Nation,* August 29, 2004.

32. Musharraf has written that in 1999 Pakistan's nuclear capability was not operational, and that any talk of preparing for a nuclear strike is "preposterous." *In the Line of Fire,* p. 98.

33. Ibid., p. 137.

34. Benazir Bhutto, BBC interview, *World Today,* July 23, 1999.

35. *From Surprise to Reckoning: Kargil Review Committee Report* (New Delhi: Sage, 2000), pp. 70–71 (hereafter *KRC Report*).

36. Ibid., p. 226.

37. Musharraf, *In the Line of Fire,* p. 96.

38. Lieutenant General V. K. Sood (Ret.) and Pravin Sawhney, *Operation Parakram: The War Unfinished* (New Delhi: Sage, 2003), p. 66.

39. Ibid., p. 66.

40. P. R. Chari, "Introduction: Some Preliminary Observations," in *Kargil: The Tables Turned,* edited by Krishna and Chari, p. 15.

41. Jyoti Malhotra, "G-8 Doesn't Name Pak but Says Intrusion Irresponsible," *Indian Express,* June 21, 1999.

42. See Bruce Riedel, *American Diplomacy and the 1999 Kargil Summit at Blair House,* Policy Paper Series 2002 (University of Pennsylvania, Center for the Advanced Study of India, 2002) (www.ccc.nps.navy.mil/research/kargil/reidel.pdf).

43. Malik, *Kargil: From Surprise to Victory,* p. 146–47.

44. Ibid.

45. Talbott, *Engaging India,* p. 201.

46. Suba Chandran, "Role of the United States: Mediator or Mere Facilitator?" in *Kargil: The Tables Turned,* edited by Krishna and Chari, pp. 206–07.

47. The view of a senior Western diplomat interviewed for this project.

48. Tom Clancy with General Tony Zinni (Ret.) and Tony Koltz, *Battle Ready* (New York: G. P. Putnam's Sons, 2004), p. 347.

49. Ibid.

50. Mazari, *The Kargil Conflict 1999,* p. 61.

51. Tariq Fatemi, "Beyond the Line of Prudence," *Dawn* (Karachi), October 7, 2006 (www.dawn.com/2006/10/07/op.htm [January 10, 2007]).

52. Riedel, *American Diplomacy and the 1999 Kargil Summit.*

53. It would have been out of the question for the United States to share this information with India, nor is there evidence that India had better information about the Pakistani program, as General V. P. Malik suggests.

54. Singh, *Call to Honour,* p. 227.

55. Musharraf, *In the Line of Fire,* p. 97.

56. Talbott, *Engaging India,* p. 165. For an account of the Sharif visit, see also Bill Clinton, *My Life* (New York: Random House, 2004), pp. 864–66.

57. Talbott, *Engaging India*, p. 166. Clinton stuck to the position in his subsequent trip to the subcontinent. On February 16, 2000, in talking to reporters, he repeated what he had told Nawaz Sharif the previous July 4, that the United States ought to be more involved in resolving the Kashmir dispute but would refrain from doing so "unless we are asked by both parties to help." On March 17, on the eve of his departure for South Asia, Clinton said he would use the trip to rekindle the relationship with India and reduce tensions between New Delhi and Islamabad. See "Presidential Press Conference on Economy," White House Office of the Press Secretary, February 16, 2000 (www.clintonpresidentialcenter.org/legacy/021600-presidential-press-conference-on-economy.htm [November 4, 2004]); Clinton, *My Life*, p. 865; and "Remarks by President on Gun Safety," White House Office of the Press Secretary, March 17, 2000 (www.clintonpresidentialcenter.org/legacy/0131700-remarks-by-president-on-gun-safety.htm [November 4, 2004]).

58. *KRC Report*. The committee was chaired by K. Subrahmanyam.

59. See Celia W. Dugger, "Atmosphere Is Tense as India and Pakistan Agree to Talks," *New York Times*, June 1, 1999 (www.nytimes.com/library/world/asia-/060199india-pakistan.html [January 15, 2007]).

60. Raj Chengappa, *Weapons of Peace* (New Delhi: HarperCollins, 2000), p. 437.

61. Statements of senior army and air force officers during a review of an earlier draft of this book.

62. See "Address to the Nation by Prime Minister Nawaz Sharif, July 12, 1999" (http://acronym.org.uk/dd/dd39/39kash.htm).

63. Sood and Sawhney, *Operation Parakram*, p. 71.

64. Riedel, *American Diplomacy and the 1999 Kargil Summit*.

65. See Sonika Gupta and Arpit Rajain, "Interview with Gen. V. P. Malik," in *Nuclear Stability in Southern Asia*, edited by P. R. Chari, Sonika Gupta, and Arpit Rajain (New Delhi: Manohar, 2003), p. 158.

66. Mazari, *The Kargil Conflict 1999*, p. 18. These statements were made by both these interlocutors in a conference held by the Center for Contemporary Conflict, Naval Postgraduate School, Monterey, Calif., in May 2002.

67. For more detailed information on Padmanabhan's views, see Praveen Swami, "General Padmanabhan Mulls Lessons of Operation Parakram," *Hindu*, February 6, 2006 (www.hindu.com/2004/02/06/stories/2004020604461200.htm [January 15, 2007]).

68. Indian accounts of the crisis draw heavily on these tapes, treating them as damning evidence. These intercepted conversations took place on May 26 and 29, 1999, and were released by India during the crisis to reveal the complicity of the Pakistan army in mounting and sustaining the Kargil intrusions. The transcripts are reproduced in Singh, *A Call to Honour*, pp. 213–19.

69. *KRC Report*, pp. 233–38.

70. B. Raman, *Intelligence: Past, Present and Future* (New Delhi: Lancers, 2002), p. 233. The author is a former member of the Intelligence Bureau and the Research and Analysis Wing.

71. "Pak Army Alone to Blame—George," *Statesman*, May 28, 1999.

72. Ajay Singh, "Behind the Near-War," *Asiaweek*, June 11, 1999.

73. "Kargil Operation Had Approval of Sharif—The Nation," *Hindustan Times*, June 30, 1999.

74. Raj Chengappa, "Nawaz Sharif Speaks Out," *India Today*, July 26, 2004, pp. 18–24.

75. "Nawaz Sharif Is Lying: Shujaat," *News* (Lahore), August 6, 2004.

76. Ibid.

77. The incident is discussed in Singh, *A Matter of Honour*, p. 219.

78. These military CBMs included the Agreement on Advance Notice on Military Exercises, Manoeuvres and Troop Movements (April 6, 1991), the Agreement on Prevention of Airspace Violations and for Permitting Overflights and Landings by Military Aircraft (April 6, 1991), and the Joint Declaration on the Complete Prohibition of Chemical Weapons (August 19, 1992).

79. "Chronology of Events," *Mainstream* 37 (June 1999).

80. Niaz Naik's version of these talks can be seen in Robert G. Wirsing, *Kashmir in the Shadow of War: Regional Rivalries in a Nuclear Age* (Armonk, N.Y.: M. E. Sharpe, 2003), pp. 26–33. R. K. Mishra has not yet disclosed his side of the story.

81. See Talbott, *Engaging India*, pp. 163 ff.

82. Ashley J. Tellis, C. Christine Fair, and Jamison Jo Medby, *Limited Conflicts under the Nuclear Umbrella: Indian and Pakistani Lessons from the Kargil Crisis* (Santa Monica, Calif.: Rand, 2001), pp. 79–80.

83. Charles L. Glaser, *Analyzing Strategic Nuclear Policy* (Princeton University Press, 1990), p. 46, n. 69. The stability-instability paradox was originally recognized in Glenn H. Snyder, "The Balance of Power and the Balance of Terror," in *The Balance of Power*, edited by Paul Seabury (San Francisco: Chandler, 1964), pp. 184–201, and expanded in Robert Jervis, *The Meaning of the Nuclear Revolution* (Cornell University Press, 1989), pp. 19–22.

84. Text of the Clinton-Sharif statement of July 4, 1999, in the *Hindu*, July 6, 1999. See also www.acronym.org.uk/dd/dd38/38kash.htm.

85. The Simla Agreement states, in part, that the LOC "shall be respected by both sides without prejudice to the recognized position of either side. Neither side shall seek to alter it unilaterally, irrespective of mutual differences and legal interpretations. Both sides further undertake to refrain from the threat or the use of force in violation of this Line."

Chapter Six

1. Harish Khare, "A Decisive Battle Has to Take Place: PM," *Hindu*, December 14, 2001 (www.hinduonnet.com/thehindu/2001/12/14/stories/2001121400360100.htm [January 15, 2007]).

2. Special correspondent, "Police Claim 'Clinching Evidence,'" *Hindu*, December 15, 2001.

3. See Naunidhi Kaur, "A Verdict and Some Questions," *Frontline* Magazine, January 18–31, 2003; and People's Union for Democratic Rights (PUDR), "A Critique of the POTA Court Judgment on the 13 December Case" (February 2003) (www.pppucl.org/Topics/Law/2003/parliament-case [March 10, 2005]).

4. "Summary of Press Briefing by the Official Spokesperson," December 21, 2001 (www.mea.gov.in/pressbriefing/2001/12/21pb01 [March 10, 2005]).

5. See Preetam Bora, "SAPRA India: Terrorist Attack on Parliament: Striking at the Heart of Indian Democracy," December 26, 2001 (www.subcontinent.com/sapra/terrorism/terrorism20011226a.html [September 30, 2005]); Purnima S. Tripathi, "Terror in Parliament House," *Frontline* Magazine, December 22, 2001–January 04, 2002, pp. 1–5.

6. *Nation* (Lahore), April 8, 2002.

7. While speaking in the Lok Sabha on December 18, Deputy Prime Minister L. K. Advani stressed that an attempt had been made "to wipe out the entire political leadership of India." See *Keesing's Record of World Events* 47 (December 2001): 44508–09.

8. Government of India, *Ministry of Defence, Annual Report, 2002–2003* (New Delhi), p. 4.

9. Lieutenant General V. K. Sood (Ret.) and Pravin Sawhney, *Operation Parakram: The War Unfinished* (New Delhi: Sage, 2003), p. 73.

10. Jawed Naqvi, "India Had Planned Offensive," *Dawn* (Karachi), December 24, 2002, quoting a Press Trust of India report. This statement was made by General N. C. Vij, later India's chief of army staff.

11. Details of this incident may be seen in Sood and Sawhney, *Operation Parakram*, p. 80.

12. See Lieutenant General R. K. Jasbir Singh, ed., *Indian Defence Yearbook 2003* (Dehra Doon: Natraj, 2003), pp. 43–60. See also Zulfiqar Khan, "Pakistan-India Military Standoff: A Nuclear Dimension," *IPRI Journal* 3 (Winter 2003): 99–125.

13. See Celia W. Dugger, "The Kashmir Brink," *New York Times*, June 20, 2002.

14. For a detailed discussion of the theory of compellence and different types of coercive diplomacy, see Alexander George, *Forceful Persuasion: Coercive Diplomacy as an Alternative to War* (Washington: United States Institute of Peace, 1991); and for a balanced overview of deterrence and compellence in South Asia, see Rajesh M. Basrur, *Minimum Deterrence and India's Nuclear Security* (Stanford University Press, 2006), esp. chap. 4, "Compellence in a Nuclear Environment."

15. "Interview with Maleeha Lodhi," *CNN Live Today*, January 21, 2002 (http://archives.cnn.com/TRANSCRIPTS/0201/); Y. M. Bammi, *Kargil 1999: The Impregnable Conquered* (Noida: Gorkha, 2002), pp. A47–A52.

16. Lieutenant General Kamal Matinuddin, "India-Pakistan Standoff," *Regional Studies* 21 (Summer 2003): 3–62.

17. See A. G. Noorani, "Vajpayee's Pakistan Policy," *Frontline* Magazine, May 24–June 06, 2003 (www.hinduonnet.com/fline/fl2011/stories/20030606000907500.htm [September 18, 2007])

18. Khan, "Pakistan-India Military Standoff," pp. 99–125.

19. For a detailed Pakistani interpretation of India's action, see Matinuddin, "India-Pakistan Standoff."

20. See "President of Pakistan General Pervez Musharraf's Address to the Nation," Islamabad, January 12, 2002 (www.presidentofpakistan.gov.pk/FilesSpeeches/Addresses/020200475758AMword%20file.pdf).

21. For the text of the speech, see www.dawn.com/2002/01/12/speech020112.htm.

22. Interviews with midranking civilian and military officials.

23. For a detailed analysis of the erosion of secularism in India, see the short book by Khushwant Singh, *The End of India* (New Delhi: Penguin Books, 2003). See also "The Erosion of Indian Secularism," *News* (Lahore), March 17, 2002.

24. For a Pakistani perspective, see "Babri Masjid-Ram Mandir Controversy," *News* (Lahore), March 24, 2002.

25. See Pervaiz Iqbal Cheema, "UP Election and the Tension," *News* (Lahore), January 20, 2002. See also Cheema, "UP Elections and the Pakistan Factor," *News* (Lahore), February 22, 2002.

26. As claimed during an interview with an official close to Prime Minister Vajpayee. India argued that the mobilization had to continue to ensure that elections could be held in Kashmir "in a relatively calm atmosphere without the alleged interference from Pakistan supported militant organizations." See Matinuddin, "India-Pakistan Standoff," p. 20.

27. For a statistical analysis of this violence, see Praveen Swami, "Beating the Retreat," *Frontline* Magazine, November 8, 2002, pp. 14–16.

28. Robert Powell, *Nuclear Deterrence Theory: The Search for Credibility* (Cambridge University Press, 1990), p. 180.

29. Government of India, *Ministry of Defence, Annual Report 2002–2003,* p. 4.

30. See General Rashid Qureshi, statement to Agence France-Presse (www.inq7.net/wnw/2002.nov/29/wnw_4-1.htm).

31. Editorial, *Dawn* (Karachi), October 18, 2002.

32. Murali Krishnan and Chander Suta Dogra, "Operation Parakram: Burden of Peace," *Outlook,* May 19, 2003, p. 34.

33. Discussions with a corps commander. The Indian minister of defense informed parliament that 1,874 men were either killed or injured, and the cost of the mobilization was estimated to be $2 billion. See Krishnan and Dogra, "Operation Parakram," p. 34.

34. Yaqoob Malik, "Enemy Defeated without a War, Says Musharraf," *Dawn* (Karachi), December 13, 2002 (www.dawn.com/2002/12/13/top1.htm [January 15, 2007]).

35. Hasan Akhtar, "U.S. Assured Pakistan Will Not Begin War: Musharraf, Armitage Hold Talks," *Dawn* (Karachi), June 8, 2002.

36. Satish Kumar, "Reassessing Pakistan as a Long-Term Security Threat," *Strategic Digest* 33 (March 2003): 240.

37. For the text, see www.pak.gov.pk/public/presidentialaddress-27-5-2002.htm.

38. Akhtar, "U.S. Assured Pakistan Will Not Begin War."

39. Government of India, *Ministry of Home Affairs, Annual Report 2002–2003* (New Delhi), p. 18.

40. Interview with official close to Prime Minister Vajpayee.

41. Because of the usual delay in the transition from one administration to another, it took five months to swear in a new assistant secretary of state for South Asia (Christina Rocca), and it was six months before Blackwill arrived in New Delhi to assume his post on July 27, 2001. There were also problems with American representation in Pakistan: an initial appointee had to leave Pakistan on May 28, 2002, at the height of the crisis.

42. Manohar Joshi, "U.S. Ambassador Blackwill Called on Speaker of the Lok Sabha," *Hindu*, December 13, 2002.

43. U.S. Department of State, "Daily Press Briefing for December 18," December 18, 2001 (www.state.gov/r/pa/prs/dpb/2001/6895.htm).

44. U.S. Department of State, "Daily Press Briefing for December 20," December 20, 2001 (www.state.gov/r/pa/prs/dpb/2001/6949.htm).

45. According to several officials close to the embassy, American intelligence tracked closely with Indian assertions that Pakistan was behind the terrorist attacks. The United States had some independent sources, and these, where they overlapped, corroborated Indian claims and matched the interpretation of other friendly states with good information. India's sources on Pakistani plans and capabilities were, in the word of one key official, "fantastic."

46. See Michael Krepon and Polly Nayak, *U.S. Crisis Management in South Asia's Twin Peaks Crisis*, Report 57 (Washington: Stimson Center, September 2006) (www.stimson.org/pub.cfm?id=327 [February 28, 2007]).

47. See http://calcutta.usconsulate.gov/www.warn.html (July 13, 2005).

48. Thomas L. Friedman, "India, Pakistan, and GE," *New York Times*, August 11, 2002, sec. 4, p. 13.

49. Ibid.

50. Thomas L. Friedman, *The World Is Flat: A Brief History of the Twenty-First Century* (New York: Farrar, Straus and Giroux, 2005).

51. The statement of one American official intimately involved with the events, corroborated by other interviews.

52. Sood and Sawhney, *Operation Parakram.*

53. One such plane was assigned to the royal household; it had IFF (identification friend or foe) electronics that would have alerted Indian or Pakistani air defenses of its benign role.

54. "India's Missile System in Position: Fernandes," *Hindu*, December 27, 2001.

55. C. Raja Mohan, "Missile Test Was Delayed to Avoid Escalation," *Hindu*, January 26, 2002.

56. Celia W. Dugger, "India Test-Fires Intermediate-Range Missile," *New York Times*, January 25, 2002.

57. Rama Lakshmi, "Missile Test by India Raises Nuclear Ante: Pakistan Assails Firing at a Time of Tensions," *Washington Post*, January 26, 2002.

58. Faraz Hashmi, "More Tests Likely," *Dawn,* May 26, 2002 (www.dawn.com/2002/05/25/top10.htm).

59. "Pakistan Test Fires Nuclear-Capable Missile," *Hindustan Times,* May 25, 2002.

60. Rajesh Rajagopalan, *Second Strike: Arguments about Nuclear War in South Asia* (New Delhi: Viking/Penguin, 2005), p. 121, citing press reports.

61. Barry Posen, *Inadvertent Escalation: Conventional War and Nuclear Risks* (Cornell University Press, 1991), p. 3.

62. Personal interviews.

63. This is the observation of some officials who sat in on CCS meetings during this crisis.

64. General S. Padmanabhan, *The Writing on the Wall: India Checkmates America 2017* (New Delhi: Manas, 2004).

65. Sood and Sawhney, *Operation Parakram,* p. 73.

66. Sukumar Muralidharan, "General's Manoeuvre," *Frontline* Magazine, February 1, 2002.

67. Tyndall Report (www.tyndallreport.com/archive02.php3 [July 30, 2006]).

68. Sood and Sawhney, *Operation Parakram,* pp. 73–77.

69. Jasjit Singh, "Dynamics of Limited War," *Strategic Analysis* 24 (October 2000): 1219.

70. Strobe Talbott, *Engaging India* (Brookings, 2004), p. 186.

Chapter Seven

1. For a 2005 assessment by one of the authors, see Pervaiz Iqbal Cheema, "Sustaining the Composite Dialogue," paper presented at the Annual Conflict Transformation Workshop, WISCOMP (Women in Security, Conflict Management, and Peace), New Delhi, India, October 3, 2005.

2. Feroz Hassan Khan, "The Independence-Dependence Paradox," in *Arms Control Today,* October 2003 (www.armscontrol.org/act/2003_10/Khan_10.asp).

3. Kargil Review Committee, *The Kargil Review Committee Report: From Surprise to Reckoning* (New Delhi: Sage, 2000), p. 183.

4. For a more accurate description of Pakistani strategy, see Major General Mahmud Ali Durrani (Ret.), "Pakistan's Strategic Thinking and the Role of Nuclear Weapons," Cooperative Monitoring Center Occasional Paper 37 (Sandia National Laboratories, July 2004) (www.cmc.sandia.gov/links/cmc-papers/sand2004-3375P.pdf [May 2, 2006]).

5. "Roll Back Proxy War, Pakistan Told," *Hindu,* May 19, 1998.

6. See Editorial, *Times of India,* June 2, 1999.

7. Cited in Praful Bidwai, "Nuclear South Asia: Still on the Edge," *Frontline* Magazine, January 31, 2003, p. 118.

8. Rajesh Rajagopalan, *Second Strike: Arguments about Nuclear War in South Asia* (New Delhi: Penguin Books, 2005), p. 127.

9. Ibid., p. 128.

10. See S. Paul Kapur, "India and Pakistan's Unstable Peace: Why Nuclear South Asia Is Not Like Cold War Europe," *International Security* 30 (Fall 2005): 141; Kapur has since published *Dangerous Deterrent: Nuclear Weapons Proliferation and Conflict in South Asia* (Stanford University Press, 2007).

11. Satu Limaye, "Mediating Kashmir: A Bridge Too Far," *Washington Quarterly*, Winter 2002–03, p. 159.

12. "It's Seven Minutes to Midnight," *Bulletin of the Atomic Scientists*, March/April 2002, p. 8.

13. Sonika Gupta and Arpit Rajain, "Interview with Gen. V. P. Malik," in *Nuclear Stability in Southern Asia*, edited by P. R. Chari and others (New Delhi: Manohar, 2003), p. 154.

14. Lieutenant General V. K. Sood (Ret.) and Pravin Sawhney, *Operation Parakram: The War Unfinished* (New Delhi: Sage, 2003), p. 170.

15. P. R. Chari, *India-Pakistan Nuclear Standoff: The Role of the United States* (New Delhi: Manohar, 1995), p. 94.

16. Charles L. Glazer, *Analyzing Strategic Nuclear Policy* (Princeton University Press, 1990), p. 46, n. 69, citing T. C. Schelling's "Comment" in *Limited Strategic War*, in Klauss Knorr and Thornton Read, eds., *Limited Strategic War* (New York: Praeger, 1962) pp. 250–53; Glenn H. Snyder, "The Balance of Power and the Balance of Terror," in *The Balance of Power*, edited by Paul Seabury (San Francisco: Chandler, 1965), pp. 184–201; and Robert Jervis's discussion of the "stability-instability" paradox in *The Illogic of American Nuclear Strategy* (Cornell University Press, 1984).

17. Neil Joeck, "Nuclear Relations in South Asia," in *Repairing the Regime: Preventing the Spread of Weapons of Mass Destruction*, edited by Joseph Cirincione (Washington: Carnegie Endowment for International Peace, 2000), pp. 1–2.

18. Kapur, "India and Pakistan's Unstable Peace," p. 128, n. 5.

19. Ibid., p. 129.

20. For a strong defense of the agreement, see Dinshaw Mistry and Sumit Ganguly, "The Case for the U.S-India Nuclear Agreement," *World Policy Journal* (Summer 2006): 11–19; and for a view of the agreement from a realist/hawk perspective, see Bharat Karnad, "Minimum Deterrence and the India-U.S. Nuclear Deal," *Seminar*, January 2007 (www.india-seminar.com/2007/569/569_bharat_karnad.htm [March 5, 2007]).

21. For a discussion of the effects of nuclear war, see U.S. Congress, Office of Technology Assessment, *The Effects of Nuclear War* (GPO, May 1979), pp. 3–4.

22. S. Rashid Naim, "Aadhi Raat Ke Baad" (After Midnight), in *Nuclear Proliferation in South Asia: The Prospects for Arms Control*, edited by Stephen Philip Cohen (New Delhi: Lancer International, 1991), p. 59.

23. Raj Chengappa, "If Pakistan Nukes India...," *India Today*, June 10, 2002, pp. 24–32.

24. U.S. Information Service, U.S. Embassy, *Third Report to Congress: Update on Progress toward Regional Non-Proliferation in South Asia* (New Delhi, April 19, 1994), pp. 8–10.

25. Suba Chandran, "India-Pakistan Summits: A Profile," in *India and Pakistan: The Agra Summit and After,* edited by P. R. Chari and Suba Chandran (New Delhi: Institute of Peace and Conflict Studies, 2001), p. 6 (www.ipcs.org/newIpcsPublications.jsp?status=publications&status1=topical&mod=e&check=6&try=true [October 21, 2005]).

26. Chris Gagne, "Nuclear Risk Reduction in South Asia: Building on Common Ground," in *Nuclear Risk Reduction in South Asia,* edited by Michael Krepon and Chris Gagne (New Delhi: Vision Books, 2003), pp. 64–65.

27. Suba Chandran, "Indo-Pak Summits: A Profile," Article 514 (New Delhi: Institute for Peace and Conflict Studies, June 27, 2001).

28. The text of the Lahore Declaration, February, 21, 1999, may be accessed at wwww.ipcs.org/documents/1999/1-jan-mar.htm.

29. "Joint Statement, Meeting between Foreign Secretaries of India and Pakistan," June 28, 2004 (www.mea.gov.in/declarestatement/2004/06/28js01.htm).

30. Ibid.

31. For an overview of the process, see "Seek Out of the Box Solutions," *Post* (Lahore), December 10, 2006 (http://ipripak.org/articles/latest/seekout.shtml [January 15, 2007]).

32. "Joint Statement, India-Pakistan Expert-Level Talks on Nuclear CBMs," June 20, 2004 (www.iiss.org/showpage.php?mixedPagesID=99#20_June_2004).

33. "Peace Bid: Centre Drafts 9-Point Strategy for JK," *Press Trust of India,* November 29, 2004 (http://news.indiainfo.com/2004/11/29/2911jk.html).

34. International Institute for Strategic Studies, *The Military Balance, 2004–2005* (London, 2004), p. 251.

35. This argument, based on the observation of everyday phenomena, is made in Thomas C. Schelling, *Arms and Influence* (Yale University Press, 1960), pp. 69–78.

36. Michael Krepon, "Moving from Crisis to Nuclear Safety," *Hindu,* February 5, 2004.

37. Council on Foreign Relations, *New Priorities in South Asia: U.S. Policy toward India, Pakistan, and Afghanistan,* Chairman's Report of an Independent Task Force (New York, 2003), pp. 7–8.

38. Bernard Brodie, *The Absolute Weapon* (New York: Harcourt, Brace, 1946), p. 76.

Index

About the Authors

P. R. Chari is research professor at the Institute of Peace and Conflict Studies in New Delhi. His books include *Nuclear Stability in South Asia* and *Security and Governance in South Asia.*

Pervaiz Iqbal Cheema is president of the Islamabad Policy Research Institute. His publications include *The Armed Forces of Pakistan.*

Stephen P. Cohen is senior fellow in Foreign Policy Studies at the Brookings Institution. His previous books include *The Idea of Pakistan* and *India: Emerging Power.*